The Immigrant Superpower

The Immigrant Superpower

How Brains, Brawn, and Bravery Make America Stronger

Tim Kane

OXFORD
UNIVERSITY PRESS

Oxford University Press is a department of the University of Oxford. It furthers
the University's objective of excellence in research, scholarship, and education
by publishing worldwide. Oxford is a registered trade mark of Oxford University
Press in the UK and certain other countries.

Published in the United States of America by Oxford University Press
198 Madison Avenue, New York, NY 10016, United States of America.

CIP data is on file at the Library of Congress

ISBN 978-0-19-008819-4

DOI: 10.1093/oso/9780190088194.001.0001

1 3 5 7 9 8 6 4 2

Printed by LSC Communications, United States of America

For Madonna and Marcella, my wonderful sisters

Contents

Boxes, Tables, and Figures

Boxes

Tables

Figures

Acknowledgments

My campaign manager for the congressional primary in 2018 was a guy named Chris Galloway. I credit him for this book, because he's the one who encouraged me to run as a Republican with a limitless faith in the American dream.

My phone rang at 5:00 AM on election day, May 8. "You awake?" "Already shaved. Ready to rock them like a hurricane?" "Hunnert percent. See you at the radio station." And then he went missing.

Chris never says yes. And he also never admits he's wrong. His two basic responses are "Whatever" and "Hunnert percent." My odds of victory on election day were somewhere between those two.

Campaign staff, even the manager, get terrible pay. They're cynical on the outside, but deep down everyone in politics is doing it because they still believe in this thing called America. I decided to splurge on a luxury hotel room for Chris the night before the election, and it was those knuckleheads that lost his car keys. Three hours later, he tracked me down with a half dozen volunteers at a busy intersection, waving to morning traffic north of the city. Anthony Lagunzad is holding the big KANE FOR OHIO banner to my right. One of my enthusiastic college Republicans is hopping up and down shaking his sign so vigorously I worry he'll cause a crash. Rea Hederman, an old pal from the Heritage Foundation, is to my left with another poster.

Chris walks over with his luxury hotel coffee in hand and just shakes his head. "Did you ever think about going to a polling location to wave at actual voters?"

It was thanks to Chris that the *New York Times* sent out a reporter to cover the campaign and ran a feature story on my candidacy. It was titled, "Meet the Pro-Trade, Pro-Immigration Economist Running for Congress. As a Republican. In Ohio."

"The party's primary on Tuesday will feature ten candidates, including two state senators, a county prosecutor, and a local conservative activist.

"Then there is Tim Kane.

"Mr. Kane, 50, has a résumé that sounds as if he answered a casting call for a Republican congressional candidate: an Ohio native, he served in the Air Force, then earned a PhD in economics and worked at conservative think tanks such as the Heritage Foundation and the Hoover Institution. Along the way, he helped start two companies, wrote four books, and became a familiar commentator on economic issues in newspapers and on television."

The reporter, Ben Casselman, was sincere in his curiosity about what was happening at the grassroots level. Who were these crazy Trump voters? It's not that folks around here don't like immigrants, I explained. Every kid I went to high school with could tell you their family's story of coming to America, especially here in the Midwest with a thick mix of religions and homelands that had warred against one another in the Old World. What folks didn't like is being told that they're racist just because of their skin color by elites who have no idea about the hardships many midwestern families overcame. Folks here can tell you the names of ancestors who fought to free the slaves, who believe in the American dream, who gripped hands with fellow soldiers of every background as they fought for the freedom and democracy of foreigners in foreign lands.

I want to make sure to acknowledge the friends I grew up with for inspiring this book, especially the refugee who sat next to me in first grade whose family had fled Vietnam. My buddies and I helped him and his sister learn their first English words before my family moved across town. I have forgotten his name but not his face.

The writing was aided tremendously by my research assistants and interns at the Hoover Institution at Stanford University over the past few years, especially Jessica Gonzalez, Jason Lin, Anya Ku, and Andrew Friedman. Revana Sharfuddin was a superstar during the summer of 2019 when we were launching the research effort together in Hoover's DC office. Sara Browning, an insightful historian, spent a graduate internship doing all of the presidential research for chapters 5 and 6. Zach Rutledge, an econometrics guru, worked with me on the state study. And my longtime friend Aaron Smith, who literally wrote the textbook on econometrics, offered invaluable guidance early on.

The danger in naming professional colleagues is that there are so many who add real value to a book project like this that the author can never fairly identify some without neglecting others. But it would be wrong to leave out thanks for the endless intellectual inspiration I've gotten from Garett Jones, Bryan Caplan, Alex Nowrasteh, Teresa Cardinal Brown, Andrew Selee, Chris DeMuth, Ayaan Hirsi Ali, John Cochrane, David Henderson, Bob Litan, Ulrike Schaede, Charles O'Reilly, Laurie Hodrick, Andrew White, H. R. McMaster, Jim Mattis, Glenn Hubbard, Richard Epstein, Condi Rice, Tom Gilligan, John Taylor, George Shultz, and Eddie Lazear. George and Eddie passed away within weeks of one another, just before the final round of edits were complete. I'm going to miss sharing the published book with them more than words can say.

Danny Heil and Tom Church are Hoover colleagues and have been the best of friends. Both read chapters here before anyone else, and Tom read the entire manuscript a few days after I typed the last word. If any typo remains, Tom found it, but I neglected to fix it. Many friends read chapter drafts and offered suggestions, most recently Steve Payson. Thanks to all.

I have endless thanks for my agent, Jill Marsal. Jill always has time, wisdom, and kindness.

James Cook and David Pervin, my editors at Oxford, were fantastic. David pushed me to give the book the shape it has now, and to bring the stories to life. James had the unenviable task of hacking, revising, and reshaping my dreck into something that even I enjoyed reading. Thank you.

Madelaine Hanson was a tireless help in crafting every one of the chapters, and deserves more thanks than anyone for helping me make this book what it is. Thanks, too, for organizing the talks I gave at Oxford and UCL in the fall of 2019, and to the students who shared the perspectives on America in the world. Madelaine and Ollie Guillou worked with me to edit and produce the new *Why America?* podcast as a companion to the book. Likewise, thanks to Richard Caldwell, who welcomed me to the University of Denver's Scrivner School for a lecture series that served as the backbone of the manuscript.

And most of all, I want to share my deepest thanks to J-P Conte for his support of my research and this book in particular, not only by endowing a fellowship at the Hoover Institution but also by encouraging me wholeheartedly. Both of J-P's parents immigrated to the United States long ago, and I hope this book is worthy as a small legacy to the journey they took.

PART I

LIFE AND DEATH

One century ago, in 1921, as the American colossus was emerging on the world stage, a populist backlash against foreign immigration was reinforced by fears of a global pandemic known as the Spanish flu. The backlash was bipartisan, and "emergency" legislation passed the US Congress overwhelmingly. That decision was strategically myopic, undercutting the source of America's surprisingly sudden strength. Indeed, immigrants and the sons of immigrants filled the ranks of the victorious US Army coming home from Europe after World War I, and it was the sons of immigrants who would fill the ranks in World War II as well. Only during the Cold War era did America's leaders realize that its isolationist immigration laws were harmful.

In 2021, the United States is stronger than ever on the world stage, yet ironically finds itself in a situation that mirrors that of 1921: populism combined with a global pandemic. Even as Joe Biden's Democratic Party takes over the reins of the federal government, limits on foreign travel are more extreme than ever. Whole countries are all but blockaded, and the emergency justification for keeping out potentially diseased foreigners in the Covid-19 era will be hard to overcome. People, even enlightened voters in great democracies, are not very good at measuring short-term gains against long-term costs.

This first of four parts of the book provides an introductory overview in chapter 1 as well as two chapters that explore national security and the nature of threats. Immigration is far more central to the American identity and a cornerstone of its superpower than will ever be appreciated. Even though immigration tends to be at the heart of the nation's origin story of pilgrims, recent media narratives use words like "invasion" and "foreign terrorism" to justify building walls against supposed job thieves from poor countries. The consequences of the September 11, 2001, attacks on the Pentagon and New York's Twin Towers caused the shift in popular narratives in immigration, explored in chapter 2, with an emphasis on the creation of a new "homeland" mentality. The analysis continues in the third chapter's review of national security strategy.

Chapter 1
Oaths

I had always hoped that this land might become a safe and agreeable asylum to the virtuous and persecuted part of mankind, to whatever nation they might belong.

— George Washington[1]

On a dry, summer day long ago, I stood at attention in formation alongside a thousand fellow cadets on the parade field at the United States Air Force Academy and took an oath. We said, in unison, "I do solemnly swear that I will support and defend the Constitution of the United States against all enemies, foreign and domestic; that I will bear true faith and allegiance to the same," words that echo back to 1775 when soldiers in George Washington's Continental Army took such an oath. We do not fight for the soil, or for a ruler, or even for the nation. We fight for the revolutionary idea of democracy in which all human beings are equal and free.

It dawned on me during my cadet days that civilians never take an oath. Nor should they. Citizens in a free country should never be compelled with loyalty oaths, but those among us who volunteer to serve as warriors should pledge themselves to the Constitution, and be indoctrinated about its principles. The irony is that my youthful reflections were wrong, at least in part. There is a group of American civilians required to take an oath. Immigrants.

Foreign-born US citizens must study the Constitution and pass a test that native-born Americans don't face. This is the price of admission for naturalized citizenship, and the oath of allegiance is the final step taken every week by tens of thousands of foreigners from every country on Earth, a celebration of joining the American people.

Weighing fifty pounds and standing four feet, zero inches tall, a refugee from Vietnam named France Hoang took the citizenship oath when he was eight years old in the summer of 1982. It was seven years after his family fled the communist invaders in Saigon where his father had fought along-side the US Army. France wasn't even two years old when he was resettled in Tumwater, Washington. He went on to receive a nomination to West Point, graduate in the top 1 percent of the class of 1995, deploy to Bosnia, fight in Afghanistan, work in the White House as a legal counsel, and start multiple American companies that employ over 1,200 professionals across the fields of law, technology, and aerospace. France Hoang epitomizes the United States' advantages as a nation of immigrants.

France and I met long after we had both left active duty service and became friends long before I learned that he was born abroad. But we share a love of country and a frustration that a fundamental source of America's greatness is being forgotten. I credit France, uniquely, among my friends and family who are foreign-born for compelling me to tell this story. This book is my effort to share a simple insight and make this case to my fellow countrymen: immigrants are the foundation of America's great power in global affairs.

President Ronald Reagan remarked on this exceptionalism during his last full day in the White House: "You can go to live in Germany or Turkey or Japan, but you cannot become a German, a Turk, or a Japanese. But anyone, from any corner of the Earth, can come to live in America and become an American. . . . Other countries may seek to compete with us; but in one vital area, as a beacon of freedom and opportunity that draws the people of the world, no country on Earth comes close. . . . This, I believe, is one of the most important sources of America's greatness. We lead the world because, unique among nations, we draw our people—our strength—from every country and every corner of the world."[2]

Sadly, the debate about immigration is polarized, but it also focuses only on concerns about domestic affairs. My unique perspective is that without its long tradition of robust and diverse immigration, the United States would have a weaker economy, a weaker military, and even weaker innovation. Migrants bring brawn, bravery, and brains to our side of great power competition—a truth that can be seen in America's rise to great power be-fore and during the World Wars, during the Cold War against the Soviets, and in the present era as autocratic regimes in the Middle East and Asia rise. Even more surprisingly, most of the great changes in immigration policy were intertwined with foreign affairs, from the 1920s closed doors following World War I to the 1960s re-opening and diversification as a Cold War strategy.

The founding fathers had very deep insights on the nature of man and the subtle institutions of democracy. I worry often that we natives tend to forget what America is. But immigrants remember. The American ideal is why they strive to come.

Failure Is Forgetting

In the United States, the political debate over immigration has become impossibly mired in partisanship. Both sides are guilty, Republican and Democrat. Politicians are having an increasingly confused debate that mixes illegal and legal immigration while putting impractical symbolism over commonsense pragmatism. Serious legislation is nowhere in sight.

While the debate tends to be about economics as well as culture, most people forget how immigration is fundamentally related to national security—and not just in negative ways. Pundits such as Michelle Malkin are quick to paint a picture of a terrorist "Invasion" but blithely ignore the thousands of immigrants who join the US Army and fight the Jihadis. They forget who Americans are.

The hot debate is hardly original to this era. As Joe Klein wrote in the *New York Times*, "[Nativism] has almost always been a minor chord in American politics."[3] The issue will be debated decades from now, just as it has been every decade since the Revolutionary War. Modern nativists such as Mark Krikorian warn that the extraordinary prosperity of the United States means that mass, unskilled migration is no longer compatible with our economy or our people. Truly unique to this era is that the entire world is going through a technological revolution that is deeper and wider than the innovations that drove the agricultural and industrial revolutions. Sam Huntington, the eminent political scientist, warned in numerous books before his death in 2008 that America itself had changed and was no longer a "settler" country, that its classic ideal of *e pluribus unum* was being supplanted by an internal tribalism. The British economist Paul Collier suggests that globalism has lowered the costs of travel so sharply that this century will likely experience a destabilizing "exodus" of people from the poor South to the rich North, with potentially dire consequences for the institutions that made so many northern countries prosperous in the first place.

These are serious concerns, and we will take them seriously in this book. But shouldn't we begin with an accounting of the proven strength that immigrants contribute before engaging with hypothetical threats?

The first time I was asked to add my voice to the debate was in 2005 when former US attorney general Ed Meese invited me to join a group of conservative scholars at the Heritage Foundation. Our objective was to find common ground. My role was to be the voice of economists, who tend to make up the more libertarian wing of the conservative coalition. At the time, George W. Bush was starting his second term as president, and Heritage wanted to help him craft a comprehensive immigration reform bill.

We failed.

With frustration and bemusement, I have now witnessed firsthand three presidents and many more Congresses try and fail to reform the deeply dysfunctional rules and regulations that are known as the US immigration system.

I can tell you exactly why the effort keeps failing. Frankly, many legislators want reform to fail because unsolved problems are invaluable for election campaigns. It may be cynical to suggest disingenuous politicians pretend to advance legislation by nodding seriously during hearings and asking serious questions while secretly slow-rolling the process and sabotaging complex bills with not-so-innocent amendments, but that's the political game. And anyone who really wants to fix US immigration has to understand the political game in order to win.

Meanwhile, the tone of the immigration debate has grown darker, and not just in the United States. Refugees from Syria's civil war (which displaced around half of the country's population of 22 million people) and Africa (plagued by civil wars, terrorism, corruption, and poverty) started flooding into Europe in 2011, exposing the European Union's (EU) weak borders. The inability of governments throughout the continent to control that surge added to a sense among many Europeans that they were losing control of their own societies, an unease that sparked a revolt by the British people to abandon the surprisingly unstable European Union in a vote known as "Brexit." In the United States, the presidential election of 2016 exposed the immigration debate as increasingly ugly, alarmist, and even paranoid.

Curtailing illegal immigration makes sense. But I've come to worry that the backlash poses a danger because it might easily lead to draconian restrictions on legal migration. That is precisely what happened when the US immigration debate turned ugly and paranoid in the 1920s. At the time of this writing, the US Senate is considering a bill that would slash legal immigration by half, or worse.

If the world's democracies actually turn inward, particularly if Americans become sharply isolationist, I believe a global recession is sure to follow. Worse, the nature of the American identity will change, and over the long term that may well end the country's exceptional role in the world.

Two Facts About American Exceptionalism

President Trump often asked why the United States is "the only country in the world" that has "ridiculous" immigration policies. During a speech in October 2018, he threatened to end birthright citizenship with an executive order even though it is enshrined in the Constitution. He said, incorrectly, that the United States is the only country that recognizes every child born on its soil as a full citizen. Even though most countries in the Western hemisphere have birthright citizenship, Trump was right that America is unique, even exceptional, but not in the way he thought. Two facts about American exceptionalism must be reconciled to understand the immigration issue.

Fact 1: The United States is the richest nation in the world. It also happens to be the richest nation in history. And the word "rich" has many meanings here: money, yes, but more than that. America's powerful economy serves as the foundation of its superpower status and funds its dominant military strength. There are many, many factors that explain economic growth and many, many books about it (including one I co-authored with Glenn Hubbard called *Balance: The Economics of Great Powers from Ancient Rome to Modern America*), but take my word for the time being that there is no debate about American economic dominance at this moment in history.

Fact 2: The United States welcomes more immigrants than any other country, just counting the legal immigrants. One million. Every year. Yet relative to population, the United States is not the most open. European citizens are moving across the open internal borders of the EU, making its nations appear more open. But in absolute numbers of permanent new citizens, and global diversity, no other country comes close. American openness to global immigration mirrors the Great Powers of history, notably ancient Rome and Ottoman Turkey. If only the United Kingdom had opened its citizenship and representation in Parliament to the colonists in North America and its subjects in India, it would be the subject of this book. Alas.

Are these two exceptional features related? I think so. The premise of this book is that they are far more than a coincidence. I argue that being a nation of immigrants is a fundamental cause of extraordinary prosperity and military power for the United States. Not only is immigration central to American identity, but it is also what military strategists call a force multiplier. Unlike others who narrowly look at migration patterns as a demographic or economic question, I make the case that immigration is an essential ingredient in the grand strategy that makes the United States a dominant superpower.

Despite contentious newspaper headlines casting America as cold and indifferent, the reality is that every year, 1 million people born elsewhere are granted permanent legal residency and the right to take the oath as naturalized American citizens. More important, this welcoming policy is based on deep public support for immigration. Opinion polls reveal that Americans support diversity and immigration more than any other country in the world, with 70 percent expressing support for continuing the current level of legal immigration or increasing it. The next few chapters will expand on this history and how the United States developed its current legal openness.

Democratic leaders such as Barack Obama, Bill Clinton, and Lyndon Johnson understood the vitality of immigration for US power, and support for immigration has been even more central to Republican Party leaders from George W. Bush all the way back to Abraham Lincoln. Interestingly, the chief executives consistently rated at the top of presidential greatness rankings were proponents of greater immigration. They recognized that raw power needs the three things that immigrants bring: brawn, bravery, and brains.

George Washington and the other founding fathers who declared independence from Great Britain were motivated not only by trade restrictions and a lack of representation in Parliament but also because the king was restricting migration to the colonies. He feared that they were too popular and growing too quickly. It must be said that the founding fathers fought for unlimited immigration. In the early years of the American government, Congress obsessed over ways to attract more immigrants from Europe because a larger populace was the only guarantee of military strength that could protect the young country.

Let's dig into the first fact, that the economic power of the United States is unmatched. Critics of immigration on the political right and left share an assumption that the United States has become weaker in recent decades. Bernie Sanders, for example, has been mildly hostile to immigration (legal and illegal) his entire career because he and other Labor-leftists believe that migrants take jobs from natives. Meanwhile, Donald Trump and other nativists speak of immigration as an invasion with dire implications for jobs but also culture and safety. Later in the book, I'll explore the impact immigrants have on the economy, but for now, I want to emphasize how wrong the underlying premise of US economic weakness is.

The United States has a stronger economy than any country in the world, by far. Only two other societies can produce on the same scale as the United States as measured by gross domestic product (GDP): China and the European Union. Yet each lags America's total economic output, each does not invent as many technologies, and—most important—each has significantly lower

GDP per person. In the United States, GDP per capita is $59,500. England's is $44,000. Japan's is $43,000. Germany's is $50,000. And China? GDP per person in China is just under $17,000.

America isn't just rich; it is prosperous. The nation's GDP grows as if growth were something easy, but this is a relatively new phenomenon in the scope of recorded history. Economic growth was so rare as to be negligible, even unimaginable, until the industrial age erupted in the early 1800s. Growth emerged from enlightenment institutions of widespread literacy, the scientific method, and free markets, and by the middle of the 19th century, it was clearly measurable and appreciated as a modern wonder. Within a century, the vast internal markets of North America, its universities, and its openness to people yearning to be free from all around the world enabled millions of new homes for even the poorest citizens with marvels of electricity, plumbing, and hot water. The wonders continued as Americans patented their discoveries of television, batteries, air conditioning, even flight. Today, American citizens take all this and more for granted, while foreigners witness relentless technological and cultural surplus: personal computers in the 1980s, the Internet in the 1990s, electric cars, Hollywood movies, YouTube videos, Amazon markets. The US economy is not only thriving but also leading, and it seems everyone knows it but Americans.

Instead, our political system is locked in a cynical debate that assumes things are getting worse and has settled onto the question of whom to blame. Sadly, foreigners make easy scapegoats, especially for imaginary ills.

An anecdote: I was a luncheon speaker to a group of Republican women a few years ago, and my talk on immigration was warmly received. My presentation touted the positive economic effects of migrant workers and entrepreneurs while also admitting the challenges of labor market competition that scholars have documented are real concerns, especially for less-skilled, native-born workers. Most people in the audience liked the talk and some even cheered, but there were a handful of pointed questions during Q&A. Afterward, a meek lady wanted to talk to me privately. She said, "Dr. Kane, I trust you on the economic issues because you're an expert. But what about culture? Don't you worry that these immigrants from Mexico are eroding America's Judeo-Christian culture?" Her question caught me by surprise given her meek, unassuming persona. I leaned in close and whispered, "You know, Ma'am, most immigrants from Mexico are Catholic." And then she smiled and hissed, "Exactly!" She thought we were sharing a moment. I was quiet for that moment, searching for the appropriate thing to say. After a beat, I said, "Perhaps you should know . . . I'm Catholic." Moment: over.

This woman appeared to be the sweet grandmother next door, which reminded me that hate exists in surprising places. Hate is part of the human condition. But I can tell you that as a military officer, I have seen love in unexpected places that is more powerful than that hate. Men and women of every color serving together for a greater cause is something we experience in the military, and I wish every American could have that experience, too. I served alongside Jews, Muslims, and atheists. I served with southern rednecks and foul-mouthed Yankees. I served with people from every imaginable demographic. After I was given a top-secret clearance and assigned to work in military intelligence, I served with more immigrants than most civilians realize. My fellow officers who were foreign-born were very good with languages, a skill that is invaluable in the intelligence community, and they were just as committed to the Constitution as everyone else. Maybe more so.

This Book's Path

In this book, I make my case for the need to preserve robust immigration as the essential ingredient for American exceptionalism. Mine is a national security argument, and I wrote the book primarily as an affirmative case in favor of greater immigration that I hope will persuade my fellow conservatives: the only way to win the great power competition of the 21st century is by embracing America's identity as a nation of immigrants. We will not be able to match a technologically surging China with a demographically declining America. With security in mind, the first part of the book includes chapters that explore the nature of threats, and whether the United States is being "invaded" by immigrants.

The second part of the book is a historical assessment of immigration through the eyes of presidents. I'll also use data to challenge the conventional wisdom that current high levels of migration are unprecedented. There have been four distinct eras of immigration policy in the United States, and only one of them (1924–1965) was restrictive. That era was presaged by laws excluding Asian immigrants that were adopted in the 1880s. This history is retold in nearly every book on immigration, but what you'll find here is a special focus on the presidents who made it. George Washington, Abraham Lincoln, and John F. Kennedy all played key roles in winning the immigration debates of their times, and their messages deserve to be remembered. We will also take an honest look at the border wall between the United States and Mexico, as well as the polarized political wall dividing Republicans from Democrats—both are unique to our era.

Part III is the heart of the book: a three-part narrative reviewing the strategic advantages that immigrants have brought to the United States: brawn, bravery, and brains. First, immigrants add brawn, or raw population and demographic vibrancy. Second, immigrants add bravery, meaning they have been far more likely to volunteer for US military service than the native-born during times of war. For example, the North doesn't win the Civil War without immigrants, and slavery doesn't end. And they don't just serve; the foreign-born serve with distinction, and relative to their proportion of the population, they have won double the number of Medals of Honor as native-born Americans. Third, immigrants add brainpower to the United States. The numbers of patents, Nobel prizes, and startup companies are much higher thanks to immigrants, but those are just the most visible contributions. We must also recognize that the risk-taking nature of migrants, regardless of educational achievement, fits ideally the American culture of entrepreneurship and self-reliance. Simply put, immigrants add entrepreneurial zeal beyond what their raw numbers suggest. They are risk-takers by nature, and everyone benefits from the new companies they create. It is widely known that one of Google's co-founders is an immigrant, but most people are surprised to learn that Steve Jobs, founder of Apple, was half-Syrian. Or that Yahoo!, Intel, and even Levi jeans were founded by immigrants to the United States.

The final part of the book will focus on the two main objections to immigration that we must take seriously: economics and culture. Milton Friedman noted this economic paradox: a welfare state may not be able to survive if it is open to immigrants. More recently, the economist Garett Jones has challenged the feel-good naiveté that all cultural diversity is healthy. Was it healthy for California to turn so sharply from Republican to Democratic dominance at the hands of immigration? Was it healthy when foreign migrants pulled Argentina sharply toward socialism seventy years ago and transformed its economy from the fourth richest in the world into a permanent state of fiscal crisis? I'll challenge the dominant view from the Left that seems to pretend cultural shifts are an illusion—an ironically gymnastic argument from those who claim that cultural diversity is real and should be celebrated and tolerated. Migration does change the political leanings of a voting public, but the hard question is whether this is a threat.

Throughout world history, hostility toward "outsiders" was based on myths and falsehoods. Foreigners are accused of carrying strange diseases and committing crimes (when poor) or exploiting the economy (when rich). Those falsehoods are still echoed today in America's immigration debates. For example, during an August 2017 interview, Stephen Miller, the immigration czar in the Trump White House, claimed repeatedly that people who came to the United States legally with a green card (calling it a "golden ticket") caused "significant reductions in wages for blue-collar workers, massive displacement of African American and Hispanic workers, as well as the displacement of immigrant workers from previous years."[4]

Miller's worldview is rooted in what economists call the lump-of-labor fallacy, which is the idea that there is a fixed amount of work and therefore a fixed amount of labor demand. "Stealing jobs" is easy to believe because the logic is so simple and because labor displacement is real. It happens all the time, mostly when capital equipment displaces human work. Think of tractors replacing farm workers in the 1930s. Disruptive, yes. Harmful, no. Displacement is also caused by outsourcing and the domestic migration of, say, Ohioans to Texas. Displacement is caused by progress. I will take a very close look at this microeconomic question in a stand-alone chapter, but be warned that the local impact of immigration is not as positive as advocates want us to believe. It is neither positive nor neutral, but rather mixed.

Economic and cultural tensions can be resolved with smart, pragmatic policies. But who are we kidding? It's not enough for me, or any policy wonk, to lay out a plan to improve the immigration system and blithely ignore the actual politics playing out in Washington, DC. Immigration, more than any other issue, is caught up in the dysfunctions of modern elections, virtue-signaling, and identity politics. The final chapters of the book take the politics of immigration seriously and lay out a path forward based on a new in-depth survey I conducted for this book on American attitudes toward immigration reform. The results are very promising.

I'll admit that I'm excited to share a perspective on the economics of immigration that is usually ignored—the macro effect. I build on the argument that population growth is a core ingredient in economic and military strength. As I like to say, immigrants put the power in superpower. The raw size of an open economy makes it more efficient, specialized, and productive. This is why the United States and China have an unmatched economic advantage as continental powers, an advantage the nations of Europe tried to mimic in 1992 by creating the European Union with its common currency.

Nativists worry that America is becoming more culturally diverse, with particular attention to the notion of an emerging minority-majority. The term dates back to at least the 1970s when the Supreme Court invoked it as a rationale for establishing legislative districts in which a majority of voters were of a "minority" ethnicity, that is to say, African American districts. Today there are four states where non-Hispanic whites make up less than half of the voters: Texas, New Mexico, Nevada, and California. Indeed, in most major urban areas—Miami, New York, Memphis, San Diego, among others—whites comprise less than half of the population. But there's something amiss in all the celebrations of this new diversity and the breathless commentary about how it will change America. What is white? A monolithic white culture in a United States is a myth, unless white is elastically defined to pretend the tensions between Protestants and Catholics were negligible, or that Jews and Arabs (both "white" in the census) are culturally the same, or that Ben Franklin's famous hostility to swarthy (non-white) Germans is irrelevant.

As the great political analyst and demographer Michael Barone wrote, the United States was "always culturally diverse from its colonial beginnings, and each successive surge of migration has changed the cultural and ethnic and political balance of the country."[5] The very idea of constantly working toward a "more perfect union" in the preamble of the Constitution is that the country isn't perfect and, indeed, has constantly overcome ethnic, religious, racial, and other divisions in pursuit of the expansive ideal of equality for all.

If your family is like mine, you heard stories about intolerance among one grandparent's relatives toward the other. In my case, it was my Irish grandpa when he married my Polish grandma, both families Roman Catholic, yet both suspicious of the other. Diversity politics nowadays centers more on skin color, but the Left's identity obsession is rooted in a myth of whiteness. Racial identity in the United States a hundred or even fifty years ago was shaped far more by ethnicity than color, when religious divisions between the Protestant majority and Catholic and Jewish minorities were the norm. Early census records note "white" citizens, to be sure, but what the present forgets is how eastern and southern Europeans, and all people not "Nordic" were not considered truly white.

Immigration and racial identity politics have been conflated in recent years, which confuses matters more than clarifying them. Whereas most other countries have a unique ethnicity, language, and sometimes religion, the United States has only the common unity of ideas embodied in its founding documents. Japan, France, and Egypt are examples of countries that were distinct cultures long before they were countries. Immigration changes them. America is exceptional in this sense because it changes fundamentally when immigration stops.

Why Is Immigration So Difficult?

Immigration reform is hard because it mixes multiple issues (culture, economics, law, and national security) across multiple sovereignties (international, federal, and local). There is no denying that there are many problems and many kinds of problems with immigration. Conservatives tend to over-emphasize crime and drugs, which are indeed real concerns, while progressives tend to turn a blind eye to human trafficking, welfare abuse, and cultural loss unless it's an outsider's culture. But the ultimate problem is what I call political hijacking.

If you judge this issue by what you see on cable news, the immigration system in the United States is obviously broken. With the relentless shrillness of political coverage, how could you think otherwise? Millions of illegal immigrants stealing jobs. Trump shouting, "Rapists and murderers!" Caravans from Honduras. Migrant children in cages.

Indeed, a reliable trope one hears in discussions about immigration policy is that "we may disagree on the solutions, but we can all agree the U.S. immigration system is broken." I've heard this at a hundred roundtables, congressional hearings, and political speeches. But is it true?

When your car is broken, it doesn't move. When your television is broken, the screen is black. So if the US immigration system is broken, it begs the question: How, exactly? To be sure, terrorism happens far too often, but no terrorist has ever crossed the US border illegally. And there are millions of people living in the United States as illegal aliens, but the debate about what to call them (undocumented immigrants?) is oddly more contentious than the economic harm they supposedly cause. In contrast, the system for legal migration and legal non-immigrant visitors is working with a hidden, uncontroversial smoothness. Thousands of foreigners become US citizens every day, work hard, pay taxes, and integrate remarkably well into American society, far better than the many immigrants who cannot find a way to fit into other nations.

True, US immigration policy can be chaotic and confusing, thanks to numerous laws and regulations that send mixed signals and create perverse incentives. John Kelly, days after leaving his role as chief of staff to President Trump, explained the dilemma that led to a caravan of Hondurans massing along the border in Tijuana, Mexico, at the end of 2018. He said, "One of the reasons why it's so difficult to keep people from coming . . . is a crazy, often-times conflicting series of loopholes in the law in the United States that makes it extremely hard to turn people around and send them home."[6]

Time and again, federal lawmakers have offered amnesty to illegal migrants or their children residing in the country. Who qualifies for each amnesty is complicated and distorted by rumor throughout Latin America, which doesn't help matters. At the same time, policymakers in Washington, DC, erect fencing and hire more border patrol agents to keep migrants out. Then they pass laws penalizing domestic employers of undocumented immigrants, even as states and cities declare themselves sanctuaries and authorize generous welfare benefits to members of this same group. This is a mess of contradictions at odds with one another, yielding an incoherent message that could easily tilt to one extreme or the other in the coming years. Let me be clear: I think open borders are a terrible idea, as is the progressive rallying cry to abolish ICE (Immigration and Customs Enforcement, the federal agency for enforcing immigration). Extreme solutions are often worse than the problems they aim to fix.

I contend that what is broken and wholly dysfunctional are immigration politics and the endless national "conversation" about race in America. Politicians in Congress have perfected the art of wedge issues, using artificial outrage to get booked on cable television. No issue is wedged more by politicians than immigration. Look no further than the longest government shutdown in US history thanks to President Trump's request for $5.7 billion in funding for a border wall in the waning days of 2018. But the shutdown fight of 2018–2019 was less about immigration policy than about the increasing inability of US politicians and institutions to reach compromise.

I actually planned to downplay the US-Mexico border wall in this book, but current events during the writing demand otherwise. Experts will tell you that the Great Wall of America is an almost entirely symbolic, political spat that is much less important than visa overstays, E-Verify (a federal work identity verification system), or the alphabet soup of work visas, among others. But President Trump's fight with incoming Speaker of the House Nancy Pelosi in early 2019 is a microcosm of how the politics of immigration broke down.

Robert M. Gates, who served as secretary of defense to President George W. Bush and President Barack Obama, put equal blame on Republicans and Democrats for the shutdown, noting, "For too long hyperpartisanship has prevented the American government from addressing the immigration problem."[7] He's right, but Gates then called for a big, bipartisan, comprehensive bill modeled on the 2006 effort. That simply won't work for structural reasons that I'll explain later in the book. Gates has the best intentions, but the political dilemma cannot be wished away.

I am going to challenge you to think hard about what is causing hyperpartisanship. And what's a deep-thinking strategy to overcome it?

Let's recognize that politicians thrive on conflict and have stuck themselves in an all-or-nothing legislative quagmire they call "comprehensive immigration reform." I've come to appreciate that politicians and the immigration quagmire are like pigs and mud. The only difference is that pigs don't create their own quagmires, whereas the immigration mess is good for riling up voters on both sides. After repeated, drama-filled failures at comprehensive legislation during both the Bush and Obama presidencies, how about a new approach?

I'm going to make the case for Congress to go small. More elegantly, let's call this the incremental strategy. To break through the virtue-signaling and insincere bargaining, Congress should be forced to vote on the smallest immigration bill that deals with an issue of overwhelming public consensus. This is the no-brainer step.

But which sub-issue? There's the wall. There's the issue of refugee children in cages. There's the paradox of thousands of brilliant foreign engineers at US universities who are barred from working in the United States after graduation. Another tangential issue in the era of Covid-19 is the dilemma of 181 million annual "non-immigrants." How should the United States update its visa system that controls foreign visitors—tourists, students, and business travelers? Then there's the controversial lottery visa for 50,000 green cards every year—perhaps those visas should be turned into a merit-based system.

The extremes in the Democratic and Republican Parties will pull every trick to stop any reform—preserving their wedge politics—but they will be immediately isolated on the fringes if step one is a success. So the challenge is actually to identify a sub-issue with widespread support.

This isn't hard if we keep faith with the bedrock principle of self-government: the people know what they want. I've seen dozens of opinion polls that could not be clearer. I've even conducted my own public polling which is, if you'll forgive the phrase, comprehensive.

I will review these polls later in the book, but here's the key: the American people don't want open borders or mass deportations. They want robust legal migration and an end to illegal immigration. They want to welcome migrants coming to America to work as fellow citizens but not to take welfare or vote as non-citizens. I intend to expose the immigration consensus hiding in plain sight.

Incremental step two is to pass a *second* small bill through Congress, this time targeting a more controversial sub-issue. Maybe border security and E-verify? Again, it doesn't matter what the exact immigration issue is. It's the process that needs strengthening. Once that second bill becomes law, there will be a true bipartisan working coalition in Congress, and the fringes will be isolated for good.

Incremental step three is to reform the legal immigration system. The United States needs to think carefully about the composition of green card recipients. Many experts think the country should distribute green cards using some kind of merit-basis rather than the current emphasis on family reunification, but that may be too hasty. As the renowned economist Eddie

Lazear says, "Family reunification is a worthy goal, not only for humanitarian reasons but because people in intact families perform better in society."[8] In the national security context, assimilation is the priority, and there are many ways to enhance immigration that should be considered.

Ultimately, we need an immigration system that preserves American exceptionalism well into the 22nd century. The future challenges of immigration will be unprecedented. For instance, international transportation costs have already plummeted, making migration cheaper than ever. Yet demographics are shifting even faster, as populations begin to stabilize in developing countries and decline in advanced countries. What happens when societies face a global labor shortage? What happens as economies continue to converge? Can the United States maintain its leadership?

I am hopeful. The smart answers are obvious, and the American people actually get it. I just worry that democracy in this new era of instant social networks and outrage manipulation is growing weaker.

America's exceptional openness to immigrants is the key feature, not a flaw, in its role as the dominant superpower of the century. It is also the feature that distinguishes the United States from all other great powers in history. If Americans lose touch with that identity, they will see their nation's military and economic power fade. In the end, I don't know whether the popular consensus will win out over partisan extremes. What I do know is that immigration is the issue that will test American democracy and determine whether the nation's exceptionalism will persevere.

Chapter 2
Threats

Battle not with monsters, lest ye become a monster.

— **Friedrich Nietzsche**

Sixty police officers and 343 firefighters were killed during the terrorist attacks on September 11, 2001, when the twin towers collapsed in New York City. One of them was a man who had served on both forces, the New York Police Department and the Fire Department of New York, but on that morning he was in the South Tower as a firefighter with his Brooklyn-based ladder company 132. The 33-year-old man's story is a poignant one: born on the Fourth of July, engaged to be married, he was a US citizen who had immigrated from Argentina as a young boy. His name was Sergio Villanueva.

The irony of Villanueva's heroic status as police officer, firefighter, and naturalized US citizen is that the intersection of immigration and national security is normally understood as a singular concern: terrorism. This way of thinking has been reinforced in the United States in recent years, partly due to the bombastic 2016 campaign and subsequent presidency of Donald Trump. But it's mainly due to the very real rise in Islamic terrorism, including the Boston Marathon bombing in 2013, the coordinated suicide bombings and shootings in Paris in November 2015, the cargo truck rampage that killed eighty-six pedestrians in Nice during the summer of 2016, and three different automobile and knifing rampages in London during the spring of 2017. The sense of "immigration as a threat to security" is increasingly echoed in countries all around the world, according to a 2013 study by Julia Tallmeister. It's important to remember that hostility to immigration is a constant thread in human history, but that framing immigrants as a violent threat is relatively unique to our time.

After learning that the 9/11 attacks were perpetrated by nineteen young men from the Middle East, the response of many Americans and their representatives in Congress was that there should be much tighter limits on immigration. A 2002 study by Caroline R. Nagel found that "immigration control from the outset became a cornerstone of the 'war on terrorism,' closely linked in public discourse and policy to America's efforts to protect itself against an array of shadowy menaces."[1]

President George W. Bush made every effort to calm nativist fears. Six days after 9/11, Bush visited the Islamic Center of Washington where he gave what is known as the "Islam is peace" speech, emphasizing that those American Muslims surrounding him were "friends" and "taxpaying citizens." He read from the Quran. He said, "The face of terror is not the true faith of Islam. That's not what Islam is all about. Islam is peace."[2] While President Bush acted sagely in abating racial tensions, the rising fear of terrorism was inevitable in the immediate aftermath of 9/11 – and an overreaction. Yet anti-immigrant sentiments faded rather quickly. Ten years after 9/11, an overview of immigration attitudes by Joshua Woods confirmed the stabilization:

> [T]he percentage of Americans who believed that "immigration should be decreased" rose from 41 percent in June 2001 to 58 percent in October 2001. . . . The percentage of Americans who thought that "immigration is a bad thing for this country" increased from 31 percent in June 2001 to 42 percent in October of the same year. Both indicators remained above the pre-9/11 level until June 2006, after which both fell below this level.[3]

An intensive intelligence effort in the United States quickly pinned responsibility for the attacks on al-Qaeda's mysterious leader, Osama bin Laden, based in Afghanistan. The British government confirmed the analysis and offered its full support. Within a month, the United States launched an invasion alongside forces from the United Kingdom as well as local warlords.

Although the anti-immigrant public attitudes were temporary, the policy changes inspired by 9/11 were permanent. The public made a distinction between terrorists versus immigrants, but federal institutions had already shifted. In 2001, as US Army Rangers were bearing down on Taliban forces, a new Office of Homeland Security was formed in the White House.[4] That was an ominous name in a country that historically considered itself a nation of immigrants from all corners of the Earth rather than an ethnic homeland.

What followed was the largest reorganization of the executive branch in more than half a century. It began in October of 2001 when the PATRIOT Act was passed by a 99–1 vote in the US Senate, enabling the Immigration and Naturalization Service (INS) and the State Department to better screen visa applicants. Then, as Marc Rosenblum recounts, "Following a series of congressional hearings in 2002 that highlighted critical failures in the government's intelligence, foreign policy, and law enforcement performance, Congress passed the Homeland Security Act of 2002. It brought together some or all of 22 federal agencies into a new Cabinet agency, the Department of Homeland Security (DHS). The agencies included the US Immigration and Naturalization Service (INS)."

This move literally and symbolically placed immigration enforcement under a national security umbrella instead of its traditional locus under domestic policy. A half dozen additional laws were passed in 2002, 2003, and 2004 that enabled much faster and more thorough data sharing, entry-exit tracking, and collection of biometrics on tourists and other visitors. In 2006, Congress passed the Secure Fence Act, funding 700 miles of fencing along the southern border with Mexico. Despite their many efforts to espouse positive themes about immigrants, the presidencies of George W. Bush, Barack Obama, and Donald Trump have been largely defined by cementing the intersection of immigration and insecurity.

As I write, the United States maintains troops throughout the Middle East. Relentless conflict has caused a global refugee crisis, particularly due to civil wars in Libya, Syria, and Yemen. The presence of US military troops is a convenient scapegoat for the regional turmoil, even though the abrupt withdrawal of forces from Iraq in 2011 by President Obama made the turmoil worse. Regardless, it all adds to a perceived link between immigration and insecurity. Refugees from Syria and Africa have flooded into Western Europe in the past decade, raising alarms about cultural loss and rising incidents of Islamic terrorism, notably in Paris and London.

Thinking of immigration as a security threat is mostly wrong, and definitely too narrow. Specifically, immigration and terrorism are incorrectly linked. For example, in the United States, foreign-born terrorists are exceedingly rare and almost never immigrants. In fact, none of the 9/11 terrorists were immigrants. True, they were born overseas and visiting America, but they came as part of the annual flow of tens of millions of tourists, students, and businessmen. Not immigrants. Think of it this way: if you were a foreigner intent on committing a terror attack in the States, would you endure the arduous and uncertain application to become a citizen? Would you hazard the journey through the dangerous gang-controlled Mexican desert and try to cross the border illegally over a barbed-wire wall patrolled by US and Mexican agents? No, you wouldn't. You would come as a tourist to Disney World.

Contrary to what you have been told, immigrants such as Sergio Villanueva are essential to strengthening US national security. In the simplest calculus, the United States military has relied on foreign-born citizens since the Revolutionary War. They serve in disproportionately higher numbers than native-born citizens and win disproportionately more medals for valor. The diversity of the US Army allows it to be far more effective when fighting abroad—whether in Nazi Germany or the mountains of Afghanistan. But the dimensions of immigration enhancing US power go far beyond filling the ranks.

Consider again the 9/11 attacks. Nearly 3,000 people were victims, including 246 innocents on board the four hijacked planes, over 2,600 people in New York, and 125 at the Pentagon. What's too often forgotten is that 372 foreign citizens were among the victims, not counting the 19 terrorists, representing 12 percent of the total. As Secretary of State Condoleezza Rice remarked during a fifth anniversary remembrance at the State Department, "Among the many innocent victims of September 11th were hundreds of citizens from over 90 countries" including Egypt, Israel, Vietnam, and even China. Yet among the 2,400 American citizens, how many were immigrants?

I was able to confirm that dozens of the people who died in the World Trade Center were first-generation immigrants who were making contributions to American society, just like Sergio Villanueva. There was Chin Sun Wells, born in South Korea in 1976 who played basketball and softball as an Oklahoma high schooler while working at the local Walmart before enlisting in the US Army in 1998. There was Sergeant First Class Jose Calderon-Olmedo from Puerto Rico, in his twentieth year on active duty in the army, a man who had served multiple tours of duty overseas. There was Dong Chul Lee, an immigrant from South Korea who came to the United States in 1968 to study computer science, later working for the National Security Agency for fourteen years after a stint in the US Air Force. There was Amgen scientist Dora Marie Menchaca, researching medicines to treat cancer and pneumonia, a wife and mother, killed at the age of 45 on her way home. Dora scribbled a note that was recovered from American Airlines Flight 77 that crashed into the Pentagon: "Dear Earl, I love you. Please take care of Imani and Jaryd for me. Dora. 9/11/01 7:15 AM PST (I think)." She was born in Mexico and raised in Texas.

Immigrants did not attack America on 9/11. Rather, they were attacked. This is contrary to conventional wisdom, but worth remembering as we think about the different security threats facing the United States.

Dangerous Outsiders?

The Covid-19 pandemic showed the difficulty of assessing risk under uncertainty. Every day during 2020, Americans were told that the novel coronavirus was killing thousands of people, as mainstream news sources reported the rolling death count. Somewhere around 400,000 Americans died because of Covid-19 during the year, yet lost in the sensationalism was any sense of context. Ten times that number die in a typical year in the United States from all causes. There were an estimated 3,358,814 deaths in the United States in 2020, up from 2,854,838 in 2019. Some, not all, of those half million excess deaths were caused by Covid-19. Lockdowns were an excessive response with costs that exceeded benefits in terms of economic damage, mental health, and educational setbacks for poorer children. The 2020 lockdowns have resulted in "a 3.0% increase in mortality rate and a 0.5% drop in life expectancy over the next 15 years for the overall American population," according to the first in-depth analysis published by the National Bureau of Economic Research (NBER). The debate will rage for years, and I do not mean to resolve it here. The point is that threats to society are very difficult to assess, calmly or otherwise.

When it comes to immigration, people instinctively perceive threats first and foremost in terms of potential, not likelihood. They worry immigrants will take jobs, commit crimes, and corrode the culture. The threat of increased criminal activity is an old trope that has haunted immigrants for centuries, far beyond this era and this country. But the lack of criminality among American immigrants in recent decades—brought to light through the miracle of modern social science data—helps dispel instinctive fears. A review of the academic literature by the American Immigration Council found that "immigrants are less likely to commit serious crimes or be behind bars than the native-born, and high rates of immigration are associated with lower rates of violent crime and property crime."[5] For example, half as many young immigrant males are incarcerated than young native-born males. This isn't just a compositional issue. If you consider only young males ages 19–39 with low levels of education, natives are three or four times more likely to be in jail.

To be fair, there are many questions about the burdens of immigrants. Three of the more famous scholars known to be immigration skeptics I consider friends, and I believe their hopes for a stronger America are sincere. George Borjas is a Harvard professor whose research shows some negative consequences of recent, low-skill immigration to the United States; he's also a former professor of mine, a gentleman, and an immigrant himself. It's wrong of anyone to think of this issue as black and white. Likewise, I've broken bread with Mark Krikorian, an affable midwesterner who leads a think tank in Washington that raises important concerns about low-skill immigration into a United States that has changed radically over the past 100 years into a high-skill country. Reihan Salam is another think tank friend who was recently recruited to lead the Manhattan Institute, surely because his thoughtful writings about the challenges of assimilation vex naïve commitments to open borders. These men are arguing in good faith, arguing against extremism for the most part, and the threats they describe to the economy, cultural identity, and constitutional values cannot be dismissed lightly. While I plan to address those threats in forthcoming chapters, my main emphasis throughout the book is on national security.

Unlike those scholars, too many politicians use overheated rhetoric about immigrants. Congressman Tom Tancredo made his name in politics in the early 2000s with apocalyptic warnings about immigrants, calling for a moratorium on legal immigration and an end to high-skilled temporary workers. Congressman Tom McClintock claimed in a 2017 speech on the floor of the House of Representatives that "illegal aliens murdered 1,800 Americans," an explosive claim with no basis in fact.[6] Sadly, the mischaracterization of new immigrants is a constant in American history, whether from Ireland or Mexico or Iraq, and it is directly related to the way human brains perceive risk and, in particular, threats from people they think of as alien.

The Nature of Threats

"Which is more likely to kill you this year," Colonel Bill Casebeer asks, "a terrorist attack or a bee sting?"

When Casebeer, a cognitive scientist and Air Force veteran, talks to audiences about designing terrorist screening models for the US government, he often begins with a riddle. He is tall and folksy, the son of a poor Oklahoma farming family who became a celebrated philosopher and director of numerous neuroscience labs. Casebeer won countless trophies as captain of the Air Force Academy debate team during the 1990s, so he knows how to command a room when speaking in public.

Most people think terrorists are far deadlier than bees. Don't you? Yet if we limit ourselves to foreign-born terrorists, there have been just over 3,000 fatalities since 1975, which amounts to far fewer than 100 in an average year.[7] And if we exclude the 9/11 attacks, there have been only fifty-eight total fatalities since 1975, which amounts to fewer than two deaths per year. Bee stings, on the other hand, kill around sixty people per year. Bees are far deadlier than sharks, alligators, and dogs combined.[8]

A similar argument about the misperceived threat perception of terrorism was made by Conor Friedersdorf in a controversial 2013 *Atlantic* essay. He wrote, "Irrational cowardice is getting the better of our polity" by making Americans surrender civil liberties not for security, but for a *sense* of security. He compared the roughly 3,000 fatalities from terrorism over a twelve-year period that included 9/11 to preventable deaths due to gun violence (360,000) and drunk driving (150,000).[9] Friedersdorf didn't mention the top killers—heart disease (647,000 fatalities per year) and cancer (599,000)—which aren't comparable because they aren't caused by humans. He did, however, make the mistake of citing a *Reason* magazine article by Ronald Bailey that flippantly compares the 1 in 20 million odds of being killed by a terrorist to the 1 in 800,000 odds of drowning in a bathtub. This bathtub argument was used routinely by Nicholas Kristof, a *New York Times* columnist who penned an entire column in 2016 about President Obama, who "frequently suggests to his staff that fear of terrorism is overblown, with Americans more likely to die from falls in tubs than from attacks by terrorists."

Critics call this the bathtub fallacy. Bathtubs serve a useful purpose, and humans rationally weigh the risks against the utility. The same innate calculus allows us to utilize cars, airplanes, and butcher knives. Terrorism has no utility.

In 2017, two members of Obama's National Security Council—Jennie Easterly and Joshua Geltzer—explained why democracies are right to devote so many resources to preventing terrorism even though it kills fewer Americans than bathtubs. Unlike other crimes without utility, terrorism causes irrational fear that leads people to enter into irrational wars. And worse, terrorism can destabilize whole regions. They wrote that allowing ISIS to emerge in Iraq and Syria "has changed the direction of much of the Middle East for at least a generation, setting back development in large swaths of territory, altering alliances throughout the region, and producing thousands of children raised to embrace barbaric violence and intolerant extremism."[10]

Bloomberg columnist Jeffrey Goldberg, in a 2013 article, offered a similar critique of the bathtub fallacy. He explained that the fear of terrorism is not motivated "solely by what terrorists have done, but what terrorists hope to do." Leaders of al-Qaeda were explicit in their goal of killing many millions of Americans, Europeans, and Israelis, ideally with nuclear, biological, or chemical weapons. The libertarian columnist Megan McArdle agreed, pointing that deterrence is the key element that differentiates terrorism from accidents. Just because nuclear terrorism hasn't happened yet is a flawed rationale for ignoring it until it happens. Jihadists have an intent to kill at a scale far beyond bees and bathtubs, and they would do so unless defensive measures were taken. Surely, Covid-19 requires us to update our pre-2020 threat perceptions, as the threat of bioterrorism is now more understandable as well as more likely.

This all matters for immigration because the categorization of people as potential terrorists, no matter how unlikely at the individual level, muddies the psychological instinct to perceive utility. Applying the framework of cost-benefit analysis (CBA) to various fatality threats, the rational side of our brains can quantify the positive utility of risky things. Bees pollinate. Guns deter crime. Open fires warm homes. Even heart disease overlaps with fine dining, right?

Friedersdorf and Kristof hardly neglected those points. But the trade-offs in rights and treasure are not the only costs to eradicating terrorism. One academic analysis questioned the benefits as well, concluding that it is unlikely that "much terrorism has been deterred by security measures."[11]

What if countering terrorism too aggressively creates more animosity, alienation, and ultimately terrorism? Kristof's larger message is not that the United States should ignore Jihadism but that the bathtub fallacy is a rhetorical trick. He wants Americans to think less about bathtubs and more about climate change and other subtle, longer-range threats. "Unfortunately, our brains are not well adapted to most of the biggest threats we actually face in the 21st century," he concludes.

And this is where Dr. Casebeer commands our attention again. "Perhaps the biggest problem with the way our brains work is something known as recall bias," he says. "Evolutionary responses to immediate threats like snakes and violent humans in the next tribe are natural, but that alone doesn't explain the deep impact of modern terrorism as opposed to, say, terror attacks fifty years ago." The mind tends to focus on things it has seen or heard most recently, he says, images that are easiest to recall. And modern media are distorting the social fabric when it plays and replays high-quality violent video imagery. Today, unlike any previous era, people see ubiquitous gory images after every terror attack. They see pictures of angry, young men of Middle Eastern descent, and they make the link. Terrorists = Immigrants (Table 2.1).

The Covid-19 pandemic put death in the headlines like never before. For most of 2020, the daily conversation centered on Covid-19 death tallies and made obscure medical terms such as "infection fatality rate" and "R0" common lingo. In contrast, media coverage given to the most fatal conditions is slight, close to nil. An analysis of death reporting by Owen Shen and a team of scholars shows how skewed coverage can be. They analyzed three public media: Google searches during 2004–2006, the UK's *Guardian* newspaper during 1999–2016,

Table 2.1 Deaths in the United States, 2017

Cause	Number
All causes	2,813,503
Heart disease	647,457
Cancer (i.e., malignant neoplasms)	599,108
Accidents, poisoning	64,795
Accidents, motor vehicle	40,231
Accidents, falls	36,338
Alzheimer's disease	121,404
Diabetes	83,564
Liver disease, alcoholic	22,264
Homicide, firearm	14,452
Homicide, terrorism	95
Homicide, firearm, school shootings	43

Sources: National Vital Statistics Summary, Centers for Disease Control, the Global Terrorism Database, and the *New York Times.*

and the *New York Times* article database from 1999 to 2016.[12] Relative to thirteen types of fatalities in Centers for Disease Control (CDC) data, terrorism was the focus of 6 percent of the Google searches, 30 percent of the *Guardian* articles, and 31 percent of the *Times* coverage. Heart disease, despite being the cause of 30 percent of deaths, got 2 percent of the media attention. The authors concluded, "Kidney disease and heart disease are both about 10 times underrepresented in the news, while homicide is about 31 times overrepresented, and terrorism is a whopping 3,900 times overrepresented."

We can imagine a mathematical model of actual threats as a function of potential threats and an array of actions. For example, an alligator bite is a potential threat when you swim across a river, but actions such as riding in a boat and crossing during daytime will lower the actual threat. In a democracy, we need a larger threat model because policymaking is shaped not just by actual threats but by perceived threats. The mathematical model of perceived threats is a function of potential threats, the array of actions taken, and two other variables: visibility and time. As Bill Casebeer and Owen Shen might tell us, more visible and recent threats will be much larger in this perceived threat model.

One of the interesting discussions the dual models raise is that some actions may do a great deal to reduce threat perceptions but nothing to lower the real risk. This may seem harmless, perhaps even necessary. If a countermeasure makes the public feel more secure, why not do it? The answer is that some actions are counterproductive.

How many hours do we stand in line at airports, for example? The head of the Transportation Security Administration (TSA) testified to Congress that "ninety percent of the traveling public is waiting 30 minutes or less."[13] Thirty minutes doesn't seem like much until you multiply it by 700 million passengers each year. Do the math and that equals 350 million hours, or the equivalent of 501 lifetimes.[14] It's an exaggeration to say that the TSA is killing 501 American lives but not an exaggeration to say it wastes exactly that much lifetime. That's a tremendous sacrifice, all because of a basic misunderstanding of risk.[15]

A study by economists Adrianna Rossiter and Martin Dressner calculated that increased wait times nudge people to drive their cars instead of fly, which tends to be more dangerous.[16] Factoring in the small increase in highway fatalities, Rossiter and Dressner calculated that ten extra minutes of airport screening wait time along with additional security fees leads to "an additional 66.2 lives lost per year due to the diversion."

Cornell economists Garrick Blalock, Vrinda Kadiyali, and Daniel H. Simon found a much higher substitution effect[17] leading to over 2,000 driving deaths in the first few years after 9/11—something Nate Silver memorably described as the equivalent of "four fully loaded Boeing 737s crashing each year." However, Blalock's team also concluded that the effect was mostly a psychological response that weakened over time and had dissipated a few years after 9/11. The substitution effect waned, but wait times did not. Wait times at airports have increased for two decades, leading to the persistent cost of what we can conservatively and confidently say is 100 traffic fatalities every year.

There are other costs to enhanced security, but the ones that relate to immigration are most easily seen with the reduction of foreign tourism and student visitors to the United States. As frustrating as post-9/11 airport security is to American citizens, the frustration of foreign travelers is far worse. "The openness of [the US] higher-education system has traditionally generated enormous good will around the world," said Josh Taylor, head of global programs for New York University.[18] Foreign student travel has gone through ups and downs since 9/11, and Taylor confirmed the crackdown during the Trump administration denied admission to many potential students even though they had been accepted by US colleges. Academic studies confirm that "international student migration to the U.S. dropped after the 9/11 attacks when it became the focus of anti-terrorism and immigration reform."[19]

Twenty years ago, roughly one in four foreign students was studying at US universities, but after the tightened security measures were put in place, that fell by 50 percent. Even though the world market for university education has doubled and more foreign students are in the United States than ever in absolute terms, the losses are severe. If the trajectory pre-9/11 had continued, there would be 2 million foreigners getting their education in America instead of 1 million. That's a loss of 1 million young adults learning our values and making friends, not to mention putting billions of dollars into the US economy every month. The Trump administration made it harder, slowing down visa approvals and creating uncertainty that drove promising young men and women away. The pandemic of 2020 made it even worse.

Let's recognize that the probability of airline terrorism in the form of hijacking dropped to essentially zero on the day after the 9/11 attacks. There have been almost no hijackings since that terrible day. Cockpit protocol for pilots and crew to surrender the airplane changed dramatically after September 11, and the new protocol is to never allow passengers into the cockpit for any reason. The protocol isn't merely to protect passengers; it is to eliminate the ability of terrorists to use a heavily fueled airliner as a weapon. Cockpit doors were hardened, airport screenings tightened, in-flight procedures were revised to limit loitering, and more. As a result, there have been zero hijackings in the United States since 2001 and very few internationally. According to the Aviation Safety Network, an average of only two to three airplanes have been hijacked globally since 2001, but these include diversions to different airports due to bombing threats that were conveyed to the pilots, not a surrender of control of the aircraft (Figure 2.1).[20]

As Georgetown professor Daniel Byman likes to remind his students, "In the late 1960s and early 1970s, there was an average of more than one airplane hijacking per week globally, and those two decades saw hundreds of bombings in the United States" by domestic terrorists.[21] The operating assumption pre-9/11 was that airplane hijackers wanted a spectacle and a free flight to Havana. That possibility disappeared after cockpits were hardened, post-9/11. Hijackings are no more, regardless of TSA screenings, yet the TSA screenings continue. Why? You might say that they stop bombings from happening in airports, but bombers could just as effectively stage attacks—with greater visibility—outside of airports, or inside of train stations, or at shopping malls. So, why?

The answer in part is due to what critic Bruce Schneier famously called security theater, the practice of investing in countermeasures intended to enhance the *feeling* of improved security rather than actual security. Even TSA officials at the highest levels use the term when discussing which practices are inefficient, such as the ban on cigarette lighters. The passenger screening process creates an illusion of safety that can only be justified in terms of crowd safety, not airline safety. That logic quickly becomes circular because there are

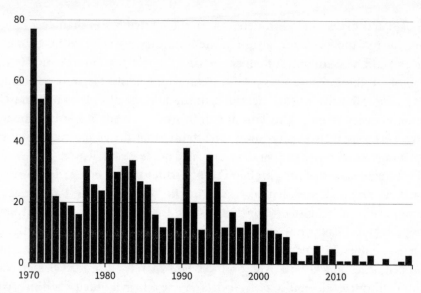

Figure 2.1 Number of airplane hijackings worldwide. Data from Aviation Safety Network.

larger crowds at shopping malls, schools, and amusement parks than there are at airports.

The lesson is not that the federal government should stop trying to prevent terrorism. Rather, the government should focus its efforts, pulling back on wasteful spending on TSA and perhaps reducing the attention given to small-scale acts of terror. The media may want to replay scenes of a deadly car rampage for hours, but that's no excuse for politicians to follow the herd. Commenting on low-scale violence is the opposite of what leadership in a democracy is about.

Professor Byman points out that the fears of terrorist escalation during the years after 9/11 to include "chemical, biological, and radiological attacks, have not materialized." The persistence of small-scale terrorism such as car rampages, knifings, and lone-wolf shootings continue, but those all but prove the point about escalation. The goal of eradicating terrorism comes with real trade-offs. Some of the actions in the model discussed above—actions that lower perceived threats but do nothing to lower actual threats—have major negative costs.

Accepting Kristof's argument about the need to balance near-term and long-term threats, accepting McArdle's insight that we should focus on threats we can pragmatically do something about, and finally accepting Casebeer's argument that our brains will be distracted by media attention, what do we get?

Increasingly, the Pentagon's strategic thinkers are reaching consensus that America's greatest potential threat is China, not terrorism, and certainly not immigration. China is the most populous nation on Earth and also has a fast-growing economy. And it is guided by increasingly aggressive and hostile authoritarianism in Beijing.

With an economy that has grown larger than the United States' in purchasing-power-parity terms, the ideological threat Beijing represents is perhaps more dangerous than the physical threat of outright conflict. Chinese communism isn't really communism at all; rather, it's a wholly original mix of centrally managed capitalism, hard-hearted authoritarianism, and a vast array of Orwellian technologism. I worry that the Sino-American Cold War will cause Washington policymakers to fall into a Nietzschean trap ("Battle not with monsters, lest ye become a monster"). Can senators and congressmen keep faith with the constitutional principles, values, and economic institutions that fueled their nation's rise to global dominance? It's not so hard to imagine a policy set that excludes entry of tens of thousands of foreign-born engineering students in the act of blocking a handful of phantom spies and terrorists, or a TSA-like agency that screens all workers and students for paperwork authorizing who is allowed to work for which companies.

Truth be told, we already see security theater in immigration policy that is far out of proportion to any potential threat from immigration. Building a wall? Cutting the number of refugees admitted by 90 percent? Limiting the number of foreign-born computer scientists? As just one example, the Covid-19 pandemic was used to justify completely shutting down foreign visitors for months on end—millions of citizens from allied countries with lower infection rates than any state in the United States—while allowing unfettered domestic travel. It makes no sense. Yet it worked as a thinly veiled justification for isolationism that will haunt the Biden administration's goal of reasserting America's global leadership.

The trillion-dollar question is this: what role does immigration play in this existential conflict between Washington and Beijing? What role does it play in the evolutionary tension between America's constitutional roots and the lure of protectionism? Far from being a threat, immigration is the key to victory in the great power conflict of this century—economically, technologically, militarily, and even culturally. The United States could use a million more Sergio Villanuevas.

Immigration, let us remember, is what built up the United States as something exceptionally different from every other nation. As for the moral of the story told by Colonel Casebeer, it turns out that Alzheimer's disease has a far greater chance of killing you than terrorism, gun homicides, bathtubs, and bees combined. It's a sad but perfect metaphor for the real threat to US national security: forgetting who we are.

Chapter 3
Invasions

A simple way to take the measure of a country is to look at how many want in and how many want out.

— Tony Blair

During the summer of 2018, when 100,000 immigrants per month were surrendering themselves to American custody at the southern border, US officials were overwhelmed. The threat of an immigrant invasion seemed very real to American viewers watching their televisions. A few politicians in Washington played word games and denied it was a "crisis" but the situation became impossible to ignore when rioting migrants outside San Diego were met with tear gas. Nobody could deny that a mob of foreigners was attempting to force its way into the country.[1] This was a clear threat to the United States.

Or was it?

Over 5,000 migrants from Central America had joined a caravan during the weeks prior to Thanksgiving. They choked roadways while marching north through Mexico. Video footage showed many throwing stones at Mexican police and breaking through roadblocks. Local officials struggled to care for the throng of families and young men, particularly at the border town of Tijuana.

Broadcast images of the caravan's journey were followed intensely by the American people, giving weight to the perception that the government was losing control. Pete Hegseth, a co-host for a FOX News morning show, reflected what many Americans were thinking when he said the caravan "looks a lot more like an invasion than anything else."[2] This echoed Trump's mid-October description of the situation as "the assault on our country."[3]

When the mob of migrants rushed the fence on Thanksgiving weekend, families across America agreed the scene was disturbing, but these families were often divided about the reason. Some condemned the use of tear gas on women and children, calling it a chemical weapon whose use was the equivalent of a war crime. Others saw the same scene and expressed dismay at the lawless, violent assault on border agents.

Homeland Security Secretary Kirstjen Nielsen defended the use of tear gas, saying that some of the migrants "sought to harm [border patrol] personnel by throwing projectiles at them." President Trump was so upset about the assaults that he ordered the border shut to all traffic, including motor vehicles and economic trade. Within days, Mexican officials responded by sending their own federal troops to help. They kept a close watch on the Tijuana camps, preventing large groups from assembling.

President Trump framed the border situation as a threat to national security. His rhetoric on that point was consistent and unequivocal, describing illegal immigration as an existential threat to the nation. "We have no country if we have no border," Trump often declared, a line that was a constant during his 2016 campaign and in the final presidential debate with Hillary Clinton.

Thousands of poor, largely illiterate, Central Americans did not strike most US citizens as likely terrorists. Lawless in the loosest sense of the term, but not killers. Rather, the crisis seemed more humanitarian- than security-related. Yet there's something disconcerting about the idea of mobs assaulting the border. What if thousands become millions? Does the utilitarian calculus change then?

Trump, Trumpism, and Immigration

As president, Donald Trump spoke about immigration incessantly, took executive actions to make entry harder, and slashed refugee admissions by nearly 90 percent. Yet his administration also proposed a merit-based legislative reform that kept legal immigration levels very high. Many of Trump's executive actions will be overturned easily by the Biden administration, but the new president will be unable or unwilling to undo all of his predecessor's constraints. In the weeks before his inauguration, Joe Biden warned that "guardrails" were needed: "The last thing we need is to say we're going to stop immediately the, you know, the access to asylum the way it's being run now and end up with 2 million people on our border."[4]

The single term of Trump's presidency was an anomaly in some ways, but his rhetoric will cast a long shadow over immigration policy during the Biden presidency and beyond. What the real estate tycoon gave voice to had been bubbling up in public attitudes for years. And there should be no doubt that the border crisis will only deepen when Joe Biden sits in the White House because the thicket of policies and pressures were worsening long before 2020, indeed long before 2016. The Obama administration failed to cut through that thicket and, like the Trump administration, simply managed the problem. Caging unaccompanied immigrant children caught crossing the border into a makeshift warehouse in Arizona with chain-link walls was initiated in 2014. Taunting Biden during one of their 2020 presidential debates, Trump asked incessantly, "Who built the cages, Joe? Who built the cages?"

One key to understanding this era is this: there is no Trumpism, only Trump. By that, I mean to say there is no great ideological depth or lasting principles that will be credited to the forty-fifth president. His economic policy was a jumbled mixture of corporate tax cuts, profligate spending, regulatory libertarianism, and monetary activism that borders on bank bullying. Likewise, foreign policy had little consistency from 2016 to 2020, despite the efforts of Secretary of State Mike Pompeo and a parade of national security advisers and Pentagon bosses. Trump lurched outward and inward with troop deployments and foreign engagement. The one exception, the one consistent instinct of Donald Trump, was his outspoken skepticism of the "new world order" promulgated by President George H. W. Bush, that is, globalism. Trump was a nationalist, not an internationalist.

Trump's isolationist campaign rhetoric in 2015 struck a nerve. A handful of gruesome events involving immigration were leveraged to great success. The first occurred on July 1, 2015, when a young American woman named Kate Steinle was killed while walking in San Francisco with her father. Her death came from a random bullet that ricocheted off the ground, fired by an illegal immigrant. The man, authorities later admitted, had been deported multiple times without consequence. Just days before, Trump had declared his candidacy in New York City, warning about Mexican immigrants who were rapists and murderers. Here was blood, and who could mock it? Steinle's killing made it impossible to ignore Trump, who seized on the issue and never let go.

On December 2, 2015, the media were consumed by terrorism at a company Christmas party in San Bernardino, California, where a Muslim American husband and wife murdered fourteen people. In response, Trump called for "a total and complete shutdown of Muslims entering the United States until our country's representatives can figure out what the hell is going on. We have no choice. We have no choice. We have no choice."[5]

In June 2016, almost exactly one year after Steinle's death, a man named Omar Mateen gunned down forty-nine people at the Pulse nightclub in Orlando, Florida. The attack riveted the nation's attention for weeks and gave candidate Trump newfound fuel for the immigrant-terror nexus. He had secured the GOP nomination months earlier but had been trailing Hillary Clinton in the polls. Then, after the Orlando shooting, he was able to grab the headlines again. On June 12, he tweeted, "Appreciate the congrats for being right on radical Islamic terrorism, I don't want congrats, I want toughness & vigilance."[6] During a prepared speech one day later, Trump expressed some very kind sentiments toward the lesbian, gay, bisexual, and transgender (LGBT) community targeted by Mateen, but continued his strident hostility to immigration:

> The killer, whose name I will not use, or ever say, was born, of Afghan parents, who immigrated to the United States. His father published support for the Afghan Taliban, a regime which murders those who don't share its radical views, and they murdered plenty. The father even said he was running for president of Afghanistan. The bottom line is that the only reason the killer was in America in the first place, was because we allowed his family to come here.[7]

Alex Nowrasteh shakes his head whenever I talk to him about Trump. Alex is a longtime friend and fellow advocate for greater immigration. For years, he spent his energy emphasizing the economic benefits immigrants bring, but he shifted gears when Donald Trump gathered so much support in the Republican Party. "It's all about crime and terrorism," he told me over lunch a few years ago. "Trump was right about that. Too bad he was wrong about who is really the threat."

After painstakingly gathering data on every terrorist incident since 1975, Nowrasteh issued a major report in mid-2019. Although the threat of foreign-born terrorism isn't zero, the data show that native-born terrorists are much more common. He found that there were 192 foreign-born terrorists who planned, attempted, or carried out attacks on US soil from 1975 to 2017, compared to 788 native-born terrorists. Nowrasteh then calculated that after 9/11, "the chance of being murdered by a native-born terrorist was 4.3 times as great as being murdered by a foreign-born terrorist."

Let's remember that the 9/11 attackers such as Mohammed Atta were foreign-born terrorists, but they were not immigrants. Once Nowrasteh sorted out terrorism by visa status, the threat of actual immigrants was negligible. Only seventeen deaths had occurred at the hands of legal immigrants, and zero at the hands of illegal immigrants.

You might think that Nowrasteh's numbers fudge the identity of second-generation immigrants who were born in the United States but never assimilated—people like Omar Mateen. On the contrary, the data on the 788 native-born US terrorists since 1975 show that only 14 percent of them were Islamists, whereas 24 percent were right wingers, 22 percent were white-supremacists, 16 percent were left wingers, and the remainder were aligned with other fringe causes.

The most in-depth examination of the link between international terrorism and immigration was published in a 2016 scholarly paper that examined 145 countries between the years 1970 and 2000. The authors distinguished permanent migrants from foreign visitors and refugees which led to a surprising conclusion: "Our arguments and empirical analyses support the Migration Inflow hypothesis that immigrants are an important vehicle for the diffusion of terrorism from one country to another."[8] However, the conclusion had two distinct parts. First, immigration is a vector for terrorism because people coming from a terror-prone state such as Syria, Afghanistan, and Peru are more likely to be exposed to and willing to engage in terrorism. Second, however the overall level of immigration in a country is not positively correlated with terrorism. On the contrary, "migration as such—independent from or not weighted by the terror level in the country of origin—actually leads to a decrease in the number of terrorist attacks by 0.5%–0.6% when the number of migrants coming into a country is raised by 10%."[9] Let that sink in: more immigration is linked to less terrorism in receiving countries.

Nevertheless, once he had the broad administrative powers of the presidency on his side, Trump was able to bolster the rhetoric with official studies and fact sheets linking immigration to crime and terrorism. On January 16, 2018, the White House published a fact sheet titled "Our Current Immigration System Jeopardizes American Security."[10] It blamed immigration for international terrorism incidents in the United States, faulting the current system of diversity-lottery visas and family-based legal immigration. It claimed that "approximately three out of every four individuals convicted of international terrorism-related charges between September 11, 2001 and December 31, 2016 are foreign-born individuals who entered the United States through our immigration system." Notice the caveat "international" in front of the word terrorism—subtle yet still misleading. Not only did the fact sheet exclude domestic terrorism, but it also twisted the facts further by including foreigners who were extradited to the United States to face trial, but never executed attacks on American soil. More misleading was that many of the crimes counted as "terrorism related" in the fact sheet were minor, including petty theft and one instance of transporting boxes of breakfast cereal across state lines without a permit.

Two weeks later, on February 1, 2018, the White House issued a second fact sheet aimed at exposing the immigration-security threat. It was titled "National Security Threats—Chain Migration and the Visa Lottery System," but unlike its predecessor, it made no effort to put the anecdotes in context other than repeating the debunked claim from before. Instead, it said that the American system of legal immigration that favored family reunification was "incompatible with preserving our national security," followed by a list of fifteen individuals convicted of terrorism-related crimes. The fact sheet suggested that having relatives in the United States made these immigrants less likely to assimilate to American culture. This is an odd claim, especially without evidence, because common sense suggests that an immigrant with no friends or family in a host country is more likely to become alienated. No matter, the White House was attempting to spur legislation in Congress.

This Time is Different

For decades, Congress had been wrestling with an immigration compromise, and the latest version of that struggle in early 2018 had wisely eschewed a broad comprehensive approach in favor of a narrow bill that would accomplish two vital reforms: fund the border wall with $25 billion and also grant legal status to the Dreamers, children who had immigrated illegally into the United States with their parents in the recent past. Lindsey Graham, a Republican senator who was close to President Trump, urged him to back the legislation, but he was unable to overcome the hardliners in the West Wing, notably Stephen Miller. Trump announced that he would veto any legislation that continued family-based legal migration, which he pejoratively called "chain migration" and blamed for terrorism.

Negotiating over reform was overwhelmed in subsequent weeks by a renewed surge of migrants at the Mexican border that grew larger as the winter cold gave way to the spring of 2018 and what eventually became the year of the caravan "invasion." Unlike the long-standing pattern of irregular migration at the southern border involving single male workers from Mexico who attempted to enter illegally (that is, without being caught by US authorities), the 2018 migrants were from the poorest countries in Central America, such as Honduras, El Salvador, and Guatemala, as shown in Figure 3.1. Another difference was that the irregular immigrants tended to travel as families with small children, as shown in Figure 3.2. This shift is one of the least appreciated changes to immigration inside the stagnant political debate in America, and so it's worth emphasis. Apprehensions of Mexican citizens averaged over 1 million per year before 2008 but dropped to an average below a quarter of a million after 2011. Simultaneously, apprehensions of non-Mexicans attempting to cross the southern border rose dramatically from near zero in 2012. That was the year that the Obama DACA policy was initiated.

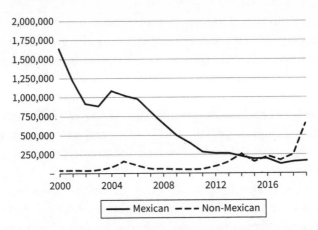

Figure 3.1 Apprehensions by nationality at the US southern border, FY 2000–2018. Data from US Customs and Border Protection.

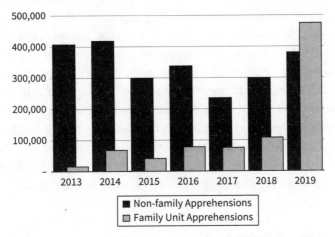

Figure 3.2 Total apprehensions at the US southern border, FY 2013–2019. Data from US Customs and Border Protection.

Unlike the Mexican men of the 1990s and 2000s, this new group of Central American families was not trying to cross illegally into the United States but was instead turning themselves over to American customs officials at the first opportunity, asking for asylum. And instead of attempting to sneak across the border in small packs, they assembled in large caravans. During the past decade, annual apprehensions by the Border Patrol floated between 300,000 and 500,000 before spiking to 851,000 in FY 2019. Yet during that time frame, family units rose as a percentage of the total from just 4 percent in 2013 to 56 percent in 2019.

So what? Families seeking asylum are clearly less a threat than young men. The problem is that the American public is allergic to lawlessness, and the rising chaos at the southern border is likely to lead to a populist backlash against legal immigrants, not just asylum fraud and illegal immigration. Chaos enhances the political campaigns of populist candidates.

An immigration backlash happened once before in US history, a century ago to be exact. Congress passed restrictive immigration laws in 1921, tightening them further in 1924. That backlash led to thirty years of isolationism against immigration of all kinds.

There's another reason to dislike the caravans: chaos at the border is harmful to the migrants themselves. The revenues from smuggling humans across the US-Mexico border are an estimated $5 billion annually, with prices ranging from $4,000 to $12,000 per head in the Americas. The costs are much higher for overseas migrants.[11] People are selling their hopes of a better life to a ruthless network of human traffickers. US Immigration and Customs Enforcement (ICE) arrests over 1,000 human traffickers per year.[12] Unfortunately, politicized news reports have exploited the deaths of the rare individuals detained after crossing the border, such as an NBC analysis in early 2019 that "22 immigrants died in ICE detention centers during the past 2 years." The reality is that every detainee death is due to extremely ill migrants who were sickened en route, and those numbers pale next to routine fatalities during the journey.[13] Every year, somewhere between 250 and 450 migrants die while trying to cross the US-Mexico border illegally, usually from heat exhaustion and often from drowning in the Rio Grande.[14] We cannot blame the migrants for wanting a better life, but some responsibility must be assigned to the perverse incentives in US policy.

Are they really refugees?

Over the decades, the strict definition of a refugee as "persecuted for reasons of race, religion, nationality, membership of a particular social group or political opinion" morphed into a generic sense of sympathy for people fleeing their home country for other reasons—gang violence, domestic violence, climate violence, even simple poverty. When it comes to the immigration courts, however, most refugee applicants are rejected because the definition of refugee plainly does not apply to economic migrants. This leads naturally to asylum fraud.

During the Obama presidency, federal authorities cracked down on so-called asylum mills that coached foreigners on how to fraudulently obtain official asylum recognition. Their clients used boilerplate language about persecution and invented fictional stories to memorize for interviews and hearings. More than thirty lawyers and translators in New York were rounded up and prosecuted for helping thousands of fraudulent but successful applicants.[15] Similarly, coyotes—people who smuggle immigrants across the US-Mexican border—coach their trafficked customers on what to say when they make contact with the US border patrol: "I have a credible fear of persecution." The sad reality is that abuse of asylum sympathies has swamped immigration systems worldwide and led to calls for a major overhaul by no less than Ayaan Hirsi Ali, a former refugee from Somalia who faces death threats from Jihadi terrorists and is now a famous feminist intellectual residing in the United States. The "distinction between a migrant and a refugee has blurred to such an extent that it is no longer useful," Ali says.[16]

This was a strange crisis for the United States because on the one hand, the caravan migrants aligned with the archetype of "huddled masses yearning to breathe free," but on the other hand, they presented a baffling question. Why not take refuge in places closer to home? Why not take refuge in Mexico, a relatively safe country and much wealthier than Honduras?

One can be pro-immigration and skeptical of the 2018 caravans claiming asylum. And one should wonder, why was there a surge in 2018? There are conspiracy theorists in both political parties who speculate that the caravans were secretly organized in order to foment a crisis at the US border. Some say violence and poverty in Central America have surged, pushing up the supply of refugees. While violence and poverty are high relative to the United States, both factors have been on the decline across Central America. GDP per capita has grown in every country in the region for nearly a decade, and homicides peaked back in 2012. As an example, the GDP of Honduras was $15 billion in 2009 and $25 billion in 2019. Likewise, the World Bank's database shows that the homicide rate in Honduras did spike above 83 homicides per 100,000 people in 2001 and 2012, but collapsed quickly afterward. These "push" factors simply do not explain the sudden surge of outmigration. You have to look at "pull" factors.

Mexican gangs that profit from human trafficking advertised that America had become newly open to immigrants claiming asylum, so long as they traveled with children. The Obama White House issued an "executive action" called Deferred Action for Childhood Arrivals (DACA) in June 2012 that granted a temporary legal status without citizenship to individuals who had been brought to the United States as children by their parents. While DACA applied to an estimated 800,000, it did not apply to newcomers. But try telling that to illiterate Central American mothers who hear that America is giving amnesty to children. The special status for children was enshrined by a judicial ruling known as the Flores Settlement, which says that minors cannot be detained for more than two weeks by US immigration authorities. That means an adult seeking asylum can be held indefinitely while their asylum case is being considered, but that same adult will be released to live freely inside the country if and only if they arrive with a child in their care. Flores was intended to protect children who were already settled, not new arrivals, but the interpretation was broadened as circumstances changed. When a surge of people claiming to be refugees from Honduras first began to arrive after Obama's DACA action, his team in the White House wasn't ready. They tried to plug the hole, ultimately appealing in 2015 to carve out an exception for Flores for new arrivals, but the courts said no. Coyotes began to advertise and traffic more impoverished Central Americans. The hole became a floodgate. There were 54,000 apprehensions of non-Mexican illegal aliens by the border patrol in 2011, which doubled in 2012 and rose to 257,000 in 2014. Obama's DACA action led to an accelerating flow of superficial refugees in 2018.

President Trump ordered 4,000 National Guard troops to the border in April 2018, a far bolder move than any other modern president had taken. A public opinion poll by POLITICO/Morning Consult found the move was overwhelmingly popular among Republicans and also supported by one out of five Democrats.[17] Trump's dilemma wasn't political; it was legal. The use of military troops for domestic enforcement is arguably a violation of the 1878 Posse Comitatus Act, which forbids US military enforcement of domestic law on US soil, even if that soil is a borderline.[18] Many White House advisers were agitating for a strong hand, but just as many were opposed. A compromise was reached, using National Guard rather than active duty troops and limiting their activities so they had zero interaction with the immigrants.

It didn't work. The numbers of asylum seekers grew throughout the summer of 2018, as did illegal crossings. There was simply no place to house the tens of thousands asking for asylum, and the media were relentlessly describing the situation as children in cages, unsanitary conditions, and outright abuse. And so, in late October, the president authorized active duty forces for border support missions.

That didn't work, either. With frustrations boiling over as the asylum crisis deepened in early 2019, administration hawks pushed for tougher rules of engagement and mounted a whispering campaign in the White House against the Secretary of Homeland Security, Kirstjen Nielsen. According to a *Newsweek* report, "Nielsen's alleged refusal to submit an additional request for more U.S. troops" led to her forced resignation on April 7, 2019. She was reported to routinely say, "Mr. President, I would love to, but it's illegal to do so," according to *Newsweek*'s source.[19] Days later, Trump ordered an additional 3,000 army soldiers and marines to the border, with weapons.

Strategy-Free Zone

The former secretary of defense, Jim Mattis, likes to joke that "the United States can always be relied upon to do the right thing—having first exhausted all possible alternatives," a wisecrack apocryphally attributed to Winston Churchill, the revered British prime minister during World War II. Mattis is revered as well, a battle-hardened Marine Corps general. He commanded troops in combat at the battalion level, regimental level, and brigade level before his promotion to lead US Central Command (CENTCOM) from 2010 to 2013, overseeing US forces in Iraq, Afghanistan, and elsewhere in the Middle East.

Mattis was known as the "warrior monk" with killer instincts and a massive personal library of classic writings. Beloved on Capitol Hill for his nonpartisan patriotism and blunt wit, he routinely joked that coordinating warfare with officials in Washington, DC, was often a challenge because "the nation's capital is a strategy-free zone." For example, Mattis foresaw that President Obama's non-response to Syrian dictator Assad's use of chemical weapons in the face of his red line warning was "the shot not heard around the world"—a flare of American indecisiveness. In his recent autobiography, *Call Sign Chaos*, he reflected on his time leading CENTCOM. "America's lack of strategy in setting priorities that would earn their trust resulted in a growing sense that we were proving unreliable. This would cause a series of challenges for me in the Middle East and would later concern me on a global scale." Uncomfortable with the general's blunt perspective, President Obama essentially cut Mattis's career short in 2013. America's loss was to my great fortune, as I had the pleasure of working with "Jim" as a colleague at the Hoover Institution where he refused to let me or anyone else call him by his military rank after retirement.

As a man devoted to principles over politics, Mattis did not expect an invitation to meet privately with president-elect Donald Trump. He found himself suddenly appointed secretary of defense, completely surprised but never unprepared. According to subsequent interviews, Mattis was determined to make strategic thinking central to his time leading the Pentagon.

Eleven months after the president's inauguration, shortly before Christmas 2017, the Trump administration published the fifty-six-page unclassified summary of the National Security Strategy of the United States of America (referred to as the NSS), the first written strategy published in many years. Described as "the keystone document" from the president and his National Security Council, it was a whole-of-government product. Thousands of man hours from top officials went into crafting the NSS, weaving together inputs from multiple agencies and departments, but its godfather was Mattis. At a stroke of the president's pen, senior government leaders from ambassadors in foreign capitals to admirals in the middle of the ocean had clear guidance about threats to and key objectives of the United States. It is that specificity that helps our own investigation into the way immigration policy should be understood in foreign affairs.

Most foreign policy analysts were impressed by the clarity and audacity of the NSS. Terrorism is no longer defined as an existential threat but rather a persistent condition in the 21st century. Indeed, the importance of terrorism is best understood by its location in the NSS, which is far behind the opening emphasis on the pillars of American strengths in economics and technology, the competitive world defined principally by "China and Russia," and the long-term need to provide peace through strength that includes nurturing alliances.

What's original and valuable is the inclusion of the blatantly economic concern with promoting US prosperity. Even though the NSS doesn't offer a coherent model of prosperity, it does stab at a few policies that are related, such as "fair and reciprocal" international trade and the vital importance of technological progress. Models of economic growth are easy enough to find, given the handful of textbooks on the topic from Chad Jones's introductory textbook (now in its second edition) to Oded Galor's more advanced treatment, which references the hundreds of papers published in the *Journal of Economic Growth* that Galor edits. Almost every economist would agree that a basic model of growth would define a nation's total output as a function of five things: capital, labor, human capital, technology, and the optimal mix of institutions. Naturally, that last item is a topic of ongoing disagreement and debate, but there's more consensus than outsiders might appreciate between Larry Summers (dean of Democratic economists) and Glenn Hubbard (dean of Republican economists) about the basics—property rights, contract law, progressive and stable taxes that lean more on consumption than saving, stable money, and so on.

The irony is that immigration is mentioned explicitly in the NSS more than a dozen times in relation to the first theme (the homeland), almost always under the shadow of border security and terrorism, while its link to the other three themes is ignored. This is ironic because increased immigration, as I'll show in the next three chapters, will increase economic prosperity (theme 2) in numerous ways while clearly also advancing US influence in the world (theme 4). The impact is obvious, isn't it? As just one of a hundred examples, who thinks having millions of thriving Vietnamese Americans instead of zero makes the United States less influential in Asia?

As the NSS was being developed, a companion effort was under way inside the Department of Defense; published a few months later, it was creatively titled the National Defense Strategy (NDS). In this document, the de-emphasis of terrorism is even sharper. There are fourteen paragraphs in the first section of the NDS, and terrorism is not mentioned until paragraph 12, which concludes, "Terrorism remains a persistent condition." What's in paragraphs 1–5?

- Paragraph 1: ". . . re-emergence of long-term, strategic competition between nations."
- Paragraph 2: "It is increasingly clear that China and Russia want to shape a world consistent with their authoritarian model."
- Paragraph 3: "China is leveraging . . ." and "As China continues its economic and military ascendance , , ,"
- Paragraph 4: "Russia seeks . . . to discredit and subvert democratic processes."
- Paragraph 5: "China and Russia are now undermining the international order from within."

I found myself reassured by the NDS, not because it gave greater emphasis to pragmatism over idealism (or vice versa) but because it was unequivocal in its emphasis on long-term thinking over short-term reactions. Terrorism abets short-termism, and the NDS puts it in its place. Jihadism isn't going anywhere, for no other reason but that rogue states Iran and North Korea will sustain it, but the NDS keeps that perspective as well.

What impressed me most, as an economist, is the tenth paragraph. It warns of "rapid technological progress and the changing character of war" naming advanced computing, robotics, artificial intelligence, biotechnology, and others. This is exactly right. Maybe the NDS writers read Chad Jones and Oded Galor after all.

In contrast, the NSS veers into tactical policy recommendations on an array of immigration and then technological competitiveness issues that don't add up. It zigs and zags. Aside from boilerplate about a secure border being essential for sovereignty, the NSS makes a wise distinction between the "contributions" of legal immigration versus the "burdens" of illegal immigration.[20] A zig. But then it zags with an overblown statement that the current system of immigration laws is "contrary to our national interest and national security."

Nobody has made a systemic analysis of the *security* impact of reforming immigration laws nor the composition of immigrants welcomed. Prioritizing family migration is current US policy, unlike any other country. What's the security impact? Nobody knows, but there's one obvious upside. Immigrants to the United States tend to assimilate well and express high levels of patriotism. Isn't assimilation the essence of a melting pot that unifies a diverse people? If you had to choose between two potential immigrants—a poor refugee from communist Cuba with a large family network in Miami or a chemical engineer from Pakistan that knows nobody in Chicago—who do you think would be a safer bet and "contribute" more in the long run? Research shows that engineers are much more likely to join violent Islamist movements—fourteen times more likely—than the typical adult male. Alienation is the main reason for the disparity according to scholars Diego Gambetta and Steffen Hertog's book, *Engineers of Jihad*.[21]

As for technological progress, the NSS mentions a handful of times how important it is for the United States to maintain its innovative edge. Unfortunately, it never makes the connection to the private sector, never says "entrepreneurship" or seems to acknowledge that patents are almost universally filed by people outside the government. Instead, almost comically, the NSS says that the government should do a better job of streamlining hiring in order to bring tech-savvy employees onto the federal payroll. That's fine, but it's not in any economic model of economic growth. I'd prefer to tip my hat to the strategic aspect of the NSS technology pillar rather than the ill-informed tactical stabs; the strategy is right and moreover it lends itself to policies that promote education and the all-important race for brainpower emerging in the 95 percent of the world's population born outside of the United States.

Although two decades have passed since the 9/11 attacks, and although the nation has been engaged in lengthy armed conflicts against jihadism in Afghanistan, Iraq, Libya, Syria, and throughout the world, the American people and government have been impressively resilient and even-keeled in their worldview. Hostility toward Muslims spiked in the first few months after the twin towers fell, but that abated. Worries about immigrants as terrorists heated up but never became a panic. Instead, there is a long-standing worry that the end of history where democracy and liberty are secure from ideological competition has not been reached yet, and further, that state-on-state violence remains the primary threat to the United States.

Despite minor flaws, the National Security Strategy published in 2017 and the National Defense Strategy published in 2018 mark a wise return to careful thinking about long-term security threats, namely, their emphasis on great power competition. China, unlike any other potential threat, is an entity with the capacity and willingness to rival and existentially harm the United States. That is the context that should guide strategic thinking on all policy matters, including immigration.

When I think about immigration policy from a security perspective, I actually don't put much weight on terrorism any more. I know better—and hopefully now you do as well. There's no there there. But I do worry about two things. The first is economic growth. The second is culture. In a world where great power competition is founded on economic power, the real threat over the next century to the United States is an economic one. Will the US economy continue to grow fast, to lead the world, to innovate? Let's ask those questions when we think of cost-benefit analysis on the scale and composition of immigration. As for the second threat, I truly believe America's great power also rests on a foundation of civic culture: constitutionalism, federalism, democracy, and rights. I wonder if immigrants—sometimes which ones—will enhance rather than weaken our precious culture, but my instinct is that the poorest "huddled masses" seeking refuge from foreign authoritarians might be the best bet of all.

PART II

PEOPLE AND TRIBE

The United States is a New World country of one-third of a billion people—which isn't all that large relative to a global population of 8 billion people. Unlike the other nations on the planet, the United States was founded on the exceptional principle that "all men are created equal." This section of five chapters presents a history of America as a nation of immigrants who are forever overcoming tribal attachments and instincts of the Old World. It's a story told many times in many places, though the lazy shortcuts of memory have forgotten too much of this history. The origin story of America, for example, is remembered as a yearning by Pilgrims for religious freedom. That much is true, but clipped from the narrative is that the Mayflower Compact was written not at the behest of Pilgrims but their hired hands who demanded a voice in the governance of their new home. The demand for equality, not freedom, forced pen to founding paper.

Consequently, chapter 4 is an admittedly revisionist look at America's immigrant origins, rooted in data about the source and scale of migration over all these centuries. It is followed by two chapters that explore immigration history from a foreign policy perspective. Chapter 5 advances a thesis that presidents were the decisive agents in immigration policy, and those presidents with the most pro-immigration approach are now rated highest in presidential greatness studies. Chapter 6 then provides a straightforward account of presidential policymaking era by era. Only one of those eras, 1924–1965, can be categorized as isolationist. That puts the modern era of openness in context, not as an aberration but a return to principle. America could have been much stronger today if that era of isolationism had been avoided, and it would be weaker if it not for the Kennedy-Johnson reform.

Many people have observed the irony of the free world's goal of "tearing down" the Berlin Wall at the end of the 20th century in contrast with the bipartisan construction of a new wall along the border with Mexico in the 21st century. How did politics turn so abruptly after 1989? Chapter 7 answers this question with a retrospective on wall-building in history. I close with a none-too-subtle observation that the wall that vexes modern America is political rather than physical. The politics of immigration is haunted by hyperpartisanship in Washington, DC, a poisonous development that is not rooted in attitudes of the American people.

Chapter 4
Origins

The happy and powerful do not go into exile, and there are no surer
guarantees of equality among men than poverty and misfortune.

— **Alexis de Tocqueville**

Leaning over the table, the elderly man's hand shook as he bent to add his name
to those signatures clustered at the bottom of the page. It was a hot summer
day in Philadelphia. The year was 1776. "My hand trembles but my heart does
not," Stephen Hopkins said proudly. The other men in the chamber, elected
members of the Continental Congress now in rebellion against England,
laughed and cheered.

The one thing Hopkins has in common with the other fifty-five signers
of the Declaration of Independence was that they were all descendants of
immigrants. Hopkins was unique in that he shared a name, if not a direct
lineage, to another famous American who signed the first founding document: the Mayflower Compact.

One hundred fifty-six years before, another man named Stephen Hopkins
landed at Plymouth Rock with the Pilgrims as one of their hired guides. Born
near England's southern coast, this Hopkins was the only *Mayflower* passenger who had previously visited the New World. Back in 1609, on a voyage to
Jamestown, Virginia, the ship he served on was blown off course and wrecked on
a Caribbean island. The passengers and crew survived for ten months on turtles,
birds, and wild pigs before building a small boat that brought them, finally, to
Jamestown. There, they found the colony destitute but not yet destroyed. Years
later, Hopkins was able to return to England, filled with the same rebellious determination for freedom that would drive many of those fleeing persecution.
His experience attracted the interest of a new group of explorers.

The *Mayflower* voyage that launched from England in 1620 had 102
passengers. A third were Puritan Separatists seeking to create a new society,

whom we know today as the Pilgrims; the remainder were hired hands called Strangers. Stephen Hopkins was a Stranger, and he agreed to travel on a contract to return to the Virginia coast where he would aid the Pilgrims in establishing a new home. He even agreed to bring his wife and three children.

Precisely because he *wasn't* one of the leaders of the colony, Hopkins is the man the world can thank for the existence of the Mayflower Compact. Why him? Simply put, he was the first American rebel. In fact, his rebellious attitude during those arduous six months as a castaway in the Caribbean had led to a charge of mutiny and a sentence of death, which he narrowly escaped.

When the *Mayflower*, buffeted by storms on the Atlantic, arrived far north of its target, Hopkins and other Strangers grumbled about the bitter cold of Massachusetts. The northern winds raced around the ship, and already the rations were running low. They argued that their contracts were no longer within the jurisdiction of the charter granted in England and threatened to abandon the mission when they set foot on shore. To stave off desertions by such rebellious thinkers, or perhaps a mutiny, Pilgrim leader William Bradford called together all the male colonists, as well as two indentured servants, to create and sign a new legal contract. Historians describe the 200-word Compact as "one of the most important contributions ever made to the civic thought of the world"[1] and the aboriginal constitution for liberal democracy. It was signed on board the *Mayflower* on November 21, 1620. Hopkins joined the first party ashore on the next day.

The Compact bound everyone to "covenant and combine ourselves together into a civil Body Politick" and thereby "do enact, constitute, and frame, such just and equal Laws, Ordinances, Acts, Constitutions, and Officers, from time to time, as shall be thought most meet and convenient for the general Good of the Colony." Its purpose was as clear as its brevity: the American system was established in a precedent of self-government, of obedience to law for the general welfare rather than to individual authority.

Like the Declaration of Independence, the Mayflower Compact establishes a precedent for what it meant and means to be American—membership in a society organized on the basis of common rights where people were allowed to live under laws that "delivered a fatal blow to class distinctions" in the words of Frederick Alphonso Noble's definitive 1907 history.

They Meant No Harm

After a month of exploring, the Pilgrims chose the site of their new colony and brought the passengers ashore onto Plymouth Rock. Hopkins took part in all the excursions around Cape Cod while others set to work on building the camp. The Plymouth colony was being built on what seemed to be an abandoned village, and initial explorations along Cape Cod had generated rare, fleeting encounters with native Indians. The first encounter was a surprise sighting of a half-dozen terrified Native Americans who ran away into the woods.

Four months later, as winter was finally breaking, a dark-skinned man wearing nothing but a leather belt with fringe that hung loosely about his waist strolled into the colony. He approached Hopkins boldly and greeted him in English, offering his name as Samoset and extending his hand in a formal greeting. The village stared at the unlikely rendezvous unfolding before them. Slowly developing confidence that the strange man meant them no harm, Hopkins and the colonists led Samoset to the shady area beneath a tree and began questioning him. Samoset explained that the grounds had four years before been filled with the Patuxet tribe, nearly 2,000 strong, all but one dead from a strange epidemic plague. As evening approached, Samoset agreed to stay in Hopkins' home, though his overnight presence was for many in the colony "a nerve-shaking business."[2]

A rose-tinted interpretation would frame Stephen Hopkins's welcome of Samoset as a willingness to accept others regardless of race or background and a desire to live with all people as equals. What is wholly forgotten is that Hopkins's attitude was framed by his experience in Jamestown, a failed colony in which the English had abused local natives, damaged essential links for resources and food in an unknown landscape, and made enemies. What Samoset found were not proud Englishmen seeking treasure but refugees. Half of the Plymouth colony had died that winter.

Samoset returned to the village a week later, on March 22. He was accompanied by another Indian who spoke fluent English. The man was named Squanto, and he was the last surviving Patuxet. Indeed, Squanto had survived only because he had been enslaved by English traders a decade before and even taken to Europe. With Squanto as interpreter, the leaders of Plymouth quickly signed a treaty and negotiated a trade agreement with the local sachem (chief) Massasoit and the Wampanoag Confederation. According to historian Glenn Swygart, Squanto lived with the Pilgrims for the remainder of his life:

"From the first day, he tied his life and fortunes to those of the English settlers. He taught them the basic survival skills needed to be successful in New England. He told them when and how to plant. The settlers followed his instructions, planting when the leaves on the trees were the size of squirrel's ears, putting several seeds in a small hill, and including a fish for fertilizer. Squanto even taught the women how to cook the corn. Squanto helped the men build warmer houses and taught them to hunt and fish."[3]

When President Abraham Lincoln proclaimed Thanksgiving as a holiday in 1863, it was to commemorate the successful first harvest of the Pilgrims in 1621, a harvest made rich thanks to the kindness and peace offered by the Native Americans.[4] What is commemorated as the first Thanksgiving feast was organized by the surviving fifty colonists who were joined by the Indians' "greatest king Massasoit, with some ninety men, whom for three days we entertained and feasted," according to a letter written decades later by one of the Pilgrims named Edward Winslow.[5]

Despite the many critiques of imperial conquest, the origin story of American culture was long celebrated as one of refugee emigration, as the newcomers were fleeing oppression in the Old World for freedom in the New. To be sure, the decimation of the Patuxet tribe by disease opened the land to colonists. The revisionist view of the past, however, is keen to ignore the inevitability of European migration to the Americas, a continuation of the constant flux and movement of peoples for all of recorded history and indeed prehistory. What makes the American story unique is not violence and injustice—those are human constants throughout every millennia of our existence—but the birth of a new culture based on ethnic and ideological tolerance and diversity. I find it fascinating that the culture of wide migration was already present among the natives in North America. Samoset, for example, was from Maine. Indeed, there were thousands of diverse native cultures across North America, and hundreds of different tribes in New England alone, ranging in type from complex feudal agricultural communities to small hunter-gatherer nomadic groups. The patterns of tolerance among them, sometimes violent, but generally not, are a central thread in the institutions that developed in the United States.

Local tribes in Massachusetts were generally governed by a single "sachem" or chief. These men associated with one another through a confederation under the light touch of a grand sachem. This kind of organization seems entirely natural, what we might expect from basic principles of self-organization that Francis Fukuyama traces in his masterpiece, *Political Order and Political Decay*. However, an interesting feature in the confederation of sachems is the principle of individual migration among the tribes. People who disliked their current sachem (or village) were allowed to leave for another village.

Today, US cities and states are open to frictionless migration from other cities and states. It wouldn't occur to Americans to act any other way. This right of movement was not common throughout other cultures around the world; often, it was forbidden and punished. Contrast the American roots with feudal Europe. The English Statute of Labourers in 1351 made it illegal for a peasant to leave their lord's land to seek higher wages elsewhere. If a man refused to serve and pay tithes and rent to his lord and master, he could be jailed. Still today, many countries limit internal migration, particularly authoritarian countries such as mainland China.

In the United States, however, the culture of free movement was codified in law early on. Indeed, the Revolutionary War might never have started if King George had not attempted to limit the population of the colonies.

The Declaration of Immigration?

The conventional view is that rebellious colonists were angry about taxation without representation, and that King George was abusive of his authority. The burgeoning potential of the British Colonies, from New Hampshire to Georgia, was increasingly obvious to people on both sides of the Atlantic Ocean. For example, Adam Smith's magnum opus *The Wealth of Nations* proposed granting American colonists' rights as full British citizens else they would continue to rebel. In fact, Smith anticipated that "the rapid progress of (America) in wealth, population and improvement" would produce more than Britain "in the course of little more than a century" and that the "seat of the empire would then naturally remove itself to that part of the empire."[6] Those words were published in 1776, and by then, the war was on. What he foresaw was seen by others in London who hoped to prevent that exact future from happening.

Restricting the flow of immigrants to America was a centerpiece of imperial Britain's strategy to weaken the colonies. The British reasoning behind this was pretty simple: the colonies relied on immigration for labor, construction, and growth, and the growing independence of the colonies presented an uncomfortable challenge to rigid class and monarchist rule on England's shores. Their success, if not carefully tapered and controlled, would be disastrous not just for the British aristocracy but for aristocracies across Europe. It is important to remember here that the Declaration of Independence was drafted in the early summer of 1776 by a committee of five led by Thomas Jefferson. It was the first time in history that ordinary people had made the case for their independence, and they did so with the noblest aspirations. "We hold these truths to be self-evident, that all men are created equal," they declared, and more as well. The substance of the document is a lengthy list of grievances that justify rebellion against the British crown. The first six grievances concerned laws, legislation, and legislative authority that "He" (King George III) had overseen. The seventh concerned immigration:

> He has endeavored to prevent the population of these states; for that purpose obstructing the laws for naturalization of foreigners; refusing to pass others to encourage their migration hither, and raising the conditions of new appropriations of lands.

Stephen Hopkins, Thomas Jefferson, and the other founding fathers understood something about immigration that modern politicians take completely for granted: migrants are a key to national power. They knew that a larger population is vital for more industry, for filling up the great frontier, and not least of all, for standing up a larger military.

Foreign-born soldiers, especially officers, were vital to the ragtag American army's success against British forces. German natives Baron Von Steuben and Baron Johann de Kalb were trusted generals under Washington's command, as well Polish-born Casimir Pulaski and Tadeusz Kosciuszko, and the French Marquis de Lafayette. When the war was won in 1781 and the final redcoats decamped in 1783, the significance of migrants for the victory was tangible for the future president. Celebrating with the soldiers of the Continental Army inside the Fraunces Tavern at the corner of Pearl and Broad Streets in Manhattan, days after the last British vessel had departed, Washington rose and offered a round of toasts. "May America be an Asylum to the persecuted of the earth!" Washington shouted as his men cheered.

Once there was a time America was referred to in the plural, as in *the United States are* rather than *the United States is*. Given the cultural roots of America's openness, the place was not conceived during the founding as something singular but something diverse. The country's motto was, of course, *e pluribus unum*, Latin for "Out of many, one." Walt Whitman wrote in the preface to *Leaves of Grass*, "The United States themselves are essentially the greatest poem. . . . Here is not merely a nation but a teeming nation of nations."[7] But even Whitman was giving way to the inexorable bend of language, for the word "nation" did not mean then what it means now, nor even what it meant when the Constitution was written. The word nation is absent from the document. Regardless, as Tom Gjelten notes in his book whose title was inspired by Whitman, "No country on the planet would be as associated ideologically with immigration as the United States."[8]

True Numbers

In the present, citizens in first world nations are stunned by television images of bedraggled refugees clambering over ditches and walls, trekking across deserts, or washing up dead on the shores of Europe. Many Americans today believe that their country is being flooded by immigrants like never before. A bit of reflection reveals this concern to be curious, and perhaps nonsensical.

North America appeared thinly populated when a wave of European settlers arrived in the 16th century. Indigenous peoples had no immunity to Old World pathogens brought by the first Europeans and Africans. Waves of smallpox, then influenza, then measles ran rampant up the coasts and trade routes, killing an estimated 56 million people throughout the Americas during the 16th century, with a net mortality rate that was potentially as high as 90 percent.[9]

As the 2020 census began, there were an estimated 45 million immigrants in the United States. Roughly 1 million have arrived per year since the turn of the century. Those sound like remarkably large numbers until put in context with the existing population of 331 million Americans. The key insight in understanding American power is that the current large population is the result of dramatic growth from a very small base.

The very first census, taken in 1790, enumerated 3,929,214 inhabitants, not counting native Indians. Most of those Americans were born on American soil. The truly shocking numerical story of the birth of the American people is that during the many years from 1492 to that first census in 1790, some 300 years, the best estimate is that a grand total of 1 million people migrated from foreign lands. That's 3,000 or 4,000 people per year, which is bracing context for the 1 million per year arriving at present. This begs the question: how thinly populated was North America before Columbus? The best estimate of historians is that there were 2.5 to 3 million American Indians.[10] That population was decimated by pox and appeared thin indeed to the Europeans, and notably to the Pilgrims.

The economist Richard Easterlin estimated that immigration inflows were relatively sparse until the Great Hunger in Ireland in the 1840s. Immigrants were, by his count, responsible for 3.3 percent of population growth during 1800–1810, 2.6 percent during the next decade, and 3.8 percent in the decade of the 1820s, then accelerating to 12 percent, 23 percent, and 31 percent in the following three decades thereafter.[11]

Conventional wisdom across the political spectrum in our era holds that immigration to the United States has rarely been higher than it is now. People disagree about whether that's a good or bad trend, but they take the trend as unquestioned truth. The *Atlantic*'s David Frum warns, "By 2027, the foreign-born proportion of the US population is projected to equal its previous all-time peak, in 1890: 14.8 percent. Under present policy, that percentage will keep rising to new records thereafter."[12] This consensus is probably wrong.

Modern America receives fewer migrants from abroad than during the first half of its existence. Even a quick glance at data on immigrant inflows, presented in Figure 4.1, clearly shows that arrivals in modern times are far lower in number compared those in the 19th century.

Yet the sense of an unprecedented wave fuels populist anxiety. And it's not merely a right-wing concern. "Border at Breaking Point," warned the *New York Times* in March of 2019 when the surge of asylum seekers overwhelmed processing capacity.[13] President Trump routinely couched his immigration policies with tweets and statements emphasizing "record" levels of migration to the United States.

The high level of refugees seeking asylum is not, however, the whole picture. The inflated headlines imply that immigration overall is setting records (as if that were a bad thing), as Frum suggests. This is probably an exaggeration, and I use the word probably because there are two competing data sources. One source, the census, is a once-a-decade national headcount that did not even assess place of birth before 1850.[14] The other source is an annual count of arriving immigrants at ports of entry that began only after Congress ordered it in 1819. And the two sources tell very different stories.

Although census takers were charged with asking about citizens' birthplace in 1850, the quality of records in that era is far below that of modern times. A fairly laissez-faire approach to recording dates of birth, marital status, and even basic names makes historical sociology a headache for even the

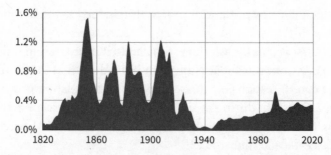

Figure 4.1 Legal migration to the United States, 1820–2018, as a percentage of population, annual 4-year average. Data from US Department of Homeland Security, *Yearbook of Immigration Statistics*.

best-intentioned social scientist. It wasn't uncommon for women to knock a few years off their reported age to census takers when marrying a new spouse, or for a man to take on a new name and identity after a spell in jail. The great unknown is whether foreign-born Americans were willing to give honest answers about their origins, skeptical that such information would harm their prospects and progeny. Just as likely, vagueness and brevity of laws made for uneven application. For example, an 1819 law requiring the national origin of all immigrants to be recorded was understood by most officials to mean country of last residence, which resulted in inbound Irish being categorized as Canadians since travel via Canada was half as expensive as direct berths to New York and Boston.[15]

Pundits typically cite the number of the foreign-born population reported in the census as a percentage of the total population. This is taken as proof that the country is now approaching a new peak, which is a good thing according to advocates and an alarming thing for the skeptics. The implication is that the United States is full, or more ominously, that the culture is at risk of dilution. Census data show that the foreign-born population fluctuated between 13 and 15 percent from 1860 to 1920. On the heels of restrictive policy in the 1920s, the foreign-born population dropped to fewer than 10 million by 1970, representing just 4.7 percent of the population. Today it is much higher: nearly 45 million, which is about 14 percent of the population.

History is not as clear-cut as the census data imply, and the data are more problematic than is conventionally understood.

In fact, there is an alternative view coming from a more consistently defined data set. The Office of Immigration Statistics, now part of the Department of Homeland Security (DHS), compiles a data series that goes back to 1820, which is three decades before the census planners began thinking about the issue. The DHS data count all foreign nationals who arrive in the country: refugees, tourists, temporary workers, and a wide array of visa recipients. Those who are conventionally described as immigrants are formally counted as lawful permanent residents (LPRs for short), nicknamed green card holders. Not all LPRs become citizens, but they have the right to do so under US law.

In Figure 4.2, I present a moving average of the five-decade tally of LPRs relative to the current-year population, side-by-side with the census numbers. It shows that LPRs peaked in 1910 and 1920 at 24.8 percent of the population.

Foreign-born levels reported in the census are nearly the same in 1910 and 2010, whereas DHS arrivals tell a strikingly different story: arrivals are less than half of what they were a century ago. Can these figures be reconciled? Is one of the series simply wrong? The most likely reconciliation is that the census data are flawed, and the reasons are numerous. Questions about

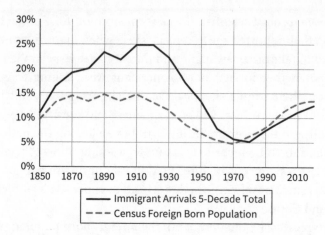

Figure 4.2 Immigrants relative to the US population, 1850–2020. Data on arrivals are maintained by the US Department of Homeland Security; the US Census Bureau has historically recorded foreign-born residents and citizens with evolving definitions.

citizenship and nationality at birth were revised incessantly from one census to the next, and the fidelity of responses is surely clouded by confusion and dishonesty. Even now, there are political controversies over what questions will be allowed and difficulties with administration of the surveys.

Fifty years prior to 1910, DHS reports there were inflows of 13.5 million and a population of 92 million in 1910. Compare that to the fifty years prior to 2010, with inflows of 34.5 million relative to the population of 309 million in 2010. Recent arrivals during the so-called *wave* of Latin American and Asian immigration represent just 11 percent of the population. Immigrant inflows were three times higher a century ago.

Inflows of LPRs summed over five decades produce an admittedly imperfect metric because life spans are much longer today than in the second half of the 19th century. Life expectancy for all Americans in 2017 was seventy-nine years, whereas in 1910 it was fifty years.[16] However, that means the current LPR-population ratio is overstated in comparison to the past, not understated.

Migrant inflows are arguably a better gauge of migration relative to population than the census, with one large caveat. What about the outflows? The godfather of immigration sociology, E. G. Ravenstein, laid out seven "Laws of Migration" in 1885 that have held up very well against the test of time. The fourth is, "Each main current of migration produces a compensating countercurrent."[17] Some migrants return to their country of origin. However, those countercurrents increase as the cost of transportation decreases. As a case in point, in recent years, net migration between the United States and Mexico is negative. There have been calculations of remigration rates based on data from the 1920s, ranging between 4 and 40 percent for the largest ethnic groups at the turn of the century. However, remigration of the Irish during the 19th century was uncommon, we know, based on the permanent depopulation of Ireland itself. The millions of Irish migrants who escaped the potato famine in the 1840s tended to stay in America, whereas Ireland's census counted 8.2 million people in 1841, 6.6 million a decade later, then just 4.7 million in 1891.[18]

Both DHS and census data capture some truth, and the discrepancies between them for the 19th century may never be reconciled. They may indicate a census undercount of foreign-born citizens due to non-response, miscounts, or respondent misidentification when the pressure to assimilate was higher. On the other hand, we cannot discount the fact that not all LPRs wanted or were able to become citizens. Regardless, the inflow of migrants today is indisputably half of what it was a century ago. America is far from full.

Cartograms for Context

From the Pilgrims to the founding, immigration was the dominant factor in the rise of a new nation. Understanding the scale of it, as we turn our attention to the 250-year history of the United States, is vital. For our purposes, as we examine presidential decision making in the next chapter, what stories do those data tell that other narratives miss? My own historical quest was an effort to identify the turning points in immigration flows, and further, to identify which presidents went beyond rhetoric in shaping immigration policy.

The challenge with such an exercise is deciding which dates to use to define the eras. Since origin-country data are organized in decades by DHS, it was easy enough to choose 1880 as the first turning point given the importance of the 1882 Chinese Exclusion Act. We can only imagine how much larger the population might have been if the people of China and Japan had been welcomed openly and how that welcome would likely have drawn immigrants from other Asian nations.

Isolationism grew in popularity, culminating in immigrant quota legislation in 1921 and 1924, but the effect of these laws was muted initially as they were described as temporary emergencies. National quotas slashed immigration from southern and eastern European countries by about 80 percent, but allowed migration from northern Europe to continue apace. Perhaps more important, the quotas did not apply to wives and families of foreign-born males already residing in the country, and subsequently those family flows grew rather than declined in the short term. The total number of immigrants was 6.3 million in the 1910s and 4.3 million in the 1920s, but barely half a million in the 1930s, so I mark 1930 as the beginning of the Restrictive Era

Since I often lecture about this history, I designed a series of cartograms to showcase the four different eras in the context of one another. A cartogram is a stylized map that presents statistical information in diagrammatic form.[19]

My cartograms in Figure 4.3 use a pixelated map of the United States with 2,000 squares. Each square represents the contemporary population, and the white block of squares in the center of the national silhouette represents the

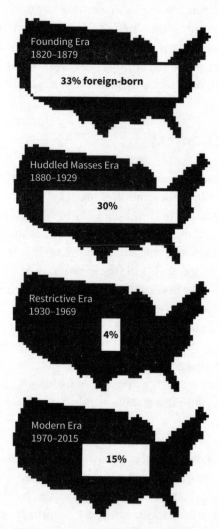

Figure 4.3 Cartograms of the four eras of US immigration; immigrant arrivals relative to the population (each square represents 0.05% of the total population during that era). Data from US Census and US Department of Homeland Security.

sum of arriving immigrants (LPRs) during each era relative to population. There are different ways to treat the denominator, using the national population during either the final year or the initial year, but my calculations use the average population during all of the years. Some of the cartograms I lecture with are colorized and show different blocks for source countries and regions, which allows students to see how dominant the Irish and German inflows were in the 19th century, and how diversified modern inflows are, with far fewer migrants from Mexico relative to Asia than the popular press appreciates.

The cartograms in this book highlight how large the inflows of foreign migrants were during the first two eras, 30 and 33 percent, respectively, and how small the inflows were in the restrictive era of 1930–1969. The cartograms are like a picture worth a thousand words; they are numbers that only begin to tell the story. They tell us what happened, in the broadest strokes, but do not tell us why. What we know so far is this: the first colonists in the New World and the founding fathers conceived of a nation of immigrants. They struggled to survive as strangers in a strange land, and they authored a revolution based on the right to grow strong through immigration. And for 250 years after the founding, some presidents and national leaders aimed to preserve that legacy, some abided by it with rhetoric of inclusion and unity and tolerance while doing nothing of substance, and some sought to reshape who was allowed in. The next chapter tells their stories.

Chapter 5
Presidents

> We the People of the United States, in Order to form a more perfect Union, establish Justice, insure domestic Tranquility, provide for the common defense, promote the general Welfare, and secure the Blessings of Liberty to ourselves and our Posterity, do ordain and establish this Constitution for the United States of America.
>
> **— Preamble to the US Constitution, 1787**

This chapter offers a simple hypothesis: the greatest American presidents are those most open to immigration. And a corollary is that the vision of those great American presidents—Washington, Lincoln, Wilson, Johnson, Reagan, and Bush especially—was essential in growing and preserving America's economic, military, and cultural power.

There are only 4,543 words in the Constitution. It is brilliantly designed to limit the power of the federal government, secure the sovereignty of the states over domestic affairs, and maximize the rights and privileges of the people. The brevity of words increases the compact's clarity, and power. Importantly, there are essentially no limits on foreign immigration in the document other than a seven-word clause in Article I granting legislative authority "To establish an uniform Rule of Naturalization."

Yet the ideal of equal openness to foreigners in the Constitution was just another aspirational star in the constellation of the American creed. The practical rules made by legislators and executives were in constant tension and sharply disrupted by two surges of nativism. The first erupted in the economically transformative 1880s and the second in the 1920s following the War to End All Wars. In 1882, the Chinese Exclusion Act banned an entire ethnicity from citizenship. A wave of "non-white" Italians and Jews arriving in the ensuing decades was resented by some, but those sentiments were held in check until an outbreak of a worldwide war in 1914 and global pandemic in 1918.

Many presidents resisted popular nativism expressed periodically in the Congress, but the pressure boiled over with the passage of two restrictive quota laws, temporarily in 1921, then permanently in 1924. The quota laws inaugurated forty years of near-isolation from foreign migration, including the shameful turning away of Jewish refugees fleeing Nazi persecution during Franklin Roosevelt's presidency. In fact, it wasn't until after President John Kennedy's assassination in 1963 that his successor Lyndon Johnson (LBJ) led a major reform to end immigration quotas. The open, color-blind structure of the Immigration and Nationality Act of 1965 holds today, a system welcoming more legal immigrants than any other country in the world.

Looking back at presidential campaigns and administrations around those key turning points, great presidents stand out, as do what historians call the "failures." Polls of historians and surveys of the public routinely rate Abraham Lincoln and George Washington as two of the greatest presidents. Both stand out in word and deed as part of the club of aggressively pro-immigration chief executives. On the other side of these rankings stand Millard Fillmore and Warren Harding, two of the most restrictionist presidents. Harding signed the 1921 law that slashed legal immigration, fulfilling his promise made during the "America First" election campaign of 1920. Fillmore infamously enforced slavery across state lines and inflamed tensions that led to the Civil War during his brief tenure in the White House, then went on to head the ignominious American Party ticket (home of the Know Nothing movement) in 1856.

The model I propose for understanding immigration history is this: the core identity of the United States is founded on the creedal ideal that "All men are created equal." The founding documents and institutions aspired to that creed, knowing that they and their society at the time did not meet it. The paradox of slave-owning Thomas Jefferson who railed against slavery succinctly represents the soul of the new nation. They set the ship of state on a course for something better. Contemporary immigration laws reflect each era's ideals of equality, especially when tested by ever-expanding ethnic diversity. The counterweight to this creed is nativism, always lurking in the hearts of mankind, an anthropologically universal suspicion of the other—other villages on the opposite side of the mountain, other religions, other races.

My colleague at Stanford, the historian David Kennedy, opened my mind to understanding how immigration represents the continual test of the American creed, more so than race. Kennedy tells the story of General George Patton's pep talk with his troops just before the invasion of Sicily during World War II: "Many of you have in your veins German and Italian blood, but remember that these ancestors of yours so loved freedom that they gave up home and country to cross the ocean in search of liberty," in contrast to those ancestral relatives who stayed in Europe to live as "slaves."[1] There it is. And the model of American immigration is one of incessant testing whether the new alloy of diverse peoples melted together is strong enough to continue. Some generations fail the test, but time seems to continually advance the next generation toward a more perfect acceptance of the creed, more tolerant, more diverse.

A Theory of Presidential Greatness

Who are the greatest American presidents?

For better or worse, each nation understands its history through the stories of its great rulers, accepting the duality and complexity of our past through no small amount of revisionism. The English fondly recall King Richard the Lionheart (albeit heavily revised as he only spent six months in the country) and King Henry V, war-fighting monarchs who ruled for a single decade. They also celebrate war-avoiding Queen Elizabeth and Queen Victoria, who ruled over prosperous eras of half a century apiece. France celebrates the self-crowning Napoleon Bonaparte as well as the regal Louis XIV. China has its greats in Zhu Di, the great Ming emperor, and Deng Xiaoping, the transformative free market Maoist. Russia celebrates the revolutionary Lenin as well as the famed czarina, Catherine the Great.

The United States has a far shorter history than most nations, but a longer list of leaders as a result of the four-year presidential term. Forty-five men have served as president, including one who served in the office twice, since the inauguration of George Washington in 1789. Celebrated as "first in war, first in peace, and first in the hearts of his countrymen," Washington set the standard for greatness—a standard of competence, integrity, and foresight that remains an active measure against which all presidents are held.

All cultures love a founding hero, someone to anchor concepts of good or bad leadership. Even the ancient Romans measured their emperors against great leaders of their past. The Roman Senate welcomed new emperors with the words "Sis felicior Augusto, melior Traiano" (Latin: "Be more fortunate than Augustus, better than Trajan"). Augustus was the first true emperor, a teenager thrust into the game of thrones when his adoptive father, Julius Caesar, was assassinated. Unlike the old generals vying to rule the crumbling Republic, Augustus was an intellectual rather than a warrior, but no less cunning. After establishing singular control, he engineered an economic boom that enabled him to boast after many decades that he had found Rome a city of bricks and left it a city of marble. Trajan, who ruled exactly a century later, pushed the empire to its largest geographic reach and arguably its economic peak. Then, as now, history and reality fray at the seams of how we understand ourselves.

If Washington is America's Augustus, who is our Trajan? Our Nero? Our Caligula? Most Americans would say Abraham Lincoln is the greatest president, in every category, but Franklin Delano Roosevelt has a worthy claim. Competition for the worst president is sadly far more crowded, ranging from apocryphal audacity to bumbling fool. That title, and the ranking of widely unremembered chief executives such as Martin Van Buren and Millard Fillmore, comes from the careful reasoning of historians and also from the mathematics of modern pollsters.

Is it possible that the greatest American presidents are also those who championed greater immigration?

Greatness Rankings

Formally ranking presidents began in 1948 when Harvard professor Arthur Schlesinger had the idea to quantify greatness using a survey of historians. The year 1948 was also a presidential election year, and a remarkable one—the first held since FDR died in office during the waning days of World War II. Elites at the time considered the twangy Harry Truman fated for certain defeat, and they had science to prove it. Public opinion polling had captured the nation's imagination that year, and all of the leading pollsters predicted that President Truman would lose to a man whom almost nobody remembers anymore. Newspapers famously anticipated the outcome and had their headlines ready to go, notably "Dewey Defeats Truman" on the front page of the *Chicago Daily Tribune* that the president held aloft the morning after.[2]

Schlesinger published his poll of historians in *LIFE* magazine on Monday, November 1, the day before the election. The instructions Schlesinger sent to participants asked them to rate each president in one of five categories: Great, Near Great, Average, Below Average, and Failures, for "performance in office, omitting everything done before or after." Fifty-five academics responded, and they considered six presidents to be great: Lincoln, Washington, Roosevelt (FDR), Wilson, Jefferson, and Jackson, in that order. It must be said that Schlesinger did not detail his methodology or report average ratings.

The *LIFE* story became a sensation, generating widespread public interest and ultimately academic interest as well. It was a powerful combination of science and pop culture, though many people questioned the methodology and the composition of the so-called experts. Why did Schlesinger use historians instead of political scientists, military officers, or distinguished law professors? Why not economists?

When Schlesinger repeated the exercise in 1962, a Stanford professor named Thomas Bailey wrote a critical book using the Schlesinger rankings as a lens on a myriad of issues in presidential scholarship such as character, personality, fortune, popularity, bias, and "measuring the unmeasurable" under the title *Presidential Greatness*. Published in 1966, Bailey's book serves as an enduring rebuke of the weaknesses in the parlor game of historical rankings. He argued that the presidency has evolved over time, and more important, "no two incumbents were ever dealt the same hand." Perhaps his most potent argument was to remind readers that any poll is indelibly a consequence of the respondents. Schlesinger's hand-picked participants were never meant to be representative, but Bailey made the point that they were worse than unrepresentative. They were biased: too Harvard, too northern, and too Democratic. "The truth is that an overwhelming majority of those who teach history in colleges and universities are Democrats, and one should not be surprised to find this bias among the Schlesinger pollees," he wrote.[3] Some say FDR's exalted reputation today is a function of that initial *LIFE* essay.

Regardless, Schlesinger Sr. inspired copycats (including his son's survey in 1996), an academic literature, and dozens of books. In 1982, Penn State political scientists Robert Murray and Timothy Blessing raised the academic rigor with an in-depth poll that collected responses from nearly 1,000 American academics. Their book, *Greatness in the White House*, identified a handful of factors that are correlated with greatness, notably, whether a president served in wartime. After examining the rich set of response data from their multifaceted, sixty-seven-question survey, the authors concluded, "The historians saw most of the significant domestic achievements of any administration revolving around four distinct themes: socioeconomic policy, federal versus state and local concerns, enforcement of the law, and the *expansion of civil rights* (emphasis added)."[4] The Murray-Blessing ratings—alongside more recent versions such as the politically neutral 2004 rankings sponsored by the *Wall Street Journal* and public opinion rankings done by Rasmussen, Gallup, Quinnipiac, and the Siena College Research Institute—are a staple of college political science classes.

The intriguing question is what factors are correlated with greatness? I've found a strong correlation with wartime service, though the main influence seems to be what might be called anti-recency bias. The presidents who served earliest in history have a massive ranking advantage. However, my theory about a greatness-immigration link has never been investigated. Looking through a half dozen books on the topic of presidential greatness, from Taranto and Leo's *Presidential Leadership* to Alvin Felzenberg's elegant *The Leaders We Deserved*, there is nary a mention of immigration.

Which greatness survey should be used as a reference point? We could use the recurring annual Siena College project or the most recent C-SPAN survey of presidential scholars, though it may not matter. As Murray and Blessing noted: "The general consistency with which professional historians have rated all the presidents since the first Schlesinger poll in 1948 suggests that the rankings of most of the past presidents are, within relatively narrow limits, rather firmly fixed."[5] To be sure, there are notable exceptions. Andrew Jackson slid to #18 in the most recent C-SPAN survey. In his book-length review of the field, Robert Merry sympathized with contemporary conservatives' frustration that Ronald Reagan was underrated in surveys taken soon after he left the White House, "just as Republicans in 1962 justifiably fumed over Eisenhower's low ranking in the second Schlesinger, Sr. poll."[6] But look what happened. President Eisenhower was rated #22 in the 1962 survey that appeared a year after his second term ended, then rated #8 by C-SPAN in 2009 and #5 by C-SPAN in 2017.[7]

Statistical analysis confirms a high degree of correlation among different greatness rankings. I compared the 2000 *Wall Street Journal* project to the 2017 C-SPAN survey experts and found that the two studies' numeric rankings have a correlation of 90 percent. Rankings are just a count from top to bottom, so that correlation really is high. The more detailed rating scores have a correlation of 94 percent.

To see if there is a relationship between immigrants coming to the United States and presidential greatness, I organized the official immigrant inflow numbers from the US Department of Homeland Security into presidential terms, and further divided them by the US population at the end of each presidential term.

The five presidents who oversaw the most immigrant inflows were Barack Obama, George W. Bush, Theodore Roosevelt, Bill Clinton, and George H. W. Bush. The elder Bush's presidency is the most impressive given that his time in office lasted just one term, whereas the others were able to tally such large numbers over two full terms.

However, relative to the national populations, the presidents who welcomed the most immigrants are some of the least remembered: Millard Fillmore (5.7%), Chester A. Arthur (4.7%), and Franklin Pierce (4.3%), whereas the presidents who oversaw the fewest immigrant arrivals are famous. For example, during FDR's presidency, one immigrant per 1,000 Americans was

Table 5.1 Presidents with the fewest immigrant arrivals (% of population)

John Quincy Adams	0.55%
Herbert Hoover	0.52%
Harry S. Truman	0.45%
James Monroe	0.28%
Franklin Roosevelt	0.13%

allowed entry during each of his first three terms. His successor, Harry Truman, welcomed four times as many (Table 5.1).

When we consider instead the ratio of foreign-born citizens relative to the total US population, the nadir occurred in the 1960s during Lyndon Johnson's presidency. Does this mean that he was less welcoming than any other president? No, exactly the opposite. Rather, this contrast teaches us that the level of immigrants during every presidency is primarily driven by the laws and policies set in the prior decade.

Here's the surprise: the relationship between immigration numbers and presidential greatness is actually negative. The negative correlation between immigration *inflows* and greatness (–36.6%) as well as immigration *levels* and greatness (–29.9%) is significant. So a first, flawed glance at the data suggests that the greatest presidents welcomed the fewest immigrants. We know this is flawed because President Lyndon Johnson championed and signed what is universally acclaimed as the most expansive federal immigration reform, the effects of which took more than a decade to be fully felt. Johnson is ranked consistently as a "near great" and is also clearly one of the most pro-immigration policymakers, but the raw numbers on immigration fail to tell his story. A purely quantitative approach is also stymied by data limitations: no arrivals data were recorded before 1820 and the first census to account for foreign births of citizens was in 1850, meaning presidents from Washington to Polk are not included in the correlations above.

Another way to test the theory is to make a qualitative ranking of presidential policies. I endeavored to do just that, contacting a handful of immigration scholars with the breadth of knowledge to offer their ratings. I did not tell the participants about my theory; I said that the project was simply to give each president a score on a 1–7 scale, with 7 representing policies "most open to immigration" and 1 representing "most restrictive."

Dan Griswold, a senior research fellow at the Mercatus Center at George Mason University, was willing to assess recent presidents with the most favorable marks given to LBJ and said, "I actually rate recent Republicans (Reagan, Bush I & II) as higher than Clinton and Obama because their rhetoric was good and they signed or supported liberalizing legislation." But Dan, like many others, didn't feel he could rate all of the presidencies going back to 1789.

Ultimately, two scholars were willing to provide ratings for the full slate of chief executives, in addition to my own. The first to respond was Tyler Anbinder, a professor of history at George Washington University and author of the monumental *City of Dreams: The 400-Year Epic History of Immigrant New York*. Anbinder rated most 19th-century presidents a neutral 4, and gave no president a score of 1 or 7.

Alvin Felzenberg, author of *The Leaders We Deserved*, also generously replied with ratings and comments, though his sense of the scale was different. He awarded a 7 rating to most of the early presidents: Jefferson, Madison, Monroe, Jackson, Van Buren, Polk, and so on. He points out that the political effect of the Alien & Sedition Acts under John Adams (rated 2 by both Felzenberg and Anbinder) activated efforts within the opposition party to organize immigrants as a voting bloc that were carefully protected by successive Democratic (then called Republican) presidents. It wasn't until Lincoln was elected to the White House that the Democratic Party lost their hold on immigrants as a voting bloc.

Among the rankings of the three of us, LBJ garnered the highest average immigration policy as "most open" to immigration, followed closely by Kennedy, then a tie between Lincoln and Obama. Other presidents with very "open" ratings are Washington, Jefferson, Wilson, and George W. Bush. The most "restrictive" are Harding, Coolidge, and John Adams.

My instinct was correct. The average qualitative ratings have a very strong, positive correlation with presidential greatness: 45.4 percent with C-SPAN scores and 37.1 percent with the *Wall Street Journal* scores. That means somewhere between a third and a half of the variation in presidential greatness rankings is explained by immigration policy. This strong relationship doesn't necessarily mean that greatness *causes* a president to be more open to immigration. There are certainly presidents considered above average who favored a restrictionist policy. However, the high correlation does affirm how history judges past leaders, and that those favoring a more open immigration policy are considered greater.

The full list of presidents and their average immigration policy rating show outliers rather clearly. Washington, Jefferson, and Lincoln were the three most open to immigration during the country's first century. These three, perhaps not coincidentally, are also famous for taking actions to strengthen the union

Table 5.2 Presidential immigration policy ratings (1–7, with 7 being most open to immigration)

President	Immigration Policy Rating	Immigrant Arrivals / Population	Foreign-Born Citizens / Population
George Washington	5.7		
John Adams	2.3		
Thomas Jefferson	5.7		
James Madison	5.0		
James Monroe	5.0	0.3%	
John Quincy Adams	4.7	0.6%	
Andrew Jackson	5.0	1.3%	
Martin Van Buren	5.0	1.6%	
John Tyler	4.7	1.6%	
James K. Polk	5.0	3.3%	4.5%
Millard Fillmore	2.7	5.7%	10.6%
Franklin Pierce	5.0	4.3%	12.0%
James Buchanan	5.0	2.1%	13.2%
Abraham Lincoln	6.0	1.6%	13.7%
Andrew Johnson	5.3	2.8%	14.2%
Ulysses S. Grant	5.0	3.1%	13.9%
Rutherford B. Hayes	4.0	1.8%	13.3%
Chester A. Arthur	2.7	4.7%	13.9%
Benjamin Harrison	5.0	3.1%	14.4%
Grover Cleveland	4.3	2.4%	14.2%
William McKinley	4.3	1.6%	13.6%
Theodore Roosevelt	5.0	4.1%	14.3%
William Howard Taft	4.7	3.7%	14.3%
Woodrow Wilson	5.7	2.0%	13.4%
Warren G. Harding	1.7	2.1%	12.4%
Calvin Coolidge	1.7	1.0%	11.8%
Herbert Hoover	2.3	0.5%	10.9%
Franklin Roosevelt	4.3	0.1%	8.8%
Harry S. Truman	5.0	0.4%	6.9%
Dwight D. Eisenhower	4.7	0.6%	5.7%
John F. Kennedy	6.3	0.6%	5.1%
Lyndon B. Johnson	6.7	0.7%	4.9%
Richard M. Nixon	4.7	0.7%	5.1%
Gerald R. Ford	4.7	0.8%	5.7%
Jimmy Carter	4.7	0.9%	6.2%
Ronald Reagan	5.3	1.0%	7.3%
George H. W. Bush	5.0	2.1%	8.6%
Bill Clinton	5.0	1.1%	10.5%
George W. Bush	5.7	1.4%	12.2%
Barack Obama	6.0	1.3%	13.2%

and defend the American creed. On the other side of the ratings, Presidents Harding and his successor Coolidge set the standard for anti-immigrant policy. Both were Republicans, and their economic policies can be described as soundly pro-business, albeit anti-trade (Table 5.2).

The American public is forever wrestling with a nativist sentiment, evidenced as early as John Adams's ignominious and politically motivated policies against French Americans. Lincoln's martyrdom and the war over slavery pushed such sentiments down for decades, but the remarkable and largely forgotten half-dozen men in the White House over the turn of the century met the test of the American creed until nativist sentiments became overwhelming. Why did Wilson stand alone as the wave crested? And why did the isolationist fever break after four long decades? Is the modern era of openness about to end?

Chapter 6
Eras

During the hot summer of 1787, there was a fierce debate at the Constitutional Convention in Philadelphia about whether immigrants should be allowed to serve as elected or appointed officials. Gouverneur Morris and Charles Pinckney asserted that "men who can shake off attachments to their own country can never love another." Alexander Hamilton disagreed, as did Benjamin Franklin, George Mason, and future president James Madison, who argued that American citizenship should be open for all who "love liberty."[1] A more practical argument was that good people across the Atlantic were rather less likely to join a republic that denied them equal rights, particularly men of great wealth and zeal.

These debates echoed across the nation but also around the world. The new republic was the first of its kind on the world stage, and it did in fact serve as a "harbinger" of liberty. As news of America spread to the Old World, the country became a beacon that drew immigrants as well as an inspiration for popular revolutions. The French Revolution happened two years after the Constitution was adopted, and that fervor spread all across Europe over the following decades. Indeed, Ho Chi Minh famously quoted Thomas Jefferson and America's founding documents as models during the struggle against imperialism in Vietnam in the 1950s.

Foreign implications were not the concern in Philadelphia that summer, other than a worry that the first attempt at self-government under the Articles of Confederation had been a failure. The country needed a Constitution that would maximize American strength. They saw a need to build a government that would attract immigrants. For that reason, most representatives at the Convention stood strongly against birthplace limits to public service, save for the presidency. How could the framers argue against such tests when so many of them were first- or second-generation immigrants themselves, and so many foreign-born countrymen had given their lives for independence from royal rule?

When the Constitution was drafted with the goal of creating a more perfect union, it included no guidelines for immigration. Mention of it in the document is sparse, which was by design for immigration and many other important topics. This is because the law of the land establishing the federal government's three branches and their balanced functions is a minimalist social contract, and a negative one. It was crafted to protect liberty through one focused strategy: limiting federal power. Powers not explicitly granted in the text to the federal government were reserved to the states, a theme that was made explicit itself in the Tenth Amendment.

Legal scholar Ilya Somin has observed: "For the first hundred years of American history, this was actually the dominant interpretation of the Constitution: that Congress did not have a general power to restrict immigration. Indeed, there is no explicit federal power in the Constitution to control immigration. The only authority granted is that Congress may establish a "uniform Rule of Naturalization," which appears in Article 1, Section 7. An Originalist reading of the text means that the federal government cannot limit who freely comes into the United States, though it can determine who is allowed to become a citizen. Thus in 1790, the first Congress passed a law that allowed any "free white person" to become a naturalized citizen after two years of residency.

The history of the most important US immigration laws is summarized in Box 6.1. Like most policies, immigration laws started with simple rules that became more centralized and restrictive as time progressed. Regardless, the founding principles are impossible to ignore and have guided policymakers toward more open policies than any other nation.

George Washington once told a group of Irish refugees that "the bosom of America is open to receive not only the Opulent and respectable Stranger, but the oppressed and persecuted of all Nations and Religions."[2] He set that tone during his two terms as president, and his policies held a powerful momentum for the next 100 years: the new nation should have no test for wealth or class when welcoming foreigners. He once declared to a minister that he "had always hoped that this land might become a safe and agreeable asylum to the virtuous and persecuted part of mankind, to whatever nation they might belong."[3]

What historian Roger Daniels calls the Revolutionary consensus for open immigration "began to break down as American politics was polarized around those two archetypical figures, Alexander Hamilton and Thomas Jefferson, and our first political parties."[4] The vice president, John Adams, along with Hamilton and the Federalists saw the influx of poorer, French migrants as an electoral challenge. Those immigrants tended to favor their rival Thomas Jefferson's party, the Republicans (which is ironically the predecessor of the

Box 6.1 History of US immigration laws

US Constitution, 1787	The Constitution grants Congress the power to establish naturalization laws, but no explicit power to control immigration. The Fourteenth Amendment and Supreme Court cases confirmed the principle of "birthright citizenship."
Naturalization Act of 1790	George Washington signed the first federal law concerning naturalization. Residency in the country for two years allows "free white persons" of good character to become naturalized US citizens.
Immigration Act of 1864	Proposed by President Abraham Lincoln, this was the first federal law to encourage foreigners to migrate to the United States.
Chinese Exclusion Act of 1882	President Chester Arthur signed this law in May 1882, banning all Chinese naturalization and prohibiting Chinese immigration for ten years.
Emergency Quota Act of 1921	After Woodrow Wilson's pocket veto, President Warren G. Harding signed this law that was passed overwhelmingly by the House and Senate. Quotas limited immigrants to 3 percent of the foreign-born persons of each nationality who resided in the United States as of the 1910 census.
National Origins Quota Act of 1924	President Calvin Coolidge signed this more restrictive version of the Act of 1921, which made the emergency quotas permanent. Quotas were lowered to 2 percent of each nationality, based on the 1890 census, aimed at cutting southern and eastern European immigration.
McCarran-Walter Act of 1952	This act repealed immigration restrictions based on race but tightened restrictions based on nationality and security concerns, enhancing the ideological scrutiny of potential communists. Sponsored by senior Democrats and resisted by younger politicians, the bill was passed with bipartisan votes in both houses of Congress over President Truman's veto.

Immigration and Nationality Act of 1965	President Lyndon Johnson championed and ultimately signed this law abolishing national origins quotas. It is the foundation for current US immigration policy, setting up channels of legal migration based primarily on family ties.
Immigration Reform and Control Act of 1986	Signed by President Reagan, this provided for a one-time amnesty, allowing resident illegal immigrants who had lived in the United States for four years to become permanent residents. It also increased border security and introduced sanctions on employers of future illegal immigrants.
Immigration Act of 1990	This law, signed by President George H. W. Bush, increased permanent visas from 290,000 to 675,000 per year, and created the diversity-visa lottery. It also softened restrictions on temporary foreign workers in the United States, and limited the government's power to deport immigrants based on their ideological leanings.
Secure Fence Act of 2006	President George W. Bush signed this bipartisan law funding the construction of more than 700 miles of fencing along the US-Mexico border (one-third of the length of the border). The fence, checkpoints, and associated security equipment were built throughout California, Arizona, New Mexico, and Texas to prevent drug trafficking and illegal immigration.

Sources: National Vital Statistics Summary, Centers of Disease Control, the Global Terrorism Database, and the *New York Times.*

modern Democratic Party). They pushed for a second Naturalization Act in 1795 that increased the residency requirement to five years.

Jefferson's faction tended to admire the French Revolution and maintained a frosty anti-British attitude whereas Adams was more conservative and favorable toward reconciliation with the British. Irish immigrants, being anti-British themselves, favored the Jeffersonian Republicans. One Federalist congressman warned of "hordes of wild Irishmen" immigrating to the new country and taking over the Congress with radical policies, a common sentiment that led to the infamous Alien & Sedition Acts of 1798 that John Adams eagerly signed into law. Adams's otherwise solid reputation as president and founding father is marred by these four laws, particularly the Sedition Act, which criminalized political speech and was used to jail nearly a dozen newspaper editors around the country.[5]

In a brazen effort to blunt Republican votes, the (third) Naturalization Act of 1798 increased the residency requirement from five to fourteen years. The law had the perverse effect of encouraging naturalization before enforcement could take effect, and was considered a mistake even among some Federalists who warned it might discourage immigration. Adams lost his re-election bid in 1800 to Thomas Jefferson, who restored the residency term of five years in 1802, where it has remained and holds today.

The Nativist Thread Begins

Hostility to Catholic immigrants was an important undercurrent of 19th-century politics. The US ambassador to England during Adams's presidency was a New Yorker named Rufus King who warned the court that America would not accept Irish "malcontents." But with Jefferson's election in 1800, the trickle of impoverished Irish migrants grew dramatically. In the 1820s, over half of the 99,000 immigrants from Europe were born in Ireland. More than triple that number came in the 1830s. Though anti-Catholic sentiment was muted for most voters until the potato famine of the 1840s, periodic violence was common. A Protestant mob burned down Boston's Ursuline Convent in 1834, and the frequency of similar attacks "was so prevalent that insurance companies all but refused to insure" Catholic institutions.[6]

Federal policy remained open and the laws unchanged until the 1870s, but the nativist undercurrent in public attitudes was constant. The election of 1816 is a case in point, a landslide victory for James Monroe, who won 68 percent of the popular vote and more than 80 percent of the electoral college. Monroe made almost no remarks or reforms regarding immigration, but that's not the story. His opponent, then senator Rufus King, ran on a platform promising to curtail Irish immigration. King's campaign was so poorly received that it served as the death knell of the Federalist Party. A King presidency would have shut off the Irish migration and set a precedent for a smaller nation in every sense of the word. Instead, the party all but dissolved, failing to even nominate a candidate for the presidency in 1820.

Monroe presided over eight years of "good feelings" during the only time in American history that federal politics were not riven by two parties. His secretary of state, John Quincy Adams, succeeded him in the election of 1824, and the seeds of regional faction grew quickly into opposing parties. Adams was the candidate of the North, Jackson of the South, and since neither achieved a majority in the electoral college, Adams was elected in a very close vote in the House of Representatives. Adams avoided his father's errors in alienating immigrant voters and probably sincerely shared the Revolutionary consensus. In a letter to a prospective German immigrant, he wrote, "Neither the general government of the union, nor those of the individual states, are ignorant or unobservant of the additional strength and wealth, which accrues to the nation, by the accession of a mass of healthy, industrious, and frugal laborers, nor are they in any manner insensible to the great benefits which this country has derived, and continues to derive, from the influx of such adoptive children from Germany."[7]

Andrew Jackson's friendliness to immigrants seems paradoxical in contrast with his enslavement of hundreds of blacks and particular brutality toward Native Americans. It makes more sense in light of his personal story. His parents, Andrew and Elizabeth Jackson, were Protestant immigrants from Northern Ireland. Only 13 during the American Revolution, young Jackson was caught running messages to the rebel army. He was slashed by a British officer while in captivity, leaving a lifelong facial scar. Jackson's brothers and mother died during the war. The point is that Andrew Jackson shared a hatred of all things English with the Irish Catholics who sought refuge in America during his and his vice president's time in the White House (1833–1845).

Politics thereafter were consumed with westward expansion and the slavery question. Anti-Catholic nativism found a home in the Whig Party. Even so, it wasn't a predominant policy concern; rather, the politics of immigration were about voting constituencies. It is notable how deeply personal the immigrant roots were for many political leaders, including President James Buchanan, whose father was an orphaned Irish immigrant.

Millard Fillmore was the one exceptional president of the era who actively disliked immigration. He was elevated to the executive office when President Zachary Taylor was felled by food poisoning (or possibly that year's pandemic) in 1850 and served out the term. Fillmore was a favorite of the nativist faction, yet his incompetence was spectacular enough that the Whigs nominated someone else for the election of 1852. When the Whig Party dissolved afterward, the nativist wing formed a new party that "burst onto the scene" in New York and within years elected eight governors and scores of congressmen. It was formally known as the American Party but was called the Know Nothings because early members of the secret society in New York pretended to "know nothing" about the group or its secrets. Although their policies were primarily anti-Catholic rather than anti-immigrant per se, the party platform called for increasing the residency requirement to twenty-one years and also to barring foreign-born citizens from public office.[8] Fillmore, an ex-president who blamed Catholics for his many defeats, was recruited for the new party's presidential nomination in 1856. in the three-way presidential race that year, he received just 21 percent of the vote; the Know Nothing Party disappeared soon after.

The Encouragement of Abe Lincoln

Abraham Lincoln's role as the foremost proponent of immigration is largely overshadowed by the Civil War. Yet Lincoln moved with both nuance and intensity in reshaping the Republican Party as the home for all immigrants. This is all the more surprising because the newly forming Republicans included a large faction of nativists, roughly half of the splintered Know Nothings.

During the summer of 1854, when Lincoln was campaigning to be an Illinois state legislator, he met with "several local Know Nothings, among them Richard H. Ballinger and a Mr. Walgamot" tendering their endorsement of Lincoln.[9] According to Ballinger, Lincoln declined their endorsement: "Who were the true native Americans? Gentlemen of the committee, your party is wrong in principle."[10]

Although Irish Americans in the North were hostile to the Republicans in the 1860 election, President Lincoln quickly won them over. German American newspapers were much more favorable to the Lincoln candidacy, and many gave him their endorsement. According to historian Jason H. Silverman, Lincoln "welcomed newcomers to [American] shores long before the Statue of Liberty represented the immortal words of Emma Lazarus."[11]

During the first three years of the Civil War, immigration had plummeted. Lincoln recognized an urgent need for immigrant labor in the country. In response, he conceived of a plan to actively recruit people abroad to come to America, proposing the first such active legislation of its kind. From the Oval Office, Lincoln penned a letter to Congress:

> I again submit to your consideration the expediency of establishing a system for the encouragement of immigration. . . . Although this source of national wealth and strength is again flowing with greater freedom than for several years before the insurrection occurred, there is still a great deficiency of laborers in every field of industry.[12]

On July 4, 1864, the House and Senate passed the Act to Encourage Immigration. It allowed immigrants to make contracts pledging their wages in exchange for travel expenses. And contrary to critics who said the law was meant to bring in poor foreigners to be drafted into the Union Army, the law exempted immigrants from military service during wartime.

During his annual message that year, Lincoln praised the new law, giving what Silverman calls "Lincoln's most important and definitive statement on the importance of immigrants in the United States." To see what a fundamental change Lincoln wrought, consider that when the Republican Party convened in 1864, the platform it adopted included this as one of its eleven planks:

> Resolved, That foreign immigration, which in the past has added so much to the wealth, development of resources and increase of power to the nation, the asylum of the oppressed of all nations, should be fostered and encouraged by a liberal and just policy.

That plank was echoed unequivocally with "immigration protected and encouraged" in 1868 and 1872, then removed in 1876 when the GOP platform instead said, "It is the immediate duty of congress fully to investigate the effects of the immigration and importation of Mongolians on the moral and material interests of the country."

It was also Lincoln who championed the Fourteenth Amendment that established the first nationwide standard for automatic citizenship to be granted to anyone, of any ethnicity, born on American soil or naturalized. The amendment finally passed in 1868, long after Lincoln's assassination. Perversely, its passage led to a clarification of the naturalization laws, which were amended just four years later to confirm that naturalization was to be allowed for whites and blacks equally. But no Asians, no Indians, no Arabs, no Turks.

Era of Huddled Masses

The year 1882 marks the first major turning point against immigration, yet it also coincided with the beginning of two ethnic surges of immigration from a different direction. Jews from eastern Europe began a decades-long flight in 1881 (articulated most harrowingly in Irving Howe's World of Our Fathers). Meanwhile, a trickle of Italians from the impoverished south suddenly turned into a flood. Consider that from 1870 to 1879, there were 11,016 Czech immigrants, 34,977 Russians, 60,127 Austro-Hungarians, and 751,769 Germans (many of them Jews transiting via Germany). In the 1880s, migrant arrivals from those countries more than doubled, tripled, quintupled.

Nearly one-third of Europe's Jewish population fled to the United States in the decades after 1880s. This was a mass migration of Jews comparable in scale to numbers expelled from Spain during the Spanish Inquisition, according to Howe.

It began abruptly with the infamous Russian "pogroms" – this is actually a Russian verb meaning "to wreak havoc" and was used in English according to Webster's dictionary as a noun to describe the government-sanctioned slaughter of Jewish populations in hundreds of towns and villages across the Russian empire in the 1880 and '90s. Why so suddenly? You may think, as I did, that Jews had lived within Russia for centuries. On the contrary, there weren't many Jewish Russians because Russia itself didn't expand until whole regions of the Ottoman Empire were ceded to Moscow in the 1800s. Ethnic cleansing erupted when Jews were falsely blamed for the assassination of the Russian ruler Czar Alexander II in 1881. In Kiev, Warsaw, Odessa, Moscow, and elsewhere, terrible riots sanctioned by the government targeted Jewish men, women, and children. Murders and rapes were common. Pogroms flared up incessantly across the land for decades after, whenever a local public gathering sought a scapegoat for anything—a burglary or a bad harvest. Consider just a few events in 1905: nineteen were murdered in Kishinev, twenty in Zhitomir, a hundred in Kiev.

The exodus overland was hard, but the promise of America was great. When an imperial decree banished some 20,000 Jews from Moscow, where else could they go but west? Western Europeans were sympathetic, but not hospitable, not to such numbers. Hence, they sailed, more often than not young, impoverished, and paperless, from German ports to New York harbor.

The same year that the Russian czar was assassinated by anarchists, an American president was also assassinated. The vice president, Chester Arthur, was elevated to the Oval Office after James Garfield succumbed to a festering gunshot wound. Arthur is considered a nonentity nowadays, but his short tenure instituting civil service rules that stamped out patronage earned the admiration of contemporaries, including the great author Mark Twain.

Migration in the late 19th century was governed by treaty rather than legislation. For example, Japan and the United States agreed to a treaty in 1894 that assured free immigration. A similar treaty with China was what Congress aimed to modify rather severely in the year 1882. Foreign policy at the time recognized the benefits of economic engagement with China, but Chinese immigrants were treated with hostility by most American citizens, and that tension was strongest in the western states.

The Chinese Exclusion Act passed Congress with wide bipartisan support, but it did not become law. As drafted, the act banned the immigration of

Chinese laborers for twenty years and denied naturalized citizenship to those already residing in the states. President Arthur vetoed it on April 4, 1882, with a statement that read, "It needs no argument to show that the policy which we now propose to adopt must have a direct tendency to repel Oriental nations from us and to drive their trade and commerce into more friendly lands."[13]

Arthur's veto infuriated organized labor, so he buckled and within a month was signing a slightly modified version. Bipartisan support was overwhelming, with 97 percent of Democrats and 72 percent of Republicans voting in favor of passage in the House of Representatives. "Hereafter no State court or court of the United States shall admit Chinese to citizenship," declared the new law.[14] That outright ban was subject to ten-year renewals, made permanent in 1902, and remained the law of the land until its repeal in 1943 when China and the United States were wartime allies. However, the repeal was more symbolic than substantive. Far from a heroic opening, the 1943 reform established a quota of no more than 105 Chinese immigrants annually.

Migration out of China had grown after that nation's humiliation in the Opium Wars and harsh British rule. As an illustration, records indicate that fewer than 200 Asians sought permanent residency in the United States in the first half of the century, but over 200,000 migrated between 1850 and 1880. Sadly, the Chinese were widely perceived as unassimilable, though the real hostility came from American laborers who resented their competition for jobs. To be sure, many Americans were sympathetic to the new immigrants, but this was a minority view. Mark Twain described the Chinese immigrants in a passage of *Roughing It*, his book about life in California: "They are quiet, peaceable, tractable, free from drunkenness, and they are as industrious as the day is long. A disorderly Chinaman is rare, and a lazy one does not exist."

Grover Cleveland, the only president elected to two non-consecutive terms, was the only Democrat elected president for the half century after Lincoln. His idealistic stubbornness is fondly remembered by historians of the era. For example, to protect long-suffering and frequently displaced American Indians, Cleveland deployed the US Army to force settlers off tribal lands. But Cleveland's better angels could not hold back isolationists in Congress in 1888, which rescinded the legal guarantee that Chinese American residents who traveled abroad would be allowed to return to the United States. The constitutionality of the 1888 law was challenged, but the Supreme Court upheld it in an 1889 decision that granted a sweeping new federal authority. Although federal power over immigration was not explicitly granted in the Constitution, the Court reasoned that it was "an inherent attribute of sovereignty—something that all governments must have."[15]

Most presidential speeches of that era present a mixed message, extolling those immigrants who assimilated while warning about those who stubbornly cling to foreign ways. Based on rhetoric alone, it is impossible to distinguish whether that era's presidents are expansionist or isolationist, especially with today's oversensitivity to racial language. Cleveland resisted populist nativism that aimed to restrict impoverished eastern and southern Europeans arriving at Ellis Island, even as his public speeches were laden with warnings about foreigners with "customs and habits repugnant to our civilization." His actions illuminate him as far more open to immigration than most Americans in his time, and his willingness to defend immigrant rights must be remembered in the context of strong nativism in both major political parties. In 1892, the written party platforms of both Democrats and Republicans called for prohibiting entry to poor foreign immigrants, those with a criminal background, and even temporary workers. New bills were constantly introduced in Congress with literacy tests that would screen out lower-class migrants at a time when one in ten Americans couldn't read. Cleveland's presidential veto messages ring with moral clarity, calling literacy requirements a "radical departure" while also arguing that America's economic growth was "largely due to the assimilation and thrift of millions of sturdy and patriotic adopted citizens."[16] Members of the House sent forward bills requiring literacy for immigrants in 1895, 1897, 1913, 1915, and 1917. These were met again by vetoes from William Howard Taft and Woodrow Wilson.

In the midst of this era of huddled masses, the nations of the world took notice of America's growing military might. The war between Spain and the United States lasted a mere three months during 1898, ending with a major triumph for the Americans and acquisition of Spain's colonial assets including Cuba, Guam, Puerto Rico, and the Philippines. The United States also annexed Hawaii, whose population was roughly half Japanese at the time. America suddenly faced a new test of its multi-ethnic creed—were these new subjects to be treated as equals?

The presidency of Theodore Roosevelt (TR) explains a great deal about the conflicted sentiments toward race and immigration at the turn of the century. His political approach was idiosyncratic even then and unimaginable today: fiercely opinionated but never ideologically rigid. He was always willing to change his mind. When he rose to the presidency in 1901 after William McKinley's assassination, TR's first State of the Union speech to Congress warned of "race suicide" as a consequence of the huddled masses of Europe who had come to the United States bearing more children than native-born Americans. His political approach was to advocate class-based screening of Asian and European immigrants, blocking the "coolies" who were unassimilable but welcoming businessmen, professionals, and students.

On principle, Roosevelt disliked hyphenated Americanism—that is, referring to a person as German-American, Italian-American, or Catholic-American. Hyphenism was very controversial at the time. As an example, one cartoon published in *Puck* magazine in 1899 shows a disgusted Uncle Sam watching hyphenated voters with the thought bubble, "Why should I let these freaks cast whole ballots when they are only half Americans?" Yet Roosevelt hated hyphenism because he loved Americanism, expounding his faith that unity under the nation's common culture was open to all races and all religions. Not everyone agreed.

Congress made the Chinese exclusion laws permanent in 1902, fueling resentment among the people of China. As news spread over the following years, the Chinese people led an anti-American trade boycott. This was a popular movement, not a government decree. Roosevelt worked for years to re-open trade ties and scolded legislators for meddling in foreign affairs. Meanwhile, politicians in California pushed in the other direction with speeches dripping with racism and state laws that were punitive to foreigners. Westerners agitated for wider immigration bans and expulsions, targeting Japanese immigrants especially. Roosevelt reacted furiously in private letters that called the California legislators fools and idiots for offending the rising empire of Japan. In an effort to defuse the situation, he negotiated the Gentlemen's Agreement of 1908 with Tokyo whereby the imperial government voluntarily restricted the immigration of future Japanese laborers in exchange for US promises to protect the rights of Japanese immigrants already living in the United States. Japanese Americans who had left the United States were allowed to return immediately, but the number of new Japanese immigrants dropped by 80 percent in 1909 and thereafter.

Roosevelt's personal journey during his service as governor of New York and as US president made him grow increasingly sympathetic toward immigrants. His friendship with the photographer Jacob Riis, a Danish immigrant to the United States as a young man, affected not only the president's crusade for food safety but also his perception that the ills of poor immigrants were rooted in their environment rather than their heritage.[17] Roosevelt began to speak more forcefully on behalf of all immigrants, no matter how poor. In 1903, the commission that he appointed to review procedures at Ellis Island rejected a literacy test but confirmed the screenings of immigrants in order to reject criminals, anarchists, idiots, prostitutes, paupers, and the diseased— but not the able-bodied no matter how poor. Indeed, he continued efforts to punish companies in the shipping industry that brought such passengers across the Atlantic Ocean. On the cultural front, Roosevelt challenged the notion of Anglo-Saxonism as unscientific, even mocking efforts to measure the ethnic purity of the Pilgrims. "Whether they are Catholic or Protestant, Jew or Gentile; whether they come from England or Germany, Russia, Japan, or Italy, matters nothing," he said during the 1906 State of the Union address.

The Restrictive Era

The sharp turn toward isolationist laws in America was a direct consequence of World War I and its aftermath when the so-called Spanish flu pandemic followed the Yanks home from Europe in 1918. Woodrow Wilson was president during the entirety of the war, an idealist whose intransigence is responsible to some degree for the sharpness of the immigration policy shifts, despite his vetoes. Wilson's legacy today is under a great deal of pressure because he was a racist by any standard, and also a southerner who wrote sympathetically of the Old South. But he was also a humanitarian, progressive, and internationalist far ahead of his time. He supported women's suffrage, which became enshrined in the Constitution in 1920. He also won the Nobel Peace Prize that year. And when it came to immigration, Wilson was exceptionally welcoming in his actions and policies, even if some of his language seems repellent today.

The pivotal year in American isolationism was 1921: that was the year Wilson left the White House and Warren G. Harding was sworn in, thanks to his successful "America First!" campaign for the presidency. Although the economy was in a boom cycle, popular opinion had turned against foreigners from just about everywhere. This was also an era of tremendous economic and social disruption as farm work was displaced by mechanization. Ironically, the mass *internal* migration from rural to urban during this era introduced many Americans to the dizzying mix of languages and cultures found in the cities.

The entry of the United States into the First World War lit a spark of nationalist unity and pride in a country that was still calling itself a union and a republic rather than a nation. The downside of the nationalism was a distrust toward foreign powers and their people. In 1917, Congress had passed the first legislation that restricted immigration across the board. The long-sought literacy test was included along with a rule that established a wide "Asiatic barred zone" blocking all Asian immigrants with the exception of Japanese and Filipinos. Even though Woodrow Wilson had vetoed the act in late 1916, large majorities in the House and Senate overrode his veto in early 1917.

After war ended, European immigration surged anew. One million migrants had arrived per year in the decade leading up to the war, and suddenly millions were arriving once again. The Speaker of the House responded to the media panic by introducing a bill directly to the full chamber in December 1920 that suspended *all* immigration for the coming year. It passed by a vote of 296 to 42.[18]

It was dropped in favor of a bill that incorporated restrictive quotas designed by a commission headed by Senator Dillingham of Vermont. President Wilson, who at that point was a lame duck, rejected it by way of the pocket veto. Newly sworn into office, President Harding called Congress into a special session where the 1921 act passed overwhelmingly by voice vote in the House and 78 to 1 in the Senate.

The Emergency Quota Act of 1921 had two main parts: (1) a numerical cap of 350,000 on the total number of immigrants allowed entry per year and (2) a quota set at 3 percent of each nationality living in the United States as of the 1910 Census.[19] So, for example, if there were 10,000 Russian-born citizens in 1910, then the new law allowed for 300 Russian immigrants per year. It escaped nobody's attention that the 1910 census was considerably more "Nordic" than the 1920 census. Despite this, the legislation put no limits on immigration from Mexico, Canada, or indeed any country in the Western Hemisphere.

The one-year "emergency" was extended by Congress for two additional years, setting up a permanent quota debate right before the 1924 presidential election. Calvin Coolidge was president then, following Harding's heart attack in 1923. Some historians such as Amity Shlaes who are sympathetic to "Cool Cal's" libertarian philosophy downplay his animosity to immigration, noting that he signed the law unwillingly and even declared the Statue of Liberty a national monument.[20] Truth be told, Coolidge was a man of his times, no worse but no better than the nativist fever that gripped all of Washington. First, let's consider why the 1924 law was so extreme, and second take a closer look at Coolidge's track record.

The Immigration Act of 1924, also known as the Johnson-Reed Act, not only lowered the nationality quota from 3 percent to 2 percent, but it also cynically shifted the baseline to the *1890* census. To put in perspective what that meant, there was a count of 728,851 citizens from eastern and southern Europe in the 1890 census compared to 4.5 million in the 1910 census.[21] The temporary quota of 135,000 annual immigrants from these countries was cut to a permanent quota of 14,577. And it had disproportionate effects since the numbers of Turkish, Polish, and Greek immigrants in 1890 were comparatively far lower than immigrants from other countries.

The act also set an overall quota of 165,000 immigrants per year for countries outside the Western Hemisphere. Furthermore, it established genuine enforcement powers such as the Border Patrol. However, the final touch was a provision—the only provision Coolidge objected to—that abrogated the Gentleman's Agreement by abruptly banning all immigrants from Japan. This action was intended as an insult to Tokyo and was received as such. The Johnson-Reed Act passed the House with 80 percent support and the Senate by even more. At the signing ceremony, Coolidge said, "Its main features I heartily approve."

When he accepted the 1924 nomination, Coolidge used a phrase that is echoed by nativists still today: "our institutions of society and government will fail unless America be kept American."[22] Consider a 1921 article that then vice president Coolidge published in the popular magazine *Good Housekeeping* titled "Whose Country Is This?" It promoted the idea of a racial hierarchy with Nordics being supreme, stressing that intermarriage between races would dilute Nordic purity. "There are racial considerations too grave to be brushed aside for any sentimental reasons. Biological laws tell us that certain divergent people will not mix or blend." Coolidge also believed that too many immigrants depressed employment and wages for natives, an idea he espoused many times while president.

The ethnic quota policies were confirmed by Herbert Hoover and FDR during the Great Depression, and were essentially made permanent. The Great Depression that began late in 1929 turned the nation's attention away from immigration policy entirely and even led to more economic isolationism in terms of tariffs and social expenditures. America's longest serving president, Franklin D. Roosevelt, was in office from 1933 until his death in 1945. He's often cited fondly for teasing 4,000 members of the Daughters of the American Revolution at their 1938 convention, "Remember, remember always that all of us, and you and I especially, are descended from immigrants and revolutionists." It was a fine bit of political rhetoric—his Democratic Party still leaned heavily on the ethnic vote—but the historical record shows that FDR's immigration policies were rather cowardly.

FDR simply accepted the status quo, saying that "immigration was a thing of the past."[23] Like the Democratic Party he led, Roosevelt believed that assimilation of people who are too alien was impossible. He rejected legislation in 1939 that would have saved the lives of 10,000 Jewish children. When the *St. Louis*, a ship carrying 937 terrified refugees, sought permission to dock in the United States, FDR said no. In the judgment of Roger Daniels, "Nothing short of a drastic revision or emergency suspension of American immigration laws could have saved a substantial number of refugees after 1938. That was a risk that FDR was not

willing to take."[24] Jews and other oppressed Europeans desperate to escape the Nazis added their names to the US visa waiting list which had 300,000 names in 1940. It was canceled altogether when the United States entered the war.[25]

Harry Truman, more than anyone, pushed to return American immigration policy to its creedal heritage. The xenophobia that rose in the aftermath of World War I did not rise again after World War II. On the contrary, troops returning from the Pacific and the Atlantic instead celebrated the memories of their multi-ethnic brothers in arms, talking lovingly of their Italian, Polish, Mexican, and other hyphenated fellow Americans. Discovery of Hitler's death camps, reported in vivid radio broadcasts and newsreels, reminded citizens from coast to coast what the racial purity of Nazism really was and that America should be its opposite. When World War II was over and the horror of the Holocaust became clear to the world, Europe was overwhelmed with tens of millions of refugees. In his 1947 State of the Union message, President Harry Truman encouraged the country to "fulfill our responsibilities to these suffering and homeless refugees of all faiths."[26]

The Displaced Persons Act became law in June of 1948 and indirectly began dismantling the quotas of the era by creating a policy for refugees as distinct from immigrants.[27] The law adopted international language—displaced persons or DPs—that future administrations used to highlight the disruptions of Soviet aggression in Hungary and Czechoslovakia, for example. Truman favored the ideals of the act but pushed to fix what he considered unjust particulars, namely, that the 200,000 visas set aside for DPs were debited from immigration quotas. He also emphasized that the law should be revised so that it was no harder for Jews to receive visas from outside the vanquished axis countries. Those amendments were adopted in 1950.

In 1952, a presidential election year, Congress took up immigration reform with an eye on both national security and the economy. Although President Truman and most liberals (Democrat and Republican) opposed anything short of ending the quota system, the McCarran-Walter Act became law with a veto-proof majority. It created the system of H-1 and H-2 temporary work visas still in place today, and broadened family reunification provisions so that female citizens could sponsor foreign husbands for the first time. Most important, it ended the exclusion of Asians or any ethnicity from naturalization. Two pillars of nativist immigration policy stood strong before Truman: naturalization bans by race and small quotas by nationality. The McCarran-Walter Act toppled the first. However, the small quotas remained. Therefore, the number of immigrants continued to be constrained. In 1954, Ellis Island was shuttered.

Historians credit the act as fruit of the Cold War. David Gerber observed that the United States had "an image problem on its hands."[28] The Soviets were

proudly advertising to newly liberated nations a communist philosophy that was based entirely on human equality whereas the Americans had a system designed by people Adolf Hitler had praised by name. Roger Daniels writes that in the "struggle for the hearts and minds of what it liked to call the Free World, the United States could no longer afford a policy that so blatantly excluded so many."[29]

The Modern Era

It was the presidency of John Kennedy, the first Catholic elected to the White House, that was the final turning point against nativism. Sadly, his agenda to reform the quota system was cut short by an assassin's bullets on November 23, 1963. Had Kennedy lived, however, there is real doubt whether his reforms would have passed Congress, or, if passed, been significant. Southern Democrats, even his Texan vice president, were unsympathetic. Meanwhile, reformers agitated against the racism of the quotas while emphasizing the harm they caused internationally. Senator Philip Hart of Michigan said, "Our laws needlessly provide grist for the propaganda mills of Moscow and Peiping."

But in death, Kennedy inspired change championed by none other than his successor, Lyndon Johnson, who pushed the slain president's agenda rather than his own, from civil rights to the Apollo missions. Hart and Congressman Emanuel Celler introduced new legislation in 1965 with strong support from the White House. Northern legislators from both parties supported it, whereas opposition came from southern Republicans and Democrats. The Hart-Celler Act scrapped the quota system entirely with a "preference system" allocating 50 percent of visas on the basis of occupational skills and family ties. Not everything was more open, as the bill introduced limits on immigration from the Western Hemisphere for the first time. The law established a larger, hemispheric quota of 170,000 for the Eastern Hemisphere (Europe, Asia, and Africa), and 120,000 for the Western Hemisphere. The last pillar of nativist policy was finally toppled, and the anomaly of isolationism was over.

The fact that Johnson staged an elaborate ceremony to commemorate the signing of the bill into law indicates the great significance he placed on the legislation. Johnson predicted that "the new law would strengthen us in a hundred unseen ways."[30] The ultimate consequences of how the new system would reshape the ethnic diversity of immigration flows were not foreseen by anyone in 1965. Ironically, skeptics were assuaged by a key provision in the law that gave priority to family reunification over any other concern. The reasoning was rooted in security concerns as much as color-blind idealism, since family members were expected to assimilate into American values more easily than foreigners with no family relationships in the United States. Skeptics and proponents alike believed that the law's allotment of 84 percent of quota slots to US residents bringing in family members would mean that the existing ethnic balance of the country would continue. In retrospect, there weren't nearly as many Europeans applying in the first place, so the slow tide of family-based migrants grew proportionally not to the ethnic balance inside the country but rather to the balance of the world.

Despite a half century of tinkering, the basic structure of immigration policy remains the same as it was in 1965. Although there was a major reform in 1990 championed by President George Bush that doubled the allotment of green cards, the bones of American policy remained the same. For all the sound and fury, current debates focus on illegal immigration which is 10 or 100 times smaller in scale than legal immigration, and the complete construction of a physical wall along the Mexican border, which is not as effective as either proponents or opponents believe. This modern era is in many ways the most open of all, which is a function of policies, economies, transportation costs, and a global network with familial connection to the United States that touch every region in every country.

Chapter 7
Walls

Mr. Gorbachev, tear down this wall.

When President Ronald Reagan uttered these words on June 12, 1987, the Cold War was still raging. He was standing in West Berlin, with the Brandenburg Gate looming over his shoulder on the other side of the Berlin Wall. For those who didn't live through the Cold War, it must be hard to imagine that the whole of Germany had been ripped in half after World War II, with the communists in charge of East Germany and a trio of Western democracies in charge of West Germany. The West was able to regain its sovereignty, whereas East Germany remained a puppet state to the USSR (Union of Soviet Socialist Republics), a barricade against Western thought, Western consumerism, and Western technology. What made the situation especially bizarre was that Berlin, the capital city, was in the heart of communist East Germany, and the Western democracies insisted on keeping its Western half free from Moscow's control.

One hundred miles inside the Soviet zone was this island of freedom known as West Berlin. In the summer of 1948, the Soviets tried to choke it off by closing all roads, canals, and trains from the West, sparking one of the first major Soviet-NATO (North Atlantic Treaty Organization) crises. The US Air Force responded by flying hundreds of thousands of resupply sorties, landing a cargo plane every thirty seconds at the Tempelhof, Gatow, or Tegel airbase. The "Berlin Airlift" finally broke the Soviet blockade in the spring of 1949, but the crisis clarified Moscow's reputation to the world as a totalitarian state. For the next decade, over 2 million citizens of East Germany escaped to the West simply by migrating from one side of Berlin to the other. The Great Brain Drain, as it is known in Europe, saw men, women, and children pack up their belongings and flee their homes for the prosperity and freedom of the West. Doctors, lawyers, and engineers disappeared overnight, causing serious structural problems in the East German state. The communists responded with the construction of the Berlin Wall in 1961. Originally made up of barbed wire, it was soon replaced by 15-foot-high concrete slabs, guarded with watchtowers, machine-gun emplacements, electrified fencing, and mines. The wall cut twenty-eight miles through the city itself and extended an additional seventy-five miles around West Berlin.

President John F. Kennedy visited West Berlin in June 1963 and gave his famous "Ich Bin Ein Berliner" speech. He drafted the speech alone because the version prepared by his speechwriters was too passive. Contrary to the myth, the translation is not "I am a jelly doughnut,"[1] and the brief remarks stand even stronger in retrospect: "Freedom has many difficulties and democracy is not perfect, but we have never had to put a wall up to keep our people in, to prevent them from leaving us."[2] Kennedy was touched by the mass of Germans who attended his speeches and was motivated by the grim image of the eastern side of the city.

Reagan's speech a quarter century later was more than an echo of Kennedy's. As Reagan prepared to travel to Europe, most national security experts did not believe the wall would come down in their lifetimes. A young speechwriter named Peter Robinson was tasked with writing a generic speech that avoided Cold War rhetoric. Robinson penned what he believed represented the hopes of the people of the city, not the cautions of American diplomats. When senior officials in the White House tried to strike the aggressive lines, President Reagan put them back in because he literally believed the wall could and would fall.[3] Consequently, the moment defined Reagan's triumphant legacy and is considered one of the great speeches in American history, as powerful in that year as it is today. Here was the Iron Curtain, erected to keep an entire people from enjoying the most basic right of all: the freedom of movement. And there were rumblings around the wall itself: young East Germans would meet at the wall to listen to their favorite Western bands being played on the other side, the constant stream of black-market tapes and records creating serious cracks in the narrative of criminal decadence in the West. As they gazed out and wondered what lay beyond the wall, curiosity grew to open discontent, then anger. The fall of the Berlin Wall in November 1989, less than a year after Reagan left the White House, was an unexpected turning point in world affairs that became a symbol for the nonviolent spread of freedom.

By then, even the figures at the heart of the Kremlin knew that it was over for the USSR. When the Soviet Union collapsed just a few years later, pieces of concrete from the Berlin Wall were celebrated souvenirs, and border walls in general were a symbol of communist despotism. Ironically, the United States never constructed a physical barrier along any of its borders from until after the Berlin Wall fell.

One year later, in 1990, there was a new beginning of wall building. American politicians who talked about the southern border shied away from describing the sporadically assembled new barrier along the California-Mexico border as a wall; instead, they euphemistically described it as a fence. The language was softer, and to be honest the politics was softer, too. Both hardened in the ensuing decades, as did the tropes, narratives, and fear for those beyond that wall.

That escalated with the 2016 presidential election. Donald Trump's campaign was the logical endpoint of a political fire that had been kindling for decades. The "big, beautiful wall" became one of the most controversial immigration reforms in recent history, sparking protests and rallies. It has become the subject of racist chants in playgrounds, far right graffiti, and countless rallies, protests, and lectures. Ironically, the passions of 2016 seemed ignorant of the basic facts, with one side claiming the wall must be built and the other claiming it must never be built; meanwhile the reality was that 650 miles of the 2,000-mile southern border wall were already standing.

It's fair to say that the end of the 20th century will be remembered for an epidemic of wall-building worldwide. Walls were erected all throughout countries in the Middle East, Asia, and Africa, even as Europe was celebrating continental integration. According to David Frye, author of an academic book on international border walls, "Only one Western nation matched the early efforts of the Asian and African countries. Well before plans had even been drawn up for the long walls of Israel, Saudi Arabia, and Egypt, a series of Clinton administration initiatives, aimed at tightening security on the porously fenced Mexican border, led to the extension or enhancement of physical barriers in California, Arizona, New Mexico, and Texas. . . . Operation Blockade and Hold the Line in 1993, Gatekeeper and Safeguard in 1994, and Rio Grande in 1997 were succeeded in 2006 by the passage of the Secure Fence Act, which saw the Clinton-era walls extended by hundreds of miles under the Bush and Obama administrations."[4]

Two questions hang over the current policy fight in the United States, one historical and one political. Have walls ever worked at controlling immigration? And, perhaps most important for a free society, does the American public actually want a border wall?

Walls in History

A wall can have two purposes—sometimes one, sometimes the other, and occasionally both: to keep people out, or to keep people in. They have been a remarkably consistent element in every human civilization, dating back 10,000 years. The human psyche is that of a tribal animal, and most of our architecture even today is built around principles of security, identity, and an almost fear of the unknown, whether that fear is a trespasser in your apartment block or an invading army. This pattern of wall-building for protection, if not population control, is visible all over the world—from China, to Europe, to the Americas. Fortification with walls to secure empires reached its peak during the medieval era when local towns grew up around castle walls, a development that occurred soon after the Roman Empire fell and locals were left to fend for themselves against invading barbarians, not to mention their neighbors.

The Romans began erecting permanent barriers along multiple borders following the death of the Emperor Trajan in AD 117 , notably Hadrian's Wall that cuts across Britain to this day. The empire reached its farthest geographic extent during Trajan's time, from the British Isles, covering the entire Mediterranean Sea, to modern-day Iraq and the Persian Gulf. His chosen successor, Hadrian, chose to scale back from the farthest frontiers, a decision as fateful as it was controversial. Hadrian thought walls and peace would last the test of time. The barbarians had other plans. Later emperors erected internal walls, even around the great city itself, to ward off eastern invaders. Two centuries of decline followed Hadrian, although in fairness that was mostly due to internal economic policy mistakes including unsustainable fiscal deficits and hyperinflations. Then in AD 300, Emperor Diocletian effectively converted the entire Roman populace into feudal serfs, making internal migration a crime in a vain effort to stabilize the chaotic economy.

Walls are conservative, in the dictionary definition of the term. The psychological impulse to protect a nation's wealth and culture from foreign contamination is an example of what behavioral economists call "loss aversion." This describes the lab-tested behavior showing individuals are more concerned about losses than gains. A lost dollar hurts more than a found dollar soothes, and the behavior affects larger social groups as well. History tells us that with great power comes great loss aversion.

Take the fate of Ming China, the world's most fabulously wealthy civilization in the 15th century. The empire cut itself off from foreign trade after the 1430s, an action urged by Mandarin bureaucrats in order to clip the power of the merchant class, their rivals at court. Court intrigue is also revealed by the extension of China's Great Wall and the abrupt termination of the voyages of Admiral Zheng He, both reflecting the Confucian attitude that foreign barbarians offered nothing of value. The following centuries saw China transform into a weak and isolated time capsule.

Despite the cautionary tales of imperial Rome and Ming China, building walls both literal and figurative has remained a habit of great powers in decline. But they haven't always been a mistake.

Consider the Byzantine Empire. When the Roman emperor Constantine re-organized governance of that vast society into two halves, a Latin West and a Greek East, he enabled the east to survive for hundreds of years when the city of Rome became unmanageable and even when western Europe collapsed. The Eastern Roman Empire came to be known as Byzantium with its capital set in the city of Constantinople (modern-day Istanbul) at the geographic intersection of Europe and Asia. The city was the richest in Europe, arguably the richest in the world, from the 5th century until the 15th century, when it finally fell to the Ottoman Turks.[5]

The reason Constantinople lasted so long is because of its wall, fourteen miles in circumference. The portions of the walls that faced water, specifically the Golden Horn inlet to the north and the Sea of Marmara to the south, were impenetrable because attackers could only come ashore in plain sight. The western walls that sheltered the city from attack by land were invulnerable. The inner fortification is surrounded by a floodable moat and an outer barricade. Inside the barricade are two successively higher walls referred to as the Outer Wall and the Inner Wall.

With the weaponry and tactics at the time, any attempt to conquer this fortress proved disastrous for the attackers. Under fire from the city, attackers could not scale the walls, and tunnels underneath the barrier would easily collapse on the sappers. Ultimately, though, Constantinople's walls met their fateful demise in the year AD 1453.

Like his predecessors, the Ottoman Sultan Mehmed II wanted to capture the cornerstone of the Christian world: Constantinople. Mehmed's militaristic desire was fulfilled by the advent of new military technologies unavailable to previous sultans: gunpowder and the cannon. Ironically, it came from an immigrant. The only man with the prowess to build such large cannons did not come from the East, rather from Europe. A Hungarian foundryman named Orban offered to craft a cannon capable of pulverizing the walls of Constantinople. After three months of construction, the cannon was dragged by oxen to the frontlines; on April 2, 1453, the walls and cannon were put to the test as the battle of Constantinople waged. As Turks began to flood Constantine's defenses, Constantine ordered the destruction of all bridges over the moat, locking the Inner Wall and resting all defenses on the strength of the Outer Walls.

Within twenty-four hours of the cannon's discharge, an entire section of the wall was destroyed, something that had not occurred for 700 years. It was beyond imagination. Women and children fought hard to rebuild it with handfuls of stones, rocks, clay, and wood, but it was too late. Turkish tactics quickly overpowered Constantinople's inner defenses as well. The final stroke came on May 29, 1453, when the "Horrible Bombard" demolished a portion of the repaired wall, allowing Turkish attackers to flood through the opening and massacre the Byzantine soldiers and citizens defending the Inner Wall. Civilians and priests cowered inside the churches and synagogues of the city, including the great cathedral of Hagia Sophia. The slaughter was so extensive that an estimated 30,000 people were killed .

News of the fall of Constantinople sent shock waves throughout Europe, a fear that was felt in every church. The Muslim invaders had not only taken the Holy Land and secured it during the Crusades, but now they had set foot in Europe itself. Hostility lingers today, particularly in the Balkan states, where bitterness toward Ottoman colonialism and the destruction of Christian sites and identity still runs high. The nature of warfare (and security) forever changed. Although the power of walls and barriers is much diminished in modern warfare, the image of "barbarians at the gate" blocked by impregnable walls lives on in our social memory.

What Are Walls Good For?

Setting aside their lack of utility against armed invasion, what are physical barriers good for? They must have some utility, because all around the world, countries are building walls again. As David Frye observed in his recent book, *Walls*, the Middle East is experiencing a renaissance of wall-building. In 2003, Saudi Arabia began installing a wall along its 1,100-mile border with Yemen and now has almost completely enclosed itself. The Saudi-Iraq border has five layers of fencing and underground motion detectors. After the Second Intifada, a Palestinian uprising that began in 2000 and lasted five years, Israel began constructing the West Bank wall that would span 450 miles and spur the creation of additional border walls around the country. Asia has experienced a similar trend after the rise of Islamic terrorism prompted India to secure its border with Pakistan with the installation of electrified barriers. We are now witnessing a similar trend in the Americas to strengthen barriers, blockades, and borders, but there is a crucial and often ignored concern in the discussion of walls: will these barriers work?

One answer comes from looking within. Gated communities have emerged in recent decades in the United States as an effective deterrent of crime. In 2005, scholars estimated that there were over 7 million "walled and fenced" communities with over 16 million residents. In a careful econometric study of Orange County, California, neighborhoods, Nicholas Branic and Charis E. Kubrin found "a 22% decrease in expected violent crimes and a 17% decrease in expected property crimes" in gated communities after factoring in demographic controls.[6] Walls are hardly impotent.

Looking back at what happened in 1990s San Diego is instructive. "It was an area that was out of control," explained Border Patrol agent Jim Henry in an interview with National Public Radio. "There were over 100,000 aliens crossing through this area a year."[7] The international border between Mexico and the United States was marked by a mere cable strung along the dirt. After local agents put up a makeshift barrier of corrugated metal sheets in 1990, federal funds began to supplement their efforts. Apprehensions dropped by 95 percent. The original makeshift fence of corrugated sheets still stands ten feet high along the fourteen-mile stretch that extends inland from the beach at the Pacific Ocean. There is a second fence, fifteen feet high, made of thick steel mesh, angled at the top to deter climbing. The two fences are separated by fifty yards that the Border Patrol sweeps with floodlights, cameras, and motion sensors.

Critics observe that migrants simply changed their routes when such barriers are erected. Unless a border is fully militarized, migrants will circumvent physical barriers with tunnels, ladders, or simply cutting holes in the fence. Using blowtorches to cut open circular gashes in the thick US-Mexico border fence happens roughly twice a day.

I have long suspected that a border wall is ineffective at stopping illegal immigration, but after visiting the border, I saw that it can be very effective at deterring drug trafficking and property crime. Having lived in San Diego as a graduate student during the late 1990s, I remember the construction of border fencing as part of the daily news. I vividly recall seeing new housing developments sprout up in the southern part of the county, particularly nice new homes in Chula Vista. Real estate agents said that after the local border fence had been constructed, property crime had gone down, allowing the development of safe, new neighborhoods.

A recent report from the San Diego Association of Governments found that the 2019 property crime rate was the lowest in forty years. The highest rate was in 1988 and 1989, when the region experienced nearly 20 percent more property crimes than the national average, but the rate fell sharply after 1990 and has been below the national average since 1995. Today, the property crime rate is one-fifth of what it was at the peak, before the border wall was built. It's unclear whether Chula Vista or other neighborhoods near the border experienced a greater relative decline in the crime data, but real estate data were easier to find.

Thanks to Zillow.com, we can compare the property values in four different regions of San Diego County. Unfortunately, this dataset doesn't go back to 1990. Zillow has median property values as far back as 1996 for eighty-seven local zip codes, which I allocated into North County, Central County, South Coastal (Chula Vista), and Border (for the four zip codes in the dataset that include the US-Mexico border). All other factors that affect property values should be roughly equal among the four regions, which gives us a fair assessment of how growth rates in real estate values changed before, during, and after construction of the border fence.

The history is relatively simple. Between 1990 and 1995, border fencing was being put up sporadically by local border patrol agents. And then in 2006, Congress passed the Secure Fence Act. Since it took time in both instances for funding and construction (and a change in perception of conditions), I used the years 2000 and 2008 as critical points in the time series data.

I was able to crunch the numbers for two series across three time periods: Pre-2001, 2001–2008, and Post-2008. The two data series are (a) median value per square foot across all home types and (b) the Zillow Index for Single Family Residences. What I found is that relative to central San Diego neighborhoods, property values along the border grew slowly before 2001. Those same border areas had equal growth in both the Zillow Index and the median value per square foot in the middle period. After 2008, there is a clear growth boost of one-third of a percentage point in Border and South Coastal neighborhoods, which is likely attributable to the border barrier.

Did immigration patterns change between the neighborhoods? Not at all. Did patterns of casual trespass change? Absolutely. It is difficult to see these results without appreciating that a wall has a deterrent effect on property crime and transient behavior.

The San Diego experience motivated construction of the "fence" all along the Mexican border. The 2006 act that passed Congress and was signed by President Bush was a start, authorizing construction of 700 miles of robust double and triple fencing. Bush, known as being supportive of legal immigration, had wanted to negotiate a comprehensive partnership with Mexico's president Vicente Fox during his first term. The 9/11 attacks set that grand effort aside, but he worked relentlessly to rekindle it during his second term that began in 2005. When he signed the 2006 act, Bush described it as "an important step toward immigration reform."[8] The law was "widely perceived as an attempt by some House Republicans to appear tough on immigration in the run-up to the elections," in the words of the American Immigration Lawyers Association, yet it passed with significant bipartisan support. The vote was 283–138 in the House, and 80–19 in the Senate with twenty-six Democrats voting in favor. Bush's later efforts to pass broader legislation were stymied by restrictionist politicians within his own party, uncompromising Democrats led by Nancy Pelosi in the House of Representatives, and certain ambitious senators as well.

The Great Wall of America is not what most people may think. It is not the border fence extending east from the Pacific Ocean and neatly winding its way toward Texas and the Gulf of Mexico. Rather, the nation's great wall is a sociological one, dividing the American people into two increasingly hostile political parties: red versus blue. Yet polling shows that the rising wall of partisanship is not emerging from the people. Both parties are losing members as tens of millions of Americans have stopped identifying as either Republican or Democrat. The largest party in the United States is "Independent." The divisiveness is being imposed from politicians and the perverse incentives of modern media. In the next chapter, we will review recent hyperpartisan immigration reform policies and media coverage of the immigration crisis that made Americans appear more divided than ever before. But is this appearance a true depiction of the American public? And how do we ensure that crossing the aisle does not become as difficult as climbing a wall?

Chapter 8
Divides

A comprehensive, single piece of legislation on any topic, but especially on immigration, is going to be very difficult to achieve. We keep talking about the same issue now for 15 years, and everybody is doing this all-or-nothing approach. And all-or-nothing is going to leave you with nothing.

— **Senator Marco Rubio**

Democracy in the 21st century strikes many observers as increasingly dysfunctional, and that's true in the United States as well as globally. Long before rioters mobbed the Capitol on January 6, 2021, civility among the political class had broken down and given way to what President Biden has described as an "uncivil war." Political animus has affected everything from presidential debates to Supreme Court nominations. In the eyes of those who have participated in politics for decades, the acrimony has been worsening year by year, decade by decade, driving many incumbents to retire in disgust. The violence of January 6 seemed impossible beforehand and somehow inevitable in retrospect.

Many will blame Donald Trump. And that will be a mistake. The Trump presidency is a consequence, not a cause, of our broken politics.

There have been low points in the long history of American democracy, notably the physical violence that took place in the halls of the Capitol in the years leading up to the outbreak of the Civil War in the 1860s, but the current intensity of partisanship has been rising in America for decades. We know because we can measure such things. As just one example, opinion polls show support for political violence rising among voters in *both* parties during the Trump presidency from below 5 percent to above 30 percent. But that too is a consequence, as the partisan hostility is coming from the top down. Party leaders in Washington, dating back to the 1970s, have used increasingly antagonistic language and tactics to get their way.

Metrics of party-line voting show an increasingly ideological gulf between Democratic and Republican legislators.[1] Before Watergate, ironically, it was common to find conservative Democrats and liberal Republicans. Republicans in the 1970s supported increasing environmental regulation, Democrats widely opposed gay marriage, and everyone worked together to keep the budget balanced.

All of the great legislative accomplishments in those days were bipartisan. For example, 80 percent of Republicans in the House and the Senate supported the Civil Rights Act of 1964, along with 70 percent of Democratic senators and 60 percent of House Democrats. That simple fact is almost unknown by students today, who have been fed a myth of partisan stereotypes. Yet it's a historical fact that GOP support routinely outpaced Democratic support for civil rights in the 1950s and 1960s. Likewise, military conscription ended in 1973 thanks to bipartisan backing for Richard Nixon's campaign promise to end the draft. Most impressively, a bipartisan effort to reform Social Security, trimming benefits and raising payroll taxes, took effect in 1983 following work by the Reagan-appointed National Commission on Social Security Reform, a group that was chaired by Alan Greenspan.[2] Those days are gone.

The popular narrative among pundits is that the American citizenry is bifurcating into ideological camps. Not true. They say there is a grassroots culture war causing hyperpartisanship in the government. Not true. This is all a mirage of television imagery, showcasing angry protestors at abortion clinics, congressional hearings, antifa riots, Proud Boy riots. They are fringe actors whom the media pretends are mainstream.

Morris Fiorina, a Stanford professor of political science, has studied the bifurcation narrative and found it wanting. Reviewing public surveys from Pew to the GSS that ask the same recurring issue questions over many decades, Fiorina finds that public attitudes haven't changed much. Interestingly, when opinions have evolved, the pattern involves a gradual shift in the *same direction* by liberals, conservatives, and independents. The bifurcation narrative persists, he says, because it is promoted by activists for their own selfish reasons, "fundraising and membership-maximizing among other things."[3] The culture war is happening in the halls of Congress and in cable television studios, not in the heartland.

Some of the best writing on hyperpartisanship comes from Jonathan Rauch, a resident scholar at the Brookings Institution and contributing editor of *The Atlantic*. Rauch's 1994 book *Demoscelrosis* was an early warning of a political problem that he sensed was growing like a cancer. His insight is that the institutional imbalances are caused by campaign finance laws. Starting in the mid-1970s, US election law mandated that big-dollar donations could only be collected by the two established parties, whereas direct donations to individual candidates became illegal. The effect was to create a duopoly over the money flow that in turn shapes the federal government.

Rauch believes the situation has been made worse by a balkanized media landscape. The pre-cable era of broadcast television, we can understand in hindsight, offered a unifying daily canon to the culture. That's gone. Moreover, the moderating influence of city newspapers and national weeklies, such as *Time* and *Newsweek*, have been undercut by social networking platforms that entrench filter bubbles. Filter bubbles allow one segment of the public to believe the 2020 election was stolen by Joe Biden and another segment to believe that the 9/11 attacks were orchestrated by George W. Bush. Grievance-based clickbait is rewarded at the expense of dispassionate journalism.

The duopoly theory got a heavy endorsement in 2017 from Harvard Business School professor Michael Porter, a renowned business scholar. He teamed up with Katherine Gehl to examine what was causing the dysfunction in federal politics. They saw an election system with competitive markers eerily similar to a duopoly, confirming Rauch's insights. Duopolists in business markets work in tandem to block entrepreneurs with new ideas that would dislodge their control of market share, which in politics is the business of fundraising. Harvard published their findings in a report that received widespread acclaim. To make sure their point wasn't missed, the authors used the word duopoly 128 times in the report's eighty pages. Gehl explained, "The core idea here is that Washington isn't broken. In fact, it turns out that Washington is doing exactly what it's designed to do."[4] Unlike duopolies such as Coke and Pepsi, which control only 70 percent of the soda market, Republicans and Democrats control 99.9 percent of elective offices in federal and state governments.

Porter and Gehl described how hyperpartisanship tends to exaggerate differences between the two sides. Can you guess which issue they believe best illustrates the failure of partisan compromise?

> In today's partisan political competition, there is actually an incentive not to solve problems. Keeping a problem or controversy alive and festering is a way to attract and motivate partisan voters, special interests, and committed donors to each side. Neither party, for example, has strong competitive incentives to solve the problem of immigration, because a comprehensive compromise solution would disappoint some of both parties' most fervent supporters and reliable donors.[5]

Immigration has become the ultimate wedge issue in American politics. If just one aspect of the immigration system is repaired, critics (in both parties) will insist that their concerns must also be addressed. Woe betide the senator who wishes to merely make green cards available to more foreign-born electrical engineers who graduate from American universities and want to work for American companies in, of all places, America! The same senator will be tied in knots by trying to address a comprehensive set of immigration issues in a single bill. That invites extremists on both sides to decry the bill's compromises. It's a catch-22. Instead, legislators seem stuck in a cycle of virtue signaling—proposing one-sided bills that cannot garner a single vote of support from the other party.

Because the US Congress has evolved into a structurally dysfunctional state, a kind of "political prisoners' dilemma," a solution is hard to imagine. Presidential leadership is necessary, but maybe insufficient, and it has faltered badly in the past decade.

Comprehensive Sabotage

President George H. W. Bush was able to unite Congress behind a major reform in 1990, a piece of legislation that is the immigration equivalent of the Louisiana Purchase. That was Thomas Jefferson's historic acquisition of nearly a million square miles of territory from France in 1803, a swath of land west of the Mississippi from New Orleans all the way to Montana, effectively doubling the geographic size of the nation. Likewise, Bush's 1990 law more than doubled the annual number of green cards granted to legal immigrants while also introducing the H1-B visa for high-skill temporary workers and the diversity lottery for 50,000 green cards open to previously marginalized foreign countries. The 1990 law's higher ceiling set at 675,000 visas for permanent legal residents bedevils restrictionists because it is the law of the land and therefore beyond the reach of White House action.

President George W. Bush also offered bipartisan, commonsense leadership on immigration reform during his 2001–2009 tenure, partnering with Senator Edward Kennedy. But the younger Bush's good faith efforts were stymied repeatedly by the hyperpartisans in Congress. His Secure Fence Act of 2006 was a smart first step toward an incremental legislative strategy. Conservatives promised to take other steps seriously if border security was addressed first. Bush honored that bargain as a down payment on the larger Comprehensive Immigration Reform Act in 2007. But Bush's effort was undermined from an unexpected quarter.

The 2007 bill was based on three earlier comprehensive proposals, a McCain-Kennedy Senate bill put forth in May 2005, another joint Senate bill proposed two months later by John Cornyn and John Kyl, and a 2006 bill sponsored by centrist senator Arlan Specter which actually passed the Senate but sank in the House. After the mid-term elections in November, President Bush was entering the final two years of his presidency and set his sights on immigration reform as his major domestic legacy. The renewed Senate effort was led by GOP maverick John McCain and liberal lion Ted Kennedy who together forged a coalition of senators. The famous "Gang of 14" promised to vote together as the bill made its way through committee and onto the floor in order to block partisan nitpicking by amendments. The legislation was filled with comprehensive bits arrayed around some core reforms: an expanded temporary worker program, enhanced border security, narrowing of the scope of family reunification as the basis for most green cards in favor of a merit-based points system, and a pathway to citizenship for illegal immigrants who passed a background check, paid a fine, and lived in the United States for eight years without any criminal incidents. It was a delicate balancing act, but ultimately proved to be a Venn diagram with no center. The summer of 2007 was fraught with failed procedural votes to advance the bill, but the administration pushed for one final Senate vote. On June 28, the Senate's cloture vote was tallied, a shocking disappointment to Ted Kennedy, with only 46 yeas, far short of the 60 needed.

The media characterized the opposition as mostly driven by Republicans, though a full third of Democratic senators were staunchly opposed as well, and the core issue for them was opposition to a guest worker program. This is the vital twist to the story. It was the robust guest worker plank that had initially attracted pro-business Republicans to support the early entreaties of President Bush. Reuters reported the day of the bill's failed vote that the bill was "opposed by some labor unions, which said its temporary worker program would have created an underclass of cheap laborers." Senator Byron Dorgan, a Democrat from North Dakota, repeatedly proposed eliminating the guest worker provision. Kennedy blocked him. That's when Dorgan cleverly approached the youngest senator in the Gang of 14, a rising star from Illinois named Barack Obama.

Years later, when asked about the ill-fated 2007 vote, Senator Chuck Schumer said, "Byron Dorgan did an amendment, and it scuttled the bill." The Dorgan amendment didn't directly eliminate the 400,000 guest work visas; rather, it sunset the program after five years. Republican senators called it a poison pill and promised to vote No if Dorgan's amendment was included. When Obama decided to support the sunset provision, despite promising to lock arms against such efforts, Kennedy unloaded on him in a private meeting, shouting, "You can't come in here and undo everything!" according to reporting by CNN's Jake Tapper.[6]

This is a story mostly forgotten in the media's narrative of virtuous Democrats and racist Republicans, but the reality is that there were deep anti-immigrant feelings in both parties. That those tensions were navigated by ambitious politicians is neither sad or shocking, but it shouldn't be forgotten. Carl Cannon, executive editor and Washington bureau chief for *RealClearPolitics*, was credited by the editorial pages of the *Wall Street Journal* as one of the lone journalists willing to remember this history ten years on. As legislators and pundits attacked Trump's policies, Cannon was bemused by the "vitriol and name-calling" of Democrats who with numerous chances "to grant 11 million immigrants access to the American dream, they instead chose, for partisan purposes, to keep them in the shadows."[7]

Barack Obama won a historic presidential election in 2008 against John McCain, and the enthusiasm for the Obama-Biden ticket was so strong that it helped Democrats control an even larger majority of the seats in the Senate and House. This "united government" could in theory pass any legislation the Democrats wanted. The US Senate requires sixty votes to overcome the minority party's traditional right to filibuster, but garnering support from a handful of pro-immigration Republicans from the Gang of 14 would have been rather easy. Unfortunately for the new president, he had something worse than a mere majority: his party actually had a supermajority in the Senate, exactly 60 Democratic senators. It would prove to be a curse to have that many votes because it made every piece of legislation a temptation to ignore moderate Republicans and go as far to the left as possible. And that's exactly what the Obama administration did.

During those first two years of the Obama administration, Congress passed a series of progressive bills. The first was a major deficit-financed stimulus bill, followed by the Affordable Care Act (known as "Obamacare"), and the Dodd-Frank Act to reform Wall Street. Congress addressed a host of other progressive concerns from equal pay protections for female workers to repealing the ban on gays in the military. But neither Obama nor Democrats in Congress took any steps to pass immigration reform, comprehensive or otherwise. They didn't vote to provide a pathway for citizenship for illegal immigrants, for dreamers, for expanded refugees. Nothing.

Why wasn't comprehensive legislation passed during these two years? Why wasn't it even proposed in committee? Some say that the White House was too busy in the first two years of the Obama presidency, but candidate Obama had promised, "I can guarantee that we will have, in the first year, an immigration bill that I strongly support." Once he was in office, he turned his back on it but made time to enact lots of other legislation, including "Cash for Clunkers." The notion that there was no time for immigration reform simply does not hold.

On election night in 2010, Democrats suffered a net loss of sixty-three seats in the House of Representative, memorable because it represented the biggest shift in seats in sixty-two years. Nancy Pelosi lost the speakership to John Boehner, divided government returned to Washington, and immigration reform was barely mentioned for the next three years. Even though the partisan gap widened, President Obama and Senate Democrats made a questionable effort to pass comprehensive immigration reform in 2013, this time with a "Gang of Eight" bipartisan senators that included the Republican rising star from Florida, Marco Rubio. Veterans of the 2007 effort were hopeful that the new Senate coalition would craft something new and appealing to Republican centrists, but that is not what happened. Instead, the Senate bill was crafted with almost perfect cynicism, designed for maximum virtue signaling and minimum appeal to conservatives. It passed the Senate 68–32 (including every Democrat and a dozen Republicans), but stalled as expected in the Boehner-led House.

John Boehner was famously moderate. He would not consider legislation that did not pass a "majority of the majority" test, meaning a bill had to have support from more than half of his fellow Republican representatives. The 2013 comprehensive bill couldn't attract more than a quarter of Republican senators, and everyone in Washington knew it was dead on arrival in the House. Meanwhile, the media heralded the Senate proposal as the biggest overhaul of immigration law in a generation—strengthening border security, mandating E-Verify, introducing a new entry-exit system, and revamping both permanent and guest-worker visas. It also dramatically shifted the basis of legal migration from families to a Canadian-style merit point system. And it had a poison pill: amnesty granted to illegal immigrants. Language in the bill was euphemistic, describing a "pathway to citizenship" for the 11–12 million illegal immigrants residing in the United States, meaning amnesty and a deal-breaker for Republicans.

The Heritage Foundation at the time published a series of studies and essays opposing such legislation, including an economic analysis that claimed the net fifty-year cost of the bill amounted to $6.3 trillion. As an economist who had worked at Heritage years earlier, I was asked repeatedly to comment on the bill and the Heritage claim. A blog I posted got quite a bit of attention, concluding that the "pileup of outlandish Heritage estimates presents a credibility hurdle." I had more interviews with political reporters than at any time in my career, with kind words in favor of the Senate legislation overall as well as my warning that the "pathway to citizenship" would doom its prospects. Why not just grant permanent legal status without citizenship?

That nuanced distinction may seem obscure, but it became a sore point when President Obama made an overtly political move in 2012 to bypass Congress and grant legal status to Dreamers. The president walked to the Rose Garden in the middle of the afternoon on June 15, 2012, and announced that because of inaction by Congress, he was taking executive action to grant legal status to illegal immigrants who had been brought to America as children. It was technically a "deferred action for childhood arrivals" (DACA):

> Effective immediately, the Department of Homeland Security is taking steps to lift the shadow of deportation from these young people. Over the next few months, eligible individuals who do not present a risk to national security or public safety will be able to request temporary relief from deportation proceedings and apply for work authorization. Now, let's be clear—this is not amnesty, this is not immunity. This is not a path to citizenship. It's not a permanent fix. This is a temporary stopgap measure.

It was high-minded. It was morally correct. And it was a smart political move to galvanize voters during the summer of his re-election campaign. But it was cynical and divisive, too. The Citizenship and Immigration Services (USCIS) began accepting applications two months later, a few weeks before the 2012 election. Obama defeated Mitt Romney with just 51 percent of the popular vote.

The Runaway Train

Two years after DACA, the Obama White House decided to push even further. The president announced an expansion, known as DAPA, that would grant legal status to an estimated 3.9 million older undocumented immigrants who were parents of legal US residents. After insisting for six years that the only path forward was a "comprehensive" piece of legislation, on November 20, 2014, President Obama issued a series of memoranda to the various cabinet secretaries responsible for overseeing the nation's immigration system. Ten distinct memoranda were published on the DHS website simultaneously, expressly described as not being changes in law. Meanwhile, Obama publicly proclaimed that "I just took action to change the law" affecting naturalization, deferred action, parole-in-place, spousal work rules, and border security.

The previous maximum age of 31 for receiving DACA relief was eliminated, affecting up to 290,000 individuals. There was even a deferral for all other nonviolent undocumented immigrants as "non-priorities for removal" which effectively blocked agents from deporting anyone who wasn't a violent criminal. Petty theft? Squatting? Voting with a fake ID? Driving without a license? Let it slide. States were told that individuals given "deferred action" were also to be granted work authorizations.

The legislation by fiat had become a runaway train.

The White House rationale for its dozen executive actions was that "Due to limited resources, DHS and its components cannot respond to all immigration violations or remove all persons illegally in the United States." Even though the memos seemed to imply more spending in plenty of areas, the actions were justified on the basis of budget constraints. Yet ten days after the announcement, the *New York Times* reported "the Citizenship and Immigration Services agency said it was immediately seeking 1,000 new employees to work in an office building to process 'cases filed as a result of the executive actions on immigration.' The likely cost: nearly $8 million a year in lease payments [for a new operations center just outside of Washington, DC] and more than $40 million for annual salaries."[8]

US District Judge Andrew S. Hanen suspended a few Obama actions after a federal lawsuit was filed by twenty-six states. The DAPA plan was ultimately blocked by the Supreme Court; someday soon DACA will be similarly found unconstitutional. There is a principle in democracy that new laws must be created by the legislature, and White House memos parading as law in the realm of domestic policy are an overreach of presidential power. Although this kind of chaos may make for good politics, it does not make for good policy.

The Obama administration never did offer a legislative package of incremental reforms, certainly nothing to make DACA a law. Where were the private meetings with Republican senators on incremental legislation? Where was the outreach to top staffers in the House and Senate to a consensus bill that granted legal status without citizenship, just like DACA? Where was the effort to re-establish a functioning legislative process? Nowhere. To be sure, President Trump followed the Obama precedent with executive actions of his own and was even more uncompromising; hyperpartisanship is a two-headed snake.

The shame of it is that immigration is an issue ripe for compromise and consensus. If President Obama had been willing to reject the false deportation-versus-citizenship choice, we would be talking about the very real benefits of a decade of success instead of serving up the same dilemma to the Biden White House.

The House Republican Implosion of 2018

A more charitable reading of Obama's decision to focus on a Democrat-only approach to policymaking rather than seeking middle ground with the opposition is that the Republican Party was truly incalcitrant in 2013. Egged on by nativists and hardliners in the Twitter era, maybe John Boehner really was powerless to control his caucus in the House. A history of his tenure as Speaker of the House will have as its main theme a frustration with trying to govern its competing factions. For better or worse, the Republican Party was the party of ideas in the new century. Too many ideas. There were libertarians, defense hawks, supply-siders, neoconservatives, Rush Limbaugh's dittoheads, Wall Street investors, Evangelicals, and small businesses, just to name some of the more active cohorts.

Congressman Eric Cantor, Boehner's protégé, lost to a Tea Party challenger in a 2014 primary election in Virginia. Cantor was a conservative centrist but suffered a defeat that shocked the political world. Despite the Speaker's ambitions to craft grand bargains with the Democrats, he was met with repeated failures on the budget, tax reform, and immigration. And every failure could be traced to resistance by the forty-odd members of the Republican Freedom Caucus. Ultimately, those members mutinied, threatening to vote no confidence against Boehner, who countered by announcing his resignation in the fall of 2015.

Finding a new leader of the House Republicans and, consequently, the Speaker, was a bizarre spectacle. To outsiders, it seemed like a game of hot potato, a job that nobody really wanted. Ultimately, the conservatives and mainstream members settled by recruiting the reluctant Paul Ryan of Wisconsin to leave his wonky role as head of the tax-writing committee. Ryan was an inspired choice, but ultimately the factions proved ungovernable for him as well. He announced his own retirement three years later, months before the 2018 mid-terms. History might have been different for Ryan and the Congress but for the tumultuous presidency of Donald Trump. The world saw the internal divisions of the GOP come to a boil in the summer of 2018.

Legislation to formalize DACA was stuck. Moderate members wanted it to get to the full floor for a vote, but conservatives in the GOP wanted it to die in committee. The only way to overcome a committee impasse is with a "discharge petition" with signatures from a majority of House members, which in 2018 required all members of the opposition Democrats and around twenty renegade Republicans. Facing this threat from the center, Ryan reconciled his factions with a strange tactic, perhaps unique in American history, that

Among Americans who primarily speak Spanish, support for making English the official language stands at 58 percent.

I'll save a broader analysis of policy reforms for later in the book. The point I want to emphasize here is that partisan divides about immigration are not found among the wider public. It is a peculiar affliction of the political class.

Powerful People, Partisan Parties

A house divided against itself cannot stand. It was true back when President Lincoln described the Civil War, and it remains true today regarding the exponential increase of hyperpartisanship in Washington, DC. How can we expect a government to function when politicians forfeit compromise in order to push policies that are destined to fail in order to appease that partisan bases? We can't.

The true wall that divides this nation is not the border wall to the south but is instead the institutional wall that divides the parties. Hyperpartisanship is quickly becoming the norm for government and one of the greatest threats to American democracy. The political aisle is meant to be crossed, but in its place, politicians have erected a barrier. It is time someone urges lawmakers to *tear down this wall!*

It's a sad state of affairs that the issue of immigration has transformed so much in two and a half centuries of American history. What was once one of the rallying cries of independence of a weak, nascent nation in 1776 is now the definitive political wedge issue in the world's great superpower. The politics of immigration have done more to fuel resentment and distrust in America than any foreign power could. It doesn't have to be this way.

Unfortunately, the hypnotic grip of "comprehensive" is hard to shake. Rarely has a reform concept so vexed actual policymaking. It's as if a surgeon couldn't just remove a ruptured appendix without also transplanting the entire digestive system. Sadly, comprehensive policymaking has failed every time it has been tried for two decades.

President George W. Bush tried in 2006 and 2007, especially supporting the McCain-Kennedy bill with a massive, extended campaign. Obama's 2013 effort was equally ambitious, if seemingly cynical. The majority parties keep pushing extreme policies masked by comprehensive and seemingly bipartisan legislation that are doomed to fail. Poison pills abound in the details after amendments. Then the majority party points fingers at the other side, claiming that they refuse to compromise, when compromise was never the goal of the legislation. Instead of recognizing the lack of legislative ac-

advanced two very different bills to the floor of the House in the third week of June.

The conservative option was considered first. Sponsored by Congressman Bob Goodlatte, it granted legal status to DACA immigrants but not a pathway to citizenship. It also slashed legal immigration by half. All Democrats and forty-one Republicans voted against it.

The moderate option was considered days later. It offered DACA-eligible immigrants a renewable six-year legal status followed by a pathway to citizenship. It also included a handful of other restrictionist provisions: $25 billion for the southern border wall, reductions to legal immigration levels, ending the diversity lottery, and narrowing family sponsorship for some legal immigrants (brothers, sisters, and adult children). All Democrats and 112 Republicans voted against it.

The dual failure was uniquely embarrassing. Republicans literally could not find common ground among themselves. Instead, comprehensive reform failed again, twice this time around.

There remains a baffling question of what might have been. Realize that Congress has never considered a narrow bill to convert DACA into legislation: a renewable three-year legal status that allows Dreamers to reside, work, and pay taxes in the United States without citizenship, welfare, or the right to vote. The wedge issue has become a self-destructive lightning rod.

You might think the Democrats watched that spectacle and prepared legislation that was truly centrist and could pass their caucus. And you would be wrong. Here is the lesson learned: Nancy Pelosi's Democratic majority did not even bother to produce an immigration reform proposal in the House after she regained the Speaker's gavel in 2019.

Trump Versus the Media

President Donald Trump put forward new legislation in a Rose Garden speech on May 16, 2019, declaring, "Our proposal is pro-American, pro-immigrant, and pro-worker. It's just common sense." It might have been seen as an olive branch extended to Democrats who by then controlled both the Senate and the House. Contrary to his reputation as an immigrant basher, the president made a proposal that surprised everyone with its centrist approach. Most notably, Trump's plan did not reduce the annual number of legal migrants; rather, it shifted the composition of green cards with an innovative merit-based system that awarded more weight to younger, more educated people with more employable skills and English proficiency. Such a shift is one of the few areas of consensus among policy wonks, and despite the immediate political resistance to the word "merit" by some of Trump's antagonists, it has been used for decades as a shorthand for employment-based immigration systems common in other countries.

Right-wingers on Twitter thought that not reducing immigration levels was a betrayal by Trump. That reaction was to be expected. What was unexpected was the elite opinion of newspaper editors, faced with a moderate proposal from Donald Trump. Since it couldn't be attacked on substance, the plan was derided for not being *comprehensive* enough. An article in the *New York Times* said the legislation "did not address protections for the so-called Dreamers . . . or the 11 million undocumented immigrants currently living in the United States." An editorial in the back pages of the same paper complained, "This proposal does not address some of the thorniest elements of the immigration debate." A lengthy front-page article in the *Washington Post* chimed: "The new proposal . . . appears destined for the congressional dustbin [and] . . . sidesteps some major components of the immigration system that can be far more complex and controversial to resolve." None of the journalists would acknowledge that the whole point of the legislation was to be incremental. The *Post*'s editorial called it an "improvement over the administration's previous bar-the-door approach . . . but the initiative omits even passing reference to the reality of 10 million or 11 million undocumented immigrants." A bemused article in the *Wall Street Journal* observed, "It doesn't address some pressing immigration policy issues."

Politicians weren't much better in their neglect of the plan's substance. Senator Chuck Schumer bizarrely called it "the same partisan, radical anti-immigration policies" as before. Of course, Schumer knew better. Trump called for preserving the legal levels of 1.1 million immigrants per year, something that deserved a nod of praise from Democrats interested in compromise.

This latest episode reveals how completely broken the political-media vortex has become. Perhaps by 2019, there was just too much bad blood between President Trump and congressional Democrats for any hopeful interactions after more than two years of the Trump era. It's still more evidence of what amounts to a political hijacking, which I mentioned in the opening chapter. The American people have a consensus for immigration reform, and it deserves more attention.

Surprises in Deep Surveys

What if the culture war is not real? What if the feverish discussions about white supremacists versus antifa rioters are just clickbait? What if, despite

the hoopla, the American people still value measured and reasoned solut on immigration reform? And what if Americans from across the pol spectrum actually agree on their preferred policies? Wouldn't that be ne somebody would ask the simple questions and report the results?

These are the questions that Stanford professor David Brady and I air answer in a public opinion poll of American attitudes on immigratio survey was fielded by YouGov in January 2020, just before the Covid-1 demic. Our web-based survey analyzed the opinions of a representative of 1,200 adults. The results confirmed that despite the hyperpartisar Washington, Americans still prefer compromise over division. On objectives was to compare the attitudes of native-born citizens, na citizens, and foreign-born non-citizens residing in the United States reached out to an oversample of 400 foreign-born adults, half citizen non-citizens.

Respondents were exceedingly disappointed in politicians' actio gard to immigration. For example, 89% of those surveyed believed would rather fight over immigration than fix it. Seventy-six per nized that the federal government is not managing immigration And hearteningly, the majority of Americans—approximately 7 want politicians to compromise on immigration policy.

There was still plenty of room for disagreement. Although respondents (26%) wanted immigration to remain at its current l quarter wanted to increase immigration (23%), while a third (to decrease it. This matched a recent Gallup poll, although Gall 34% of respondents in 2020 prefer increased immigration.[9] Thi esting because Gallup has asked the same question with vary since 1965. Historically, Americans answered the Gallup whelming support for maintaining the "present level" of imm as you know is over 1 million legal immigrants per year), whil preferred an increase. Support for "Increase" jumped into the first decade of the 2000s, then rose into the 20 percent range presidency, and now has risen to its highest level ever.

Dave Brady and I also found widespread agreement on po we surveyed whether English should be the official langu States. Seventy-eight percent of respondents agreed, but th ment is astonishing. Republicans favor the policy overwh Democrats by a 2–1 margin. In fact, YouGov's three tier tification (lean, not very strong, and strong Democrat) portive of making English the official language. Younger do Hispanics, as do immigrant citizens, as do people of e advanced two very different bills to the floor of the House in the third week of June.

The conservative option was considered first. Sponsored by Congressman Bob Goodlatte, it granted legal status to DACA immigrants but not a pathway to citizenship. It also slashed legal immigration by half. All Democrats and forty-one Republicans voted against it.

The moderate option was considered days later. It offered DACA-eligible immigrants a renewable six-year legal status followed by a pathway to citizenship. It also included a handful of other restrictionist provisions: $25 billion for the southern border wall, reductions to legal immigration levels, ending the diversity lottery, and narrowing family sponsorship for some legal immigrants (brothers, sisters, and adult children). All Democrats and 112 Republicans voted against it.

The dual failure was uniquely embarrassing. Republicans literally could not find common ground among themselves. Instead, comprehensive reform failed again, twice this time around.

There remains a baffling question of what might have been. Realize that Congress has never considered a narrow bill to convert DACA into legislation: a renewable three-year legal status that allows Dreamers to reside, work, and pay taxes in the United States without citizenship, welfare, or the right to vote. The wedge issue has become a self-destructive lightning rod.

You might think the Democrats watched that spectacle and prepared legislation that was truly centrist and could pass their caucus. And you would be wrong. Here is the lesson learned: Nancy Pelosi's Democratic majority did not even bother to produce an immigration reform proposal in the House after she regained the Speaker's gavel in 2019.

Trump Versus the Media

President Donald Trump put forward new legislation in a Rose Garden speech on May 16, 2019, declaring, "Our proposal is pro-American, pro-immigrant, and pro-worker. It's just common sense." It might have been seen as an olive branch extended to Democrats who by then controlled both the Senate and the House. Contrary to his reputation as an immigrant basher, the president made a proposal that surprised everyone with its centrist approach. Most notably, Trump's plan did not reduce the annual number of legal migrants; rather, it shifted the composition of green cards with an innovative merit-based system that awarded more weight to younger, more educated people with more employable skills and English proficiency. Such a shift is one of the few areas of consensus among policy wonks, and despite the immediate political resistance to the word "merit" by some of Trump's antagonists, it has been used for decades as a shorthand for employment-based immigration systems common in other countries.

Right-wingers on Twitter thought that not reducing immigration levels was a betrayal by Trump. That reaction was to be expected. What was unexpected was the elite opinion of newspaper editors, faced with a moderate proposal from Donald Trump. Since it couldn't be attacked on substance, the plan was derided for not being *comprehensive* enough. An article in the *New York Times* said the legislation "did not address protections for the so-called Dreamers . . . or the 11 million undocumented immigrants currently living in the United States." An editorial in the back pages of the same paper complained, "This proposal does not address some of the thorniest elements of the immigration debate." A lengthy front-page article in the *Washington Post* chimed: "The new proposal . . . appears destined for the congressional dustbin [and] . . . sidesteps some major components of the immigration system that can be far more complex and controversial to resolve." None of the journalists would acknowledge that the whole point of the legislation was to be incremental. The *Post*'s editorial called it an "improvement over the administration's previous bar-the-door approach . . . but the initiative omits even passing reference to the reality of 10 million or 11 million undocumented immigrants." A bemused article in the *Wall Street Journal* observed, "It doesn't address some pressing immigration policy issues."

Politicians weren't much better in their neglect of the plan's substance. Senator Chuck Schumer bizarrely called it "the same partisan, radical anti-immigration policies" as before. Of course, Schumer knew better. Trump called for preserving the legal levels of 1.1 million immigrants per year, something that deserved a nod of praise from Democrats interested in compromise.

This latest episode reveals how completely broken the political-media vortex has become. Perhaps by 2019, there was just too much bad blood between President Trump and congressional Democrats for any hopeful interactions after more than two years of the Trump era. It's still more evidence of what amounts to a political hijacking, which I mentioned in the opening chapter. The American people have a consensus for immigration reform, and it deserves more attention.

Surprises in Deep Surveys

What if the culture war is not real? What if the feverish discussions about white supremacists versus antifa rioters are just clickbait? What if, despite the hoopla, the American people still value measured and reasoned solutions on immigration reform? And what if Americans from across the political spectrum actually agree on their preferred policies? Wouldn't that be news if somebody would ask the simple questions and report the results?

These are the questions that Stanford professor David Brady and I aimed to answer in a public opinion poll of American attitudes on immigration. Our survey was fielded by YouGov in January 2020, just before the Covid-19 pandemic. Our web-based survey analyzed the opinions of a representative sample of 1,200 adults. The results confirmed that despite the hyperpartisanship in Washington, Americans still prefer compromise over division. One of our objectives was to compare the attitudes of native-born citizens, naturalized citizens, and foreign-born non-citizens residing in the United States. YouGov reached out to an oversample of 400 foreign-born adults, half citizens and half non-citizens.

Respondents were exceedingly disappointed in politicians' actions with regard to immigration. For example, 89% of those surveyed believed politicians would rather fight over immigration than fix it. Seventy-six percent recognized that the federal government is not managing immigration effectively. And hearteningly, the majority of Americans—approximately 75 percent—want politicians to compromise on immigration policy.

There was still plenty of room for disagreement. Although a quarter of respondents (26%) wanted immigration to remain at its current level, another quarter wanted to increase immigration (23%), while a third (33%) wanted to decrease it. This matched a recent Gallup poll, although Gallup found that 34% of respondents in 2020 prefer increased immigration.[9] This is very interesting because Gallup has asked the same question with varying frequency since 1965. Historically, Americans answered the Gallup poll with overwhelming support for maintaining the "present level" of immigration (which as you know is over 1 million legal immigrants per year), while only 7 percent preferred an increase. Support for "Increase" jumped into the teens during the first decade of the 2000s, then rose into the 20 percent range during Obama's presidency, and now has risen to its highest level ever.

Dave Brady and I also found widespread agreement on policy. For example, we surveyed whether English should be the official language of the United States. Seventy-eight percent of respondents agreed, but the breadth of agreement is astonishing. Republicans favor the policy overwhelmingly, but so do Democrats by a 2–1 margin. In fact, YouGov's three tiers of partisan identification (lean, not very strong, and strong Democrat) are all equally supportive of making English the official language. Younger Americans agree, as do Hispanics, as do immigrant citizens, as do people of every education level.

Among Americans who primarily speak Spanish, support for making English the official language stands at 58 percent.

I'll save a broader analysis of policy reforms for later in the book. The point I want to emphasize here is that partisan divides about immigration are not found among the wider public. It is a peculiar affliction of the political class.

Powerful People, Partisan Parties

A house divided against itself cannot stand. It was true back when President Lincoln described the Civil War, and it remains true today regarding the exponential increase of hyperpartisanship in Washington, DC. How can we expect a government to function when politicians forfeit compromise in order to push policies that are destined to fail in order to appease that partisan bases? We can't.

The true wall that divides this nation is not the border wall to the south but is instead the institutional wall that divides the parties. Hyperpartisanship is quickly becoming the norm for government and one of the greatest threats to American democracy. The political aisle is meant to be crossed, but in its place, politicians have erected a barrier. It is time someone urges lawmakers to *tear down this wall!*

It's a sad state of affairs that the issue of immigration has transformed so much in two and a half centuries of American history. What was once one of the rallying cries of independence of a weak, nascent nation in 1776 is now the definitive political wedge issue in the world's great superpower. The politics of immigration have done more to fuel resentment and distrust in America than any foreign power could. It doesn't have to be this way.

Unfortunately, the hypnotic grip of "comprehensive" is hard to shake. Rarely has a reform concept so vexed actual policymaking. It's as if a surgical team couldn't just remove a ruptured appendix without also transplanting the entire digestive system. Sadly, comprehensive policymaking has failed every time it has been tried for two decades.

President George W. Bush tried in 2006 and 2007, especially supporting the McCain-Kennedy bill with a massive, extended campaign. Obama's 2013 effort was equally ambitious, if seemingly cynical. The majority parties keep pushing extreme policies masked by comprehensive and seemingly bipartisan legislation that are doomed to fail. Poison pills abound in the details or in later amendments. Then the majority party points fingers at the other side, claiming that they refuse to compromise, when compromise was never the true goal of the legislation. Instead of recognizing the lack of legislative action, politicians prefer to remain stuck in this polarizing cycle of failed immigration reform.

As I wrote at the beginning of the book, Congress should vote on the smallest immigration bill that deals with an issue of overwhelming public consensus. That begs the question: which policies, exactly? That's a question we will consider in depth in future chapters. And we will start by considering what ways immigration has actually strengthened the country.

PART III
RESOURCES AND RIVALRY

This is the part of the book that America's rivals will study. An underlying theme is that the United States has a completely unappreciated advantage over rivals as the nation where the vast majority of would-be immigrants wish to go. This "destination dominance" is only possible in a multi-ethnic society with a foundation of equality under the law. Each of the following chapters will address one of the three strategic benefits that immigrants provide—brawn, bravery, and brains.

Brawn means the raw population that migrants add but also the self-selected advantages of the physical strength and ruggedness of the people willing to endure the hardships of migration. Bravery means patriotism, the devotion of those who actively choose a place in contrast with the randomness of their place of birth, a spirit that motivates so many immigrants to volunteer for military service during times of war. Last, brains mean intelligence and more. Immigrants to America are far more likely than the native-born population to get advanced degrees, to patent new inventions, and to start new companies.

Rather than just previewing the material in this overview, let's consider a bare-bones model for national power that treats the three advantages as input factors in an equation, or what a growth economist would describe as a production function. The advantages of the ultimate resource—people—can be understood more fully in a standard model of economic growth. Growth theory has been one of the main topics of academic research for half a century, emerging from the initial set of national data on inputs and outputs that was developed in the years after World War II. This will be the only equation presented in this book, but it's worth remembering:

$$\textit{Gross Domestic Product} = f(A, K, L, H)$$

Gross domestic product models are simple by design, and they include only fundamental ingredients. For example, a growth model cannot distinguish between a nation made up of 10 million homogenous Vikings and a nation made up of 10 million heterogeneous people comprising dozens of ethnicities, languages, and cultures. Likewise, these models neglect many features of economic life such as inequality, the environment, gender, ethnic diversity, religion, and human happiness. They weren't developed to explain those features internal to an economy but rather to explain the differences in the wealth of nations.

The core model is a production function with four fundamental inputs: technology (A), capital (K), labor (L), and human capital (H). There's a widespread consensus among scholars that these are the main inputs, though less of a consensus about f (the "function") itself, which stands for the way the inputs are organized. In the earliest growth models that were developed in the 1950s, the A term wasn't called technology and wasn't meant to measure technology in the way you and I think about it today. Nor did that model have an H term. Instead, it simply showed that each economy's output could be traced to a mix of capital and labor with A representing the total productivity of both those inputs. More advanced societies had larger levels of A, and that stood for everything from government regulations to telephone lines. Those initial production functions had constant returns to scale, meaning if every input were doubled, then total output would exactly double. However, each input alone would generate decreasing returns to scale such that every extra unit of labor alone would yield relatively less output. The implication is rather gloomy, as this model suggests that too much population growth can cause lower output per person, certainly in the short term. That doesn't match the historical record of radical increases in per capita income in the United States and other large countries, but skeptics could assert that growth is due to rising technology despite the drag of crowding.

Ah, but here's the rub. One of the more profound suggestions emerging from more recent developments in growth theory is that population may not have decreasing returns at all. More people means more scientists and entrepreneurs who generate more innovations. Nobel Prize–winning economist Paul Romer pioneered research into a type of "endogenous" growth model that revolutionized the field. Let's apply those insights to the way we think about immigration. Chad Jones, a professor at Stanford, continues to extend this line of research, and in a recent paper wrote, "When population growth is negative, [modern] growth models produce what we call an Empty Planet result: knowledge and living standards stagnate for a population that gradually vanishes."[1]

Chapter 9

Brawn

Immigration to the United States has not, historically, been an act of kindness toward strangers. It's been a strategy for national growth and national greatness.

— Matt Yglesias

The great copper statue of the robed Roman goddess Libertas that watches over New York is known colloquially as the Statue of Liberty. She symbolizes America's welcome to immigration, though that interpretation is challenged by some restrictionist politicians who loudly remind anyone that the statue was actually a gift from France to commemorate the 100th anniversary of America's founding, and that it was inspired by the Civil War's crusade against slavery. That's technically correct, and a fib as well.

Yes, the abolition of slavery by Abraham Lincoln is the well-documented inspiration for French author and jurist Edouard de Laboulaye, who conceived of the idea of the statue. The year was 1865, and the aftermath of America's war to end slavery inspired a world where slavery was still rampant. Look closely at the feet of the great statue: see the broken chains she is leaving behind. And when the casting of the statue was finally completed in France, the 1876 centennial had already passed. Although the torch-bearing left arm was shipped to Philadelphia in time for the 1876 World's Fair, the full statue wasn't cast until much later. The delay was caused by uncertainty about which city could afford to build the giant pedestal necessary as its foundation. A diplomatic agreement between the two countries held that the French government would fund the statue and its transportation across the Atlantic Ocean while the Americans would fund its pedestal. The final pieces arrived in New York in the summer of 1885, but fundraising for the pedestal had fallen far short.

An initial fundraising effort started in 1882, securing two-thirds of the $250,000 necessary to pay for the granite pedestal to be constructed on

Bedloe's Island (over $6 million in today's dollars). Emma Lazarus contributed a poem in 1883 that was auctioned to help construction. Titled "New Colossus," that poem is now preserved in a plaque at the base of the statue and its theme is unambiguous:

> "Keep, ancient lands, your storied pomp!" cries she
> With silent lips. "Give me your tired, your poor,
> Your huddled masses yearning to breathe free,
> The wretched refuse of your teeming shore.
> Send these, the homeless, tempest-tost to me,
> I lift my lamp beside the golden door!"

To those who would suggest otherwise, do not let them forget that the Lazarus poem came two years before the statue arrived. On June 17, 1885, the French steamer *Isère* arrived with the crates holding hundreds of pieces of the disassembled statue. Over 200,000 people lined the docks of New York to welcome her.

Even so, New York was short of funds for the pedestal by $100,000. The governor and mayor were unwilling to pay, and Congress proved ineffectual as well. Up stepped Joseph Pulitzer, remembered now for the journalism prize that bears his name. Back then, he was the publisher of the *New York World*, one of the main newspapers in the city. Pulitzer rallied his readers to send in donations so that the statue would be based in the harbor before other American cities could raise funds first. Pulitzer appealed to the huddled masses: "Let us not wait for the millionaires to give us this money. It is not a gift from the millionaires of France to the millionaires of America, but a gift of the whole people of France to the whole people of America." Pulitzer ran what the British Broadcasting Corporation has called the world's first crowdfunding campaign as it "eventually raised money from more than 160,000 donors, including young children, businessmen, street cleaners, and politicians, with more than three-quarters of the donations amounting to less than a dollar. It was a triumphant rescue effort: in just five months *The World* raised $101,091."[1]

The statue, christened *Liberty Enlightening the World*, was immediately embraced by immigrants themselves who saw the lighted torch held high as one of their first sights on arriving in the New World. One example of how poor immigrants of that era considered the statue as a landmark relevant to their journeys comes from a Greek immigrant girl named Doukenie Bacos. She was 14 years old and traveling alone in 1913 when her ship passed by: "I saw the Statue of Liberty. And I said to myself, 'Lady, you're such a beautiful!

[*sic*] You opened your arms and you get all the foreigners here. Give me a chance to prove that I am worth it, to do something, to be someone in America.' And always that statue was on my mind."[2]

There are a dozen replicas of the Statue of Liberty throughout France, four in Paris alone. The original sculptor Frédéric Bartholdi crafted a smaller version of his *Liberty Enlightening the World* in 1900 that today stands in the entrance hall to the Musée d'Orsay. A fourteen-ton replica was gifted by US citizens in Paris to France in 1889 that currently stands in the Seine near one of the city's main bridges. Bartholdi's original suffered from erosion and disrepair over the century after it was erected in New York harbor. A major restoration was undertaken by engineers and workers in preparation for the for the 1986 centennial celebration at the direction of the U.S. president who hoped to celebrate the statue and what it had come to represent. That president was, of course, the great Cold Warrior, Ronald Reagan.

People Power

China has the world's largest population with 1.41 billion citizens. India is a close second with 1.34 billion people. Who is third? The United States. Population: estimated at just under 332 million in the 2020 census. For comparison, Russia has less than half the American population with around 144 million people. Germany has about 80 million, France and the UK around 65 million, and Italy 60 million. Why does this matter for national security?

"They say that population is national power," wrote the editors of the *Korea Times* in 2011.[3] "Korea is heading toward a declining stage as it is one of the fastest aging societies with a low birth rate." Geographically isolated between its traditional rivals China and Japan, and incessantly poised for war with communist North Korea, the leaders in Seoul are acutely aware of the dangers of a relatively small population. Their concern typifies how leaders throughout history have thought of population as the fundamental parameter in the calculus of international affairs.

The classical understanding of power from Herodotus to Hans Morgenthau is defined in terms of resources. The modern scholar most respected for his analysis of power, Joseph S. Nye Jr., believes that the measurement of power will always prove somewhat elusive given the ever-evolving and dynamic nature of human affairs. Are tanks with more armor or more maneuverability superior, or is there more power in a combination of heavy infantry and helicopters? Such discussions can only be settled on the battlefield, yet make no mistake: they begin with a measure of inputs—"population, territory, natural resources, economic size, military forces, political stability, among others"—with population always listed first.[4]

For most of human history, population was synonymous with power. An empire with 10 million subjects was twice as powerful as another empire that ruled 5 million subjects because economic strength had a linear relationship with population size. There were no major technological differences between neighboring states until after the Industrial Revolution, which we can date to 1760 in Great Britain. To be sure, there were resource differences, so that a city-state or empire-state with more timber or iron ore might have a slight advantage. However, the notion that Egypt's irrigated deltas or Italy's fertile vineyards provided an agrarian advantage was mitigated by the Malthusian trap, the theory that population growth will always outpace growth in food production. To be sure, recorded history seemed to prove that economic growth always faded. Per capita incomes gyrated temporarily but never surpassed more than a few (modern) dollars per day. Any innovation, say, crop rotation or the horse harness, might enhance productivity for a few years, but the surplus was gobbled up by more children. In the absence of sustained technological growth that exceeds population growth, a population will naturally expand until it settles back to the same threshold of mere survival.

What about the Spanish conquistadors? Jared Diamond brilliantly described the great technological imbalance between the Old World explorers numbering in the dozens who defeated massive Inca and Aztec populations in his seminal *Guns, Germs, and Steel*. The conquistadors rode on horses and wore armor and fired terrifying gunpowder weapons. The technology gap was so profound that a whole continent essentially gave way to a few sailing ships full of "iron" men. Yet that was a one-time event, as the American Indians were anything but neighboring societies to Spaniards, the Portuguese, the French, and the British. Technology gaps are a historical exception to the rule, or they were until the diffusion of the Industrial Revolution. After 1820, per capita incomes began to accelerate across Europe, the British colonies, and Asia as well. Thus began a technology race and a revolution in military affairs that hasn't stopped, and perhaps never will.

Nye places population as a "critical power resource" on the top board of his conceptual model of the three-dimensional chessboard of international grand strategy, particularly valuable in 18th-century Europe and earlier eras "because it provided a base for taxes and the recruitment of infantry."[5] The classical chessboard was two dimensional, and played only at the top level, but modern times have introduced new dimensions to the game: hard technology to be sure, but also soft instruments of information and culture.

Mao Zedong said that "power grows out of the barrel of a gun" at the beginning of the Chinese Civil War in 1949. His full quote, it should be noted, is that "political power" grows from the gun, suggesting he realized there were deeper levels to grand strategy than brute force. Mao often observed that the Chinese people comprised "one-quarter of humanity." Contrary to concerns that excess density weakened the nation, he wrote in 1949: "Even if China's population multiplies many times, she is fully capable of finding a solution; the solution is production," adding that "of all things in the world, people are the most precious." Contraceptives were banned for many years in Mao's China.[6]

Technology may be the new predominant factor in warfare, but its effect is limited as the United States learned in 1950s Korea and 1960s Vietnam. The world's dominant superpower, armed with thermonuclear weapons, found itself unable to win against guerilla tactics in the jungle. The commanding US general, William Westmoreland, once told reporters that one thing that was the key to victory over the Viet Cong: "Firepower." He was wrong. Bombing the cities of North Vietnam with more explosives than the United States dropped across all of Europe in World War II was not enough.

Willpower matters. Purpose matters. And as Glenn Hubbard and I argued in our book *Balance: The Economics of Great Powers*, economic institutions matter most of all. Given all that, the reality of modern warfare is that the raw inputs matter as much as ever: urban battlespaces erode technological advantage. Thus, the classical view that population is the foundation of national power remains the consensus, even today. A RAND study published in 2000 looked at the ways demographic factors affect international security, and observed, "The majority of national security analysts can still be said to be adherents to the classical static view."[7]

Thus we are faced with a dilemma in the current century. How can the superpower status of the United States be maintained if the population ages and dwindles with ever-lower birth rates? China is ascendant, with a population four times the size of the United States', and it seems only a matter of time for its technological capacity to catch up.

Reagan's Farewell

Each president communicates with the public in their own way. FDR liked his fireside chats over the radio. Coolidge pioneered getting his photo taken for the papers for free media attention. President Trump enjoyed rallies and social media.

As a sign of the respect he had for the presidency, Ronald Reagan never took off his suit jacket in the Oval Office, which is where he preferred to address the nation through televised addresses from the Resolute desk. On January 11, 1989, he spoke from that revered spot for the final time. It was his farewell address, and two minutes into the twenty-one-minute speech, Reagan got to the one story he felt represented the best of America:

> I've been reflecting on what the past 8 years have meant and mean. And the image that comes to mind like a refrain is a nautical one—a small story about a big ship, and a refugee, and a sailor. It was back in the early eighties, at the height of the boat people. And the sailor was hard at work on the carrier *Midway*, which was patrolling the South China Sea. The sailor, like most American servicemen, was young, smart, and fiercely observant. The crew spied on the horizon a leaky little boat. And crammed inside were refugees from Indochina hoping to get to America. The *Midway* sent a small launch to bring them to the ship and safety. As the refugees made their way through the choppy seas, one spied the sailor on deck, and stood up, and called out to him. He yelled, "Hello, American sailor. Hello, freedom man."[8]

Seven percent of the US population were foreign-born during the Reagan presidency, half of the current level. The growth of immigrants in the decades since are largely thanks to Reagan-Bush Republican policies during the 1980s, which were continued and expanded by Democratic leaders Bill Clinton and Barack Obama. The signature legislation that Reagan advanced was the Immigration Reform and Control Act (IRCA), finally made law in November 1986 after nearly six years of wrangling and multiple versions passing the House and the Senate. The law was a bipartisan compromise, making it illegal for companies to hire illegal immigrants in exchange for a nationwide amnesty granted to the illegal immigrants then residing in the country, so long as they had arrived in 1981 or earlier. The president signed another law in 1986 making it unlawful to deny emergency medical care to anyone based on their residency status.

The impact of the law proved mixed. Some 3 million people applied for amnesty, and 90 percent were deemed qualified to receive it, out of an estimated population of 4 million or more. Wages and other measures of well-being rose dramatically for those affected, with little apparent negative effect on other workers. Although the enforcement penalties became operational, the flow of illegal immigrants did not abate.

In retrospect, the flaw in IRCA was its exclusive focus on eliminating illegal immigration rather than addressing the underlying cause: "the continuing and increased demand for workers in the United States, especially in the low-skilled labor market."[9] There was not enough consideration of allowing for more temporary worker visas to balance demand with supply. Interestingly, even though each of the 2.7 million amnesty recipients was free to become a naturalized citizen of the United States, fewer than half did so, according to a federal government study done fifteen years later.[10]

Lost in discussions of Reagan and immigration is the fact that refugees were arguably a larger concern than undocumented workers during the 1980s. Jimmy Carter signed a major law in 1980 that aligned US refugee policies with international standards. The Refugee Act recognized anyone fearing state-sponsored persecution, an expansion from the previous focus on refugees from communism. The Reagan administration embraced this new standard as a way to welcome people fleeing the Ayatollah's Iran, Soviet-occupied Afghanistan, and countries throughout the Warsaw Pact, although it disputed the qualification for some asylum seekers from allied Central American nations.

The point is this: Ronald Reagan's legacy is the triumph of Western capitalism over Soviet communism, and he leveraged immigration as a core element of free societies, strategically and morally. Indeed many more legal immigrants welcomed during the Reagan presidency than the Carter presidency, even more during the first four-year term 1981–85 (which had two economic recessions) than Carter's 1977–81 term. From his first speech to his last, from his vocal support of the restoration of the Statue of Liberty to his legislative success, Reagan used the bully pulpit to affirm the American creed. As he closed his farewell address, he circled back to the opening theme:

> I've spoken of the shining city all my political life. . . . And if there had to be city walls, the walls had doors and the doors were open to anyone with the will and the heart to get here. That's how I saw it, and see it still.

Destination and Destiny

On a Wednesday morning in early August 2017, speaking from a podium in the White House's Roosevelt Room, flanked by Republican senators Tom Cotton of Arkansas and David Perdue of Georgia, President Donald Trump expressed support for their immigration reform proposal.[11] Senators Cotton and Perdue had put forth a very non-Reaganesque piece of legislation that would cut the level of legal immigration by half or more. Trump said the Cotton-Perdue bill would help "minority workers competing for jobs against brand-new arrivals," a rationale for slashing legal immigration that makes sense if the labor market is a zero-sum game in which everyone competes for a finite number of jobs. I'll deal with the economic debate in a separate chapter (and warn readers that the case is not clear-cut for either side). For now, let's work through a thought experiment.

What if the United States had cut immigration by half starting 200 years ago? Intuitively, we know that our present population of 331 million souls would be smaller, but how much smaller? If we apply some social science to demographic projections, with careful consideration of birth rates and fertility rates over time, we can see the long-term impact of limiting immigration. Using data from the US census starting with the year 1820 (population 9.6 million), I calculated two alternative histories. Remember, we have to use 1820 as the starting point because that's the year immigration data were first recorded in the United States.

You may also recall that there was a presidential election in 1816. Rufus King was the Federalist candidate, genuinely opposed to immigration. In a letter, King wrote, "I certainly do not think [Irish refugees] will be a desirable acquisition to any Nation, but in none would they be likely to prove more mischievous than in mine." He lost in a landslide to James Monroe. What if he had won? A King presidency would have established a precedent that limited immigration severely with a ban on the Irish that likely would have also foreclosed German Catholics, Italians, and Spaniards, not to mention Orthodox Christians and Jews, Persians, Arabs, Indians, and Asians.

If immigration levels are held to half of the actual experience, what happens to overall population levels? This is our thought experiment. Figure 9.1 shows the results as alternative history #1, starting in 1820 and then projecting the total population. The 2020 US population would be 242 million. Basically, the United States would have 90 million fewer Americans, nearly one-third of the population. Instead of being the third largest country in the world, the United States would be the fifth largest. That's about the size of Brazil and significantly smaller than Indonesia.

My alternative history #2 considers what the US population might have become with zero immigration. This yields a present-day population of around 146 million people based on my calculations. That's 44 percent of the actual level. With a population of that size, the United States today would be exactly the same size as Russia (and much smaller than the full extent of the former Soviet Union). We can see the size of these Alternative Americas relative to other nations in Table 9.1.

How could the United States have won World War II with 25–55 percent fewer soldiers and sailors? In 1940, the actual US population was 132 million compared to Nazi Germany's 71 million. Looking back along alternative timeline #1, the United States would have had 32 million fewer people in 1940. In alternative history #2, it would have been smaller than Nazi Germany.

Table 9.1 World's largest countries
by population, 2020

1	China	1,439,323,776
2	India	1,380,004,385
3	USA	331,002,651
4	Indonesia	273,523,615
	USA (half immigration)	242,241,298
5	Pakistan	220,892,340
6	Brazil	212,559,417
7	Nigeria	206,139,589
8	Bangladesh	164,689,383
9	Russia	145,934,462
	USA (zero immigration)	145,737,058
10	Mexico	128,932,753

Sources: United Nations, Population Division, and author
analysis of USA alternatives.

America's industrial production would have been about half the actual size as well. Half the P-51 Mustangs. Half the aircraft carriers in the Pacific and merchant marine ships that reinforced Great Britain.

A smaller American population raises other doubts about grand strategy. After 1945, would the United States have been able to outgrow the Soviets economically or afford a Marshall Plan? Would Uncle Sam have dared to stop the communists in Korea in 1950? One has to wonder whether the 20th century could have been the "American Century" without immigrants, or even a great power. Instead of being one-fourth China's size in the present era, the United States would only be one-tenth China's size.[12]

Without a surge of the "huddled masses" migrating from the poorest regions of wider Europe around the turn of the 20th century, the United States would not have been able to fight in both the European and Pacific theaters during the Second World War. It would simply not have had the manpower.

On the other hand, what if the United States had avoided the xenophobia of the 1880s and isolationist lurch of the 1920s? It's easy to imagine a trajectory of Chinese immigration at the end of the 19th century that would have accelerated just like the Irish and Italians. A million per decade? Absolutely.

Consider the decennial record of Irish migration from the 1820s to the 1850s: 50,000, 170,000, 650,000, and 1 million. Chinese migration was 50,000 in the 1860s, 130,000 in the 1870s, and could easily have surged to 1 million per decade if not blocked by the 1882 ban enacted by Congress. The same can

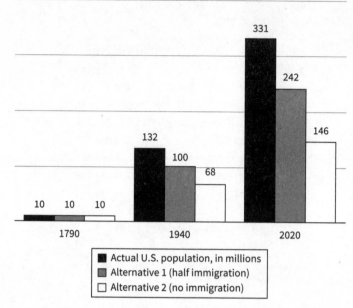

Figure 9.1 US population under different immigration scenarios. Projections by author based on US census data.

be said for two other Asian countries with similar trajectories in the nineteenth century: Japan and Turkey.

I projected an alternative history #3 to see what the US population might have been absent restrictionism. The assumptions for this thought experiment are that migrant inflows from four Asian countries (only) are allowed to continue after the 1880s, each growing at 70 percent per decade, capped at 1 million each per decade. This is actually a conservative assumption given that many other countries sourced more, notably Germany's 1.4 million in the 1880s, Russia's 1.5 million, Italy's 1.9 million, and Austria-Hungary's 2 million in 1900. Regarding the immigration flows from Europe after 1920, I assumed no growth whatsoever; rather, I projected continuous inflows equal to their 1920 or 1930 level, whichever was higher. The resulting trajectory of the United States' populace with a maximized immigration policy leads to a population of 453,699,393 in the year 2020, which is 37 percent larger than the actual level.

Interestingly, the population would not have grown much differently even up to 1920, but then would have risen dramatically after 1940. Absent the era of isolationism, America would have had 13 million more people in 1940, 75 million more in 1990, and 123 million more today. The economy would have been much larger, too, probably by 40 or 50 percent.

The thought experiment is more than an idle classroom exercise. Policymakers of this era face the same question, and the implications for choosing a Washington-Lincoln open immigration approach or a Coolidge-Roosevelt closed approach will define America's size and strength in this century as much as any other policy. The options were made rather plain in a report published by the US census in early 2020, the timing of which was unfortunate as it was overshadowed by the Covid-19 pandemic. The report presents four different scenarios: a status quo policy as well as three alternatives for high, low, and zero immigration. And the impact over the next forty years is amazingly similar to the outcomes of the past 200:

> Higher international immigration over the next four decades would produce a faster growing, more diverse, and younger population for the United States. In contrast, an absence of migration into the country over this same period would result in a US population that is smaller than the present. Different levels of immigration between now and 2060 could change the projection of the population in that year by as much as 127 million people, with estimates ranging anywhere from 320 to 447 million US residents.[13]

Population Pyramids

One cannot write of population without facing the worry of overpopulation. Although famine was the scourge of all pre-industrial civilizations, the mortalty table was overturned by the "Green Revolution" in agriculture, the dramatic increase in farm productivity in the 1950s and 1960s that eliminated undernourishment in most Western countries and enabled a population boom worldwide. For perspective, demographic historians estimate that the world's population in the year AD 1 was between 170 and 330 million, where it stayed more or less for the next millennium. World population grew slowly until 1800 but even then did not surpass 1 billion. As of this writing, global population exceeds 7 billion, and has added a net 80 million people every year for roughly half a century.

Yet human society is not running out of food. Despite the warnings of Thomas Malthus at the dawn of the 19th century that population growth would outstrip nature's capacity, echoed incessantly, humans have expanded numerically and productively. Peak pessimism manifested in a 1968 book by Stanford biologist Paul Ehrlich titled *The Population Bomb*. Ehrlich's predictions of mass starvation the following decade, revised every few years, proved false. His famous bet with Julian Simon about scarcity and price inflation for vital commodities serves as a vindication for economic science, but there was good reason to worry. The relative growth rate of the population was indeed exploding for the simple reason that life expectancy was growing rapidly thanks to countless medical innovations whereas birth rates weren't declining. Intellectuals warned about something called population pyramids, and how very wide they were becoming.

Population pyramids were created, ironically, by an American statistician in order to warn about immigration to the United States. His name was Francis Amasa Walker, a mathematical prodigy who enrolled at Amherst College at the age of 15, became an attorney, and served as a general in the Union Army during the Civil War before the age of 25. He was also a pioneer in the nascent field of economics, specializing in statistical analysis. When Walker was appointed superintendent of the US census, he developed a graphical chart that displayed the relative size of each age and gender cohort of the population. His newfangled statistical graphs highlighted the difference between native-born and foreign-born demographic patterns. The US census for 1870, overseen by Walker, introduced the world's first population pyramids, not just for the overall population but with figures for each state, ethnicity, and nativity.[14]

Walker's population pyramids presented two vertical bars for each age cohort, males to the left side of the y-axis and females to the right side. The youngest cohort (age 0–10 years in Walker's original version) had the largest bars, representing 15 percent of the population. Two slightly smaller bars representing 10–20-year-old males and females were stacked above, and then another pair for ages 20–30, and so on until the top cohort of the 80+ groups stood like a thin brick atop the pyramids of Egypt.

Walker was considered the leading American statistician of his time, although in fairness this was a time when Latin professors outnumbered economics professors by ten to one. In 1881, Walker was selected as the president of the Massachusetts Institute of Technology and also served as the inaugural president of the American Economics Association (AEA), which remains today the preeminent economics society internationally. Unfortunately, his research underpinned the notorious "race suicide" theory. Indeed, the beginnings of the AEA are marked by strident elitism of the worst kind that casts a dark shadow over the profession. One modern economist, Robert Kirby, documented the "dark days" extensively:

Francis Amasa Walker began his 1890 Presidential address to the AEA warning of the threat to the Anglo-Saxon race in the US posed by immigration. . . . Walker described these immigrants from Austria, southern Italy, Hungary, and Russia as "beaten men from beaten races, representing the worst failures in the struggle for existence," who would displace their superiors, the "native" Americans. This

anti-immigrant view was not just held by a few bad apples in the AEA; in 1888 the
AEA offered a prize for the best essay on the evils of unrestricted immigration![15]

In 1896, Walker published a lengthy anti-immigrant essay in the *Atlantic
Monthly*, warning that the country had become full and the inevitable "failure
of assimilation" was when "aggravated by the addition of some millions of
Hungarians, Bohemians, Poles, south Italians, and Russian Jews."[16] Walker
also claimed that immigrants caused lower fertility among native-born citizens, an idea that wasn't assessed or debunked until much later.[17]

Today's demographers note that population pyramids with a wide base
similar to those in 1870s America are a sign of a region that is less economically developed. A wide base of children topped by increasingly narrower bars
for older cohorts, particularly when the sides have a convex pattern, represent high levels of fertility and high levels of mortality. More economically
advanced societies tend to have age cohorts of the same size with the exception of the very elderly, resulting in figures that look more like obelisks than
pyramids. These places have gone through the "demographic transition."

In order to compare how much demographic patterns have changed in the
past sixty years, I developed a variation on the population pyramid with 1960
national population on the left side of the figure and 2020 data on the right.
I used data from the United Nations, which is consistent across countries.

The first pyramid I present, in Figure 9.2, shows Mexico's evolving population. Notice how the 1960 population of 37 million Mexicans was shaped
typically for a developing country with over half of the people under the age of
20. The Mexican population tripled and then some over the next sixty years,
but by 2020 the pyramid shape has been replaced by an obelisk. It's a stunning achievement, all because fertility has declined more than one could have
dreamed possible.

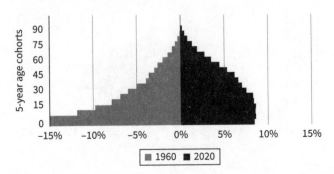

Figure 9.2 Mexico population pyramids, 1960 and 2020. Data from United Nations,
Population Division.

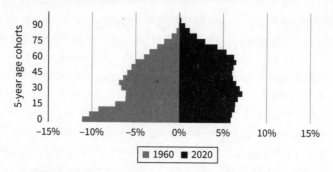

Figure 9.3 United States population pyramids, 1960 and 2020. Data from United Nations, Population Division.

The total fertility rate (TFR) is a statistic that represents the average number of live births per woman, and 2.1 is considered the level at which a population holds steady. If a country has a TFR above 2.1, then its population is growing, depending on normal mortality rates. If the TFR is lower than 2.1, then the population is in decline. For example, Japan and Italy have experienced exceptionally low fertility rates for decades, currently around 1.4, implying their populations will be halved in the next generation.

According to an analysis by the Economic Commission for Latin America and the Caribbean in 2019, "The [total] fertility rate for Latin America and the Caribbean is estimated at 2.04 live births per woman, placing the region for the first time below the level of replacement."[18] This isn't merely an average decline across all the countries in the region; rather, the TFR of every country in Central America and Latin America has dropped by four or five children per woman since 1960. Consider some examples drawn from the World Bank's dynamic database: TFR in Honduras dropped from 7.5 in 1960 to 2.5 in 2018; El Salvador from 6.7 to 2.0; Mexico from 6.8 to 2.1; and Brazil from 6.1 to 1.7.[19]

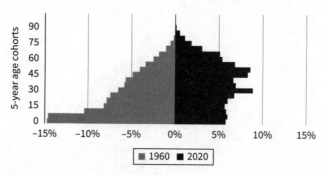

Figure 9.4 China population pyramids, 1960 and 2020. Data from United Nations, Population Division.

Population deceleration is a global phenomenon, as we can see in the stunning population pyramids for the United States and China (Figures 9.3 and 9.4). The *World Population Prospects*, a U.N. effort, said in 2019 that "global fertility is projected to fall from 2.5 children per woman in 2019 to 2.2 in 2050." The growth rate of the world's population peaked in the early 1960s and is expected to turn negative even though medical technology continues to advance life spans. However, the demographic transition is an uneven phenomenon, meaning that populations in the poorest countries in Africa and Asia grow relatively larger compared to the shrinking populations of the rich democracies of Europe.

Exodus

This population-prosperity disparity represents one of the great challenges to geopolitical security and stability of our time. The information revolution has made pretty much every human being aware of economic opportunities elsewhere, and the transportation revolution has made it cheaper than ever to move around. Do the economically advanced countries have an obligation to the huddled masses? Or is that the wrong question?

Paul Collier wrote *Exodus: How Migration Is Changing Our World*, which summarizes the population-prosperity disparity; it was published in 2013, just before the refugee crisis in Syria spilled into Europe. The main outlet for the disparity is migration, of course, and that brings profound anxieties and moral clashes over identity, law, and economics. Collier frames the question, rightly I think, not as whether immigration is "bad or good" but "how much is best?" The book implies that each country has a similar absorptive capacity, but I wonder if on the contrary there is a very wide spectrum. The oldest nations—homelands so to speak—with a homogenous ethnicity such as Japan or Indonesia or Ethiopia arguably have the lowest capacity to absorb outsiders. Larger countries such as China and Russia tend to be multi-ethnic but no more tolerant of outsiders. And then there are a few countries simply built for diversity where there is no upper bound on absorptive capacity. This begs the question: does a country founded on *e pluribus unum* have a geopolitical advantage in dealing with the new exodus?

I'd like us to consider what amounts to old-fashioned zero-sum thinking, with an eye toward seeing the potential positive contribution of each migrant. From this perspective, the question becomes this: which countries will be fortunate enough to welcome the most migrants? If I am right, there will be a war for talent in an increasingly mobile world where intercontinental transportation is ever cheaper. Masses of people around the world will want to move more than ever before.

Over 700 million people worldwide desire to migrate to a new country, according to a 2018 survey by Gallup. That represents 15 percent of the world's adults. In many countries, more than half of the people want to leave: war-torn African nations as well as the long-impoverished countries of Central America and the Caribbean such as Haiti, the Dominican Republic, Honduras, and El Salvador.

Where do they wish to go? They aspire to live in America.

As Samuel P. Huntington wrote in his seminal work *The Clash of Civilizations*: "Between 1821 and 1924, approximately 55 million Europeans migrated overseas, 34 million of them to the United States." Today, one in five potential migrants—or about 158 million adults worldwide—name the United States as their preferred destination. No other country comes close. Although the United States is home to roughly 4 percent of the world's population, it has been the top migrant destination "since Gallup started tracking these patterns a decade ago."

Thus we come to the end of our survey of the first of three strategic advantages that immigrants bring to a country. Adding to the population has been a fundamental benefit of immigrants that was recognized in the Declaration of Independence and has made all the difference in the superpower status of America. The youthful profile of immigrants makes that advantage even more powerful in an aging world. After one views immigration as a strategic asset, then the "destination dominance" the United States has held for over two centuries is precious indeed.

Will immigrants be as patriotic as the native born? That's a natural question, and it haunts all discussions in all places and eras. Perhaps in homeland-societies, the answer is no. If patriotism means fealty to a purity of religion, ethnicity, or some such. But if patriotism means a commitment to a creed of equality and liberty for all, the answer may surprise you.

Chapter 10
Bravery

To their fellow soldiers they were kikes, wops, micks, hunkies—no matter how the War Department tried, they couldn't stamp out these ethnic slurs. But after the battles fought at Soissons, Blanc Mont, Montfaucon, the Hindenberg Line, the Bois des Loges, the slurs became terms of camaraderie. As Joe Rizzi said, "You see, we were all buddies."

— **David Laskin,** *The Long Way Home*

Sergeant George Luz is trying to protect a supply of candy bars from being scavenged by his buddies in Easy Company. You have probably heard of Easy Company: the famous paratrooper unit that fought in many of World War II's fiercest battles, from the Normandy invasion to the famous defense of encircled Bastogne to the final occupation of Hitler's Eagle's Nest in the mountains of Berchtesgaden, and the candy bar scene is one of the rare light moments the men enjoyed during their terrible year fighting across the continent. It played out in the eighth episode of the HBO miniseries *Band of Brothers*.

After the bitterly cold Battle of the Bulge, the men were given a respite, arriving in the French city of Hagueneau on February 5, 1945. The shattered buildings there felt like luxury compared to the frozen foxholes in the Ardennes Forest where they'd been cut off from supply lines for weeks. In Hagueneau, Easy Company was able to live indoors for the first time on the front lines, and the supplies rolled in: —warm clothing, showers, and food.

"Oh! Hershey bars!" yells Joe Liebgott, grabbing at the pile of chocolates.

"No, there's not enough to go around!" Luz yells back.

While four soldiers pester their buddy Luz, a friendly voice greets them from across the room. "Hey bigmouth, give the kid a Hershey bar." Just inside the archway to the room stands their recently wounded friend, Frank Perconte, the smirking Italian American GI from Joliet, Illinois. Perconte was one of the very first soldiers assigned to the new paratrooper unit during basic training at Camp Toccoa, Georgia, back in the summer of 1942. His appearance that day in the shelled-out remains of a local building was a happy surprise because Perconte was back from the field hospital. Luz tosses him a chocolate bar and laughs, which is met by a complaint from Liebgott, "He gets a Hershey bar?"

"Well, he got shot in the ass," says Luz.

"I expect a little sympathy from ya," laughs Perconte.

That's when Sergeant John Martin walks over and asks, "You want me to rub it for ya?"

Tens of millions of Americans have watched *Band of Brothers*, riveted by the fact that each of the characters is based directly on a real individual. Maybe they also read the book of the same name by historian Stephen Ambrose that inspired the miniseries, or the autobiographical *Parachute Infantry* written by David Webster. The ten episodes of the miniseries were especially poignant because they were bookended by live interviews with the actual men who served and survived, notably their leader Dick Winters. The young men who busted each other's chops over Hershey bars a few hours before crossing into Germany were true heroes.

Viewers of the miniseries start remembering individual faces after a few episodes, about the time of the D-Day invasion during which Captain Winters leads the men of Easy Company on an assault of a dug-in battery of four German 105mm guns that were killing Allied troops storming onto Utah Beach. Viewers remember Sergeant William "Wild Bill" Guarnere losing his leg in a mortar attack near Bastogne. They remember the attack on Foy when Captain Ronald Spiers was sent in to take command of Easy midway through the assault. Spiers literally ran through enemy lines during the battle so that he could communicate with another company in the battalion and coordinate the joint assault. Then ran back!

People remember these things because these acts of incredible bravery to defeat Nazism and to save Western civilization really happened.

What viewers wouldn't know by simply watching the television series is that Liebgott, Luz, and Perconte were second-generation immigrants. Their parents came to America from Austria, Portugal, and Italy, respectively. Indeed, many of the young men in the band of brothers had an immigrant father, immigrant mother, or both. And some were even first-generation immigrants, notably the heroic Ronald Spiers who was born in Scotland, then emigrated to the United States in 1924. Although these individuals became famous as "everyman" Americans, their backgrounds as immigrant warriors who volunteered for military service are appropriately common in the nation's history.

Joe Liebgott survived the war and lived out his life in San Francisco as a taxi driver. George Luz returned to West Warwick, Rhode Island, and was so beloved by his fellow citizens that thousands came to his funeral. Frank Perconte returned home to Joliet, Illinois, where he worked as a postman for thirty years. Spiers stayed in the army, served in the Korean War, and retired as a lieutenant colonel after a stint as the American governor of Spandau Prison in Berlin, which held Nazi war criminals. None of them stood out in the television show with foreign accents, which was true to life and similar to most Americans from immigrant families. But we should remember.

In his book *Brothers in Battle: Best of Friends*, Bill Guarnere describes his childhood as the youngest of ten kids in a Depression-era neighborhood where nobody had a telephone and people went for days with an empty stomach. "In South Philadelphia, you didn't survive unless you learned the tricks of the streets. Food was scarce, money was scarce. . . . My pop was Joe the tailor. He worked out of our house at Chadwick and McKean. Pop was a tough old bird, came to the United States from Italy in 1891. Spoke broken English. Mom was born here, but she talked Italian."

Many other men in Easy Company were the sons of immigrants as well. Patrick O'Keefe's folks were from Ireland, as were Ed Tipper's. O'Keefe was a "replacement." Tipper was one of Liebgott's best friends, a Toccoa man who was badly wounded storming the city of Carentan when a mortar blast broke his legs and destroyed one of his eyes. Tipper lived until 2017, though he spent the remainder of his life wearing an eyepatch and using a cane to walk.

Frank Soboleski was another Easy Company soldier, the oldest of fourteen children born and raised in the United States by first-generation immigrants, his father from Poland, his mother from Austria. Awarded two Purple Hearts, a Gold Star, and a Silver Star, Soboleski was haunted by some of his wartime experiences, particularly the bombardment endured in Bastogne, but he thrived in Minnesota for over seventy years after the war.[1]

During a 2001 interview, Soboleski recounted how the attack on Pearl Harbor inspired many families like his to send their sons to volunteer for military service. "America was a great country to them, and it is to people who come from over there. And they were just flabbergasted; they couldn't believe it," said Soboleski. "My dad gave that impression. He had it tough in Poland, and they talked quite a bit about how it was over here compared with over there. And then this came, and he said it set the whole world back. It made a big impression on me. Probably wouldn't to an ordinary kid whose parents were born over here, but it did to me."

I had a chance to talk with George Luz Jr., son of Sergeant George Luz, who grew close to many of his dad's fellow soldiers in Easy Company and serves today as informal keeper of the unit lore. Young George was tasked with welcoming special individuals during annual Easy Company reunions, holding their favorite drinks for the moment they walked in the door. A screwdriver for Shifty Powers. Yuengling for Earl McClung.

"Both of Dad's parents emigrated from Portugal around the turn of the century. They were from an island in the Azores, St. Michael," George Jr. explained. "Even though my dad was born in Massachusetts, he didn't speak any English until he started school, first grade, in West Warwick. Everyone in the house spoke Portuguese."

Luz quit high school in order to start work and support his parents during the Great Depression, like many other Americans, but he volunteered for the paratroops and reported for duty in August of 1942. Assigned to Easy Company from the very beginning, he jumped behind enemy lines on D-Day, June 6, 1944, and again into Holland in September later that year. Described as "the most well-liked guy in the platoon," by Private Edward "Babe" Hefforn, Luz "was the company comedian. He could imitate people and he was always telling jokes. Good jokes, not like Guarnere. Luz was actually funny. He always told me I reminded him of his parish priest. He was a great soldier, all around 100% great American. Serious when he had to be, but he kidded with everyone he liked."[2]

The number of soldiers in Easy Company who were first- or second-generation immigrants is far more than the few recounted here. To my knowledge, an exhaustive study of this particular unit has never been done, but I was surprised how easy it was to find out with little effort that so many of the most famous members of this most famous unit were from immigrant families.

When George Luz Sr. passed away, Bill Guarnere joined the family to greet people at a local church and at the wake beforehand. According to George Luz Jr., Guarnere stood outside welcoming every person who came to pay their respects. He counted over 1,400 people. Ironically, a smaller Catholic church that Luz attended as a child was built on land secured by Luz's immigrant parents. They used their house as collateral along with two other immigrant families to pay for the plot of land where St. Anthony's Church was built in West Warwick. You can look it up on Google Maps and see the church for yourself, with a US flag flying on one side of the entrance and a Portuguese flag on the other side.

Fighting for America

Historically, immigrants have had a greater tendency to volunteer for US military service than native-born Americans. This was true in World War I and true during the Civil War. Indeed, the pattern has been true for every generation until now. I'll explain more below, but first consider the historical facts.

Every schoolchild knows the story of the Marquis de Lafayette, the French nobleman who joined George Washington's army during the American Revolution. Less well known is that 43 percent of the US military during the Civil War (1861 to 1865) were immigrants or the sons of immigrants. At the time, only 13 percent of US citizens were foreign-born whereas 25 percent of the troops in the Union Army were foreign-born. Historians have amassed evidence that "whole ethnic regiments, chiefly Irish and German, sustained the Union cause."[3] This immigrant advantage is arguably the decisive factor favoring the North, particularly because the conflict became a war of attrition.

Confederates said the immigrants were mere mercenaries, telling emissaries from European nations that such soldiers would not fight like patriots. Yet on the battlefield, migrants proved to be among the more aggressive and brave soldiers. One young Irish immigrant who served as a sergeant in a New York infantry regiment, Felix Brannigan, famously wrote that the apathy of non-volunteers among the native-born population made his "blood boil" because the United States was "a country which is looked upon by the oppressed of all nations as a haven of liberty." Not only did American immigrants volunteer for the military in disproportionately high numbers, but they were also awarded a disproportionately high number of medals. In the US military, the highest award for valor in action against an enemy is the Medal of Honor. Of the 1,522 Medals of Honor awarded during the Civil War, 369 of them were to first-generation immigrants. That is the same as the proportion of soldiers who served in the Union Army, but also far above the proportion of immigrants in the northern population.

Personal letters and testimonials from that era paint a picture of sincere commitment to the anti-slavery cause. German Americans were particularly enthusiastic supporters of Abraham Lincoln during the 1860 election and during the war. Their fervor for the United States is rooted in class-based inequality in the Old World compared to the enshrined liberties in their new country. Don Doyle recounts a speech one immigrant mother gave in 1863 to an anti-slavery convention about her son's inspiration to enlist: "I am from Germany where my brothers all fought against the Government and tried to make us free, but were unsuccessful," she said. "We foreigners know the preciousness of that great, noble gift a great deal better than you, because you never were in slavery, but we were born in it."[4]

Surprisingly, in the years before the Civil War, Irish communities in the North were hostile to Lincoln and indifferent to slavery. Irish Americans, it must be remembered, were generally destitute and crowded in the dirtiest tenements of New York and other coastal cities. Organized politically by Democrats and suspicious of the Know Nothing branch of the new Republican Party, their opposition to candidate Lincoln is understandable. Yet once the die of war was cast, Irish Americans were committed to victory for their new country. They were not alone. Tyler Anbinder's in-depth history of New York City describes in great detail how volunteer regiments sprang up spontaneously in response to President Lincoln's call:

> After the assault on Fort Sumter, members of nearly every immigrant community in the city volunteered. Scotch-born stonecutter Alexander Campbell enlisted in the Scotch American Seventy-ninth New York "Highlanders" Regiment (though his brother James, who had settled in Charleston, volunteered for the Confederate military). Many New York immigrants joined the Thirty-ninth New York Infantry Regiment, probably the most diverse military unit to fight in the Civil War. It included soldiers from Argentina, Armenia, Austria, Belgium, Bohemia, Canada, Chile, Cuba, Denmark, England, France, the German states, Greece, Granada, Holland, Hungary, Ireland, Italy, Malta, Nicaragua, Norway, Poland, Portugal, Russia, Scotland, Spain, Sweden, and Switzerland.

This wasn't the first or last time that foreign belligerents misunderstood the loyalties of America's migrant communities. King Edward of Britain never believed that British colonists would rebel in great numbers against the British Army in 1776, just as Nazi generals in 1941 miscalculated the willingness of ethnic Germans to fight under the flag of the United States.

Why didn't very many immigrants fight for the South? The simple answer is that most immigration flows had been to northern cities and states. When South Carolina and other southern states seceded, there were more immigrants in ten square miles of lower Manhattan than in over 770,000 square miles of the Confederacy.[5]

After the Civil War ended with General Robert E. Lee's surrender at Appomattox on April 9, 1865, America entered one of the greatest eras of prosperity in history. The economy grew faster than ever before. The Gilded Age, as it came to be known, was partly driven by peace, partly by surging immigration from non-English-speaking countries, and partly by the Industrial Revolution. Oil and steel and invention defined the times. Despite cycles of recession in the ensuing decades and sometimes violent labor strife that accompanied the tectonic upheaval of nascent factory-based manufacturing, everyday Americans were moving en masse from rural to urban areas, enriched like never before. They had newfound purchasing power and new technologies—indoor plumbing, telegraphs, electricity—that not only changed their lives but also propelled their country from a peripheral oddity relative to the Great Powers of Europe into the mightiest economy in the world over the years 1865 to 1914.

The era ended when the War to End All Wars began. When international tensions flared over Europe in 1914, then sparked into total warfare between the Russian-English-French alliance and the Central Powers (Germany, Austria-Hungary and the Ottomans), President Woodrow Wilson vowed to keep the United States out of it. Wilson's re-election in 1916 was in fact secured with the slogan of keeping America out of the war. His neutrality was lop-sided, however, honoring the British embargo of Germany while ignoring the German embargo of Great Britain. In hindsight, the sinking of the *Lusitania* was far more complicated than is remembered.

Unlike any war before or since, the US military was terribly unprepared. When the United States declared war in April 1917, there were only 128,000 men in the US Army and 67,000 in the National Guard. The country would rely on immigrants to fill the ranks. Congress established a national draft to select from all eligible males, ages 21 to 31. This new draft was conspicuous for including men of every ethnicity. At the time, many objected to that policy, namely, to arming "Negroes" as well as Jews, Slavs, and Italians because members of those groups were subject to racial hostility and paranoia. Consider some of the language used in a bestselling book of 1916 titled *The Passing of the Great Race*, in which the author Madison Grant wrote that a "dark Mediterranean subspecies" was diluting the white American race. "When the test of actual battle comes," Grant predicted, "it will, of course, be the native (white) American who will do the fighting and suffer the losses."

Lo and behold, 400,000 of the nearly 3 million men drafted into the ranks of the US Army in World War I were African Americans. And 1.7 million foreign-born "aliens" registered during the first year of the draft. Military historians Alexander Barnes and Peter Belmonte estimate that 800,000 immigrants served in the army during the war. Of that number, an estimated half million men born in forty-six different nations fought in combat wearing a US uniform. All told, 18 percent of the American military in World War I was foreign-born, compared to only 14 percent of the total US population. Unlike the concentrated regiments of the Civil War, immigrant soldiers were spread out among army units. This often caused a fair amount of chaos due to the multiple languages spoken. In that era, English was not yet universal in civil society let alone grade schools. The integration of inexperienced fighters who barely spoke English, had never handled a firearm, and had funny names led to a common joke that when roll was called and someone sneezed, a dozen doughboys with thick accents said, "Here."

How well did they fight? The most famous American hero of the war, Sergeant Alvin York, came to admire and praise his immigrant brothers-in-arms. York received the Medal of Honor for leading a raid on a machine-gun nest, eventually taking 132 enemy soldiers captive. He also kept a private diary that reveals an interesting evolution in his personal attitude toward his fellow soldiers. Early on, York wrote, "Those Greeks and Italians and the New York Jews! Ho ho . . . They were always asking, where was the war? They were always ready to go over the top in time of battle, almost too anxious to go over the top."[6] A later entry in his diary reveals York admiring how these fellows improved and came to fight like "wildcats" by the end of the campaign. Later still he wrote that his immigrant comrades "were sure turning out to be good soldiers. They sure kept on going."

Another testimonial comes down to us from none other than General John J. Pershing, commander of the American Expeditionary Forces during the war. Pershing was ultimately promoted to the highest rank that exists—General of the Armies—which is essentially a six-star rank. Earlier in his military career, he met a junior enlisted man named Samuel Dreben who had emigrated from an area in eastern Europe that is now part of Ukraine. Dreben was born in 1878, ran away from home, was a stowaway to London, and emigrated to the United States at the age of twenty. Six months later, he enlisted on the spot when a recruiter told him the US Army would give him a free uniform, free funeral (if necessary), a steady paycheck, and adventures around the world.

Dreben came to be known as the "Fighting Jew" because of his unflappable courage, amazing luck, and lethality with a machine gun, but he did not look the part of a great warrior. He was fat and short, even by the standards of 1880, but he enjoyed a lengthy career in the US Army and as a soldier of fortune in Mexico. Almost immediately after retiring, Dreben heard that the United States was going to enter the Great War on the side of England and France. He re-enlisted as a private in the Texas infantry in 1918, heading off to war in France at the age of 40, but he was quickly promoted up the enlisted ranks when officers recognized his experience. Sure enough, Dreben was dauntless in the trenches of France.

Awarded the Distinguished Service Cross for his valor in combat, Dreben was invited by General Pershing as his personal guest at American headquarters in Paris. Pershing also made a point to include Sergeant Dreben in the honor guard at the burial of the Unknown Soldier in Arlington National Cemetery three years after the Armistice, an honor guard that also included Alvin York. If that isn't definitive enough, General Pershing publicly proclaimed that Sam Dreben, the Fighting Jew, was "the finest soldier and one of the bravest men I ever knew."[7]

Like the other men who returned home from the devastation of World War I, Dreben recognized that America was changing. Sadly, the aftermath of the war led to a widespread resurgence of paranoia and isolationism inside the United States and other countries. Some combination of the horrors of the war, the menace of international communism, and the flu pandemic of 1918 led to an ugly national mood that saddened and surprised returning soldiers. Congress all but shut the door to non-Nordic immigrants with new quotas in 1921 and 1924.

Two thousand American Jews were killed in combat. If that wasn't proof enough of their commitment to the republic, the ratio of Jewish soldiers in combat units was much higher than the norm. Those facts didn't stop a wave of anti-Semitism in the United States that coincided with similar sentiments in Europe, sentiments that ultimately fueled Hitler's rise. Sam Dreben fought against the Ku Klux Klan's efforts to take over the American Legion post in El Paso after the war, but soon decamped for a friendlier community in California.

There's another story about Sam Dreben that is worth repeating. During his time in Paris, he crossed paths in a restaurant with the exiled Russian grand duke Nikolai Nikolaevich who had overseen years of pogroms against Russian Jews. Recognizing Nikolaevich from across the room, Dreben marched over and punched him in the face.

The end of the era of mass immigration in the 1920s was too late to slow down America's rising power, but it did change the makeup of US military forces in the next generation. Only 300,000 first-generation immigrants fought for the United States during World War II. Compared to earlier wars, the ratio serving in the ranks during the Second World War was low. The reason is that the foreign-born population was uncharacteristically old in 1941 relative to the national average. That was entirely a consequence of the 1924 law. Tyler Anbinder explains that after Pearl Harbor, "the foreign-born still made up 29 percent of [New York's] population, but they constituted only 5 percent of men aged eighteen to thirty-five. By the end of the war in 1945, 891,000 of New York's 7.5 million inhabitants had either enlisted or been drafted into the military, but only a small number of them were [first-generation] immigrants. . . . The press and Hollywood might boast that the American army was a true 'melting pot,' but the Irish, Italians, Jews, and Poles who fought side by side were almost always the children or grandchildren of immigrants rather than adopted Americans themselves."

I tend to think Hollywood has this one right. We cannot discount the military melting pot experience of second-generation veterans such as Perconte, Liebgott, Soboleski, Guarnere, Tipper, and Luz because the neighborhoods they came from across the country were much more culturally distant. Parents and neighbors often spoke little English, if at all. The wartime experience fused these men together into a united force, providing a common identity and common purpose that could not have happened absent the war. The men who fought in the Band of Brothers of the 101st Airborne were literally brothers with three times as many siblings than the average today. Bill Guarnere was famously lethal during the first days of the Normandy invasion because he had learned of his brother's death the night before D-Day. After those searing years of warfare, such men returned home with a heightened tolerance and understanding of their fellow Americans. And for the next forty years, veterans with those perspectives dominated political life. Notably, future US presidents Jack Kennedy and Richard Nixon both served on active duty in the navy during World War II and went on to promote policies that increased and diversified immigration.

Immigrant Recruiting as Grand Strategy?

Something changed about the US military in the 1990s, when the clouds of the Cold War lifted. Avoiding nuclear Armageddon was unambiguously good news, but we can look back now and see how sharply global affairs shifted before and after the fall of global communism. It wasn't long before the US federal government scaled back the size of the armed forces. The peace dividend they called it.

The downsizing seemed abrupt, but it was actually part of a trend that has continued now for seventy years. Aside from a few concentrated communities around military bases, you just don't see men in uniform like you did when FDR, Truman, and Eisenhower were in the White House. Over 3 million troops were on active duty in the 1950s. There are fewer than half that many today. A simple statistical projection implies the number will literally go to zero around the year 2060. As the army declined, the overall population boomed, meaning that the percentage of Americans in uniform has seen a dramatic reduction. One in forty-five Americans were on active duty during the Korean War, compared to one in 300 today.

The great military downsizing has more to do with the nature of warfare than budget constraints or fading patriotism. The US Army uses more technology and capital equipment than ever; more tanks and drones and code. The era of mass troops may well be ending once and for all because the demand for low-skilled battlefield labor no longer exists among advanced militaries.

Consequently, the demand for low-skilled immigrant labor in the military has collapsed. For the first time in US history, the ratio of immigrants serving in uniform is lower than in the population at large.

Does this mean the Pentagon is passively waiting for soldiers to enlist? Hardly. After President Nixon ended the draft in 1973, the brass realized it would need higher pay to attract voluntary enlistments. The Pentagon refined its personnel policies to attract and retain better soldiers who in this century are measurably smarter and stronger than their civilian peers. In fact, the complaint in this new century is that so few young people qualify mentally, physically, and temperamentally to enlist. As just one example, I analyzed military demographics soon after the invasion of Iraq and discovered the shocking statistic that there are three recruits from the wealthiest American zip codes for every two recruits from the poorest zip codes. In fact, the income and education levels of military enlistees were far higher than the average civilian in 1999 and got higher still after the 9/11 attacks.

> There are slightly higher proportions of recruits from the middle class and slightly lower proportions from low-income brackets. However, the proportion of high-income recruits rose to a disproportionately high level after the war on terrorism began, as did the proportion of highly educated enlistees.[8]

The talent managers at Human Resources Command and Naval Personnel Command work every day to identify and recruit young men and women to join the ranks. In today's world, where the United States protects freedom of movement on every ocean and is engaged in countless security treaties, its military leaders put a premium on troops with linguistic and cultural expertise. In fact, they do not passively wait for foreign-born citizens to volunteer but follow tradition dating back to 1776 of encouraging foreigners to join the American ranks. More than 760,000 non-citizens have enlisted and obtained US citizenship in the past hundred years, more than 100,000 since the 9/11 attacks.

Eastern Europeans were targeted for recruitment into the US military between 1950 and 1959 by an act of Congress, an intentional strategy to counter communism throughout the region. Many treaties went even further, namely, the Military Bases Agreement of 1947, which allowed the United States to build massive military bases in the Philippines and also gave Filipinos the right to enlist directly into the US armed forces. During the George W. Bush administration, Congress developed a special program offering expedited citizenship in exchange for service in the US military service to young individuals with linguistic or medical skills. It was called the Military Accessions Vital to the National Interest (MAVNI) program.[9] Unfortunately, the program was suspended by the Obama administration at the end of his term, and many recruits have been stuck in limbo ever since. President Trump's administration subjected new recruits to excessive scrutiny and moved to discharge numerous individuals who were already in the ranks, motivated by an unreasonable fear that some were double agents. This lone program isn't definitive, but it does symbolize how confused American policy has become, though hardly for the first time. If the Pentagon is serious about countering rivals in this new century, namely China, it will massively expand recruitment efforts throughout the Indo-Pacific region.

The German Lesson

The sudden, nationwide hostility to German Americans was a cultural turning point at the outbreak of the First World War: a profound new American nationalism that had a positive, unifying side as well as a negative "clearly antiforeign" side that associated all forms of hyphenated Americanism (e.g., German American) with "disloyalty and subversion" in the words of Roger Daniels.[10] Thomas Sowell described it this way:

> The outbreak of the First World War in Europe in 1914 brought much condemnation of Germany in the United States. German-Americans were adversely affected, in part because of a generalized hostility toward Germans and German culture, and perhaps more so because German American spokesmen tended to try to justify the actions of their ancestral homeland, which was waging a war of aggression in Europe. When the United States ultimately joined the war against Germany, feelings ran higher still among Americans in general, though German Americans loyally served in the U.S. military forces and America's leading fighter pilot was of German ancestry—Eddie Rickenbacker. Nevertheless, the German language was banished from many American high school curricula, as German music was banned from concert halls.

I have argued that the nature of America as a nation of immigrants is qualitatively distinct from every other Great Power in history since Rome. Whereas it is the nature of the Russian or French or Chinese Army to fight with a sense of ethnic nationalism, the American military is altogether different, with a spirit of uniqueness just as strong but rooted in a universalist identity. An American prisoner of war held by the Nazis during World War II makes this point, retold by his captor who survived the war:

> In Normandy, in July 1944, Wehrmacht Pvt. Walter Zittats was guarding some American prisoners. One of them spoke German. Zittats asked him, "Why are you making War against us?" I'll always remember his exact words: "We are fighting to free you from the fantastic idea that you were a master race."[11]

This universalist attitude deeply affects the way Americans fight, or more accurately, the way they conduct themselves in war. There's a reason that members of the Wehrmacht were far more willing to surrender to US troops on the Western front than to Russians "imbued with ancient and ethnic hatreds" on the Eastern front.[12] Americans treated German POWs so well— shipped stateside and made to work on farms throughout the Midwest—that it was embarrassingly better than many African American citizens were treated at home. To be sure, plenty of surrendering Nazis were killed by bloodthirsty GIs. Sometimes rules of engagement from higher up the chain of command called for no prisoners. But there is no denying the widespread magnanimity of American troops, particularly in 1945. Ambrose records the memory of German Sgt. Ewald Becker from the day he and his fellow soldiers surrendered:

> "We went out into the street to surrender. The first vehicle to come was an American jeep. I raised my hands. He waved at me and continued to drive. The second was a slightly larger American vehicle with four men. They stopped and gave me chocolate. They said something I didn't understand and drove on." Eventually other GIs arrived to take away the weapons of Becker and his men, place them under a nominal guard, and walk them to the nearest POW camp.[13]

The irony is that the US military, dedicated to the proposition that all men are created equal, has been shaped from the beginning by a certain martial character among its German-born members. Germany's northern region known as Prussia is famous for producing many military leaders and thinkers. Carl von Clausewitz, for example, is the best-known military theorist in history. The long line of German American generals begins with the Revolutionary War when officers such as General Friedrich Wilhelm von Steuben arrived to help George Washington organize the Continental Army. The US Army's supreme commanders during both world wars were of German descent: Pershing and Eisenhower. In the Pacific, it was Admiral Chester Nimitz. And one of the pioneers of the Army Air Corps was General

Carl Spaatz. Even in modern wars, the tradition continues with General Norman Schwarzkopf.

An exception to the flag officers was a prototypical German American in the Second World War from New York City by the name of Heinz Kissinger. He was drafted in 1943 even though he was a teenage non-citizen, a Jewish refugee who fled Germany in 1938. Heinz became a US citizen after Army boot camp, then served with distinction in the 84th Infantry Division and later in counterintelligence (because of his fluency with the German language). We know him today as Henry Kissinger, secretary of state to President Nixon and foreign policy guru to every president since. His attitude in a November 1944 letter home, long before he became famous, is symbolic of the nature of the American soldier. In it, young Kissinger wrote, "I think of the cruelty and barbarism those people out there in the ruins showed when they were on top. And then I feel proud and happy to be able to enter here as a free American soldier."

The Diversity Force Multiplier

Kissinger's fluency and intelligence symbolize a strategic advantage that a multi-ethnic superpower possesses over ethnically homogenous rivals. The United States has the ability, unlike any other country now or in all of human history, to fight any place in the world with an army that can connect with the local populace. We might call it the language advantage but it's more than that. Imagine the Chinese army trying to mount a major invasion abroad—in Europe, in the Middle East, or even in Japan—with no personal linguistic or cultural connection. The Chinese People's Liberation Army (PLA) will forever be seen as a purely foreign army by enemies as well as allies, but the American army has no such disadvantage. The sword cast from the ethnic melting pot is double-edged in a way. Arguably, one of the reasons Americans feel relatively more compelled to intervene in affairs beyond their borders is that they identify with the suffering of foreigners who aren't so very foreign. It's a peculiar interventionist impulse that is the inverse of colonialism.

We should be wary that the restrictions some politicians today want to place on legal immigration might hurt the long-term strength of the American military. This chapter serves as a reminder of how heavily the American military has relied on immigrants to fill the ranks during wartime. Not only have immigrants increased the population of the United States decisively—putting the power in American superpower—but a disproportionately high percentage volunteer to serve in the ranks. Furthermore, immigrant soldiers are disproportionately heroic. That's not just a claim rooted in anecdotes. Across all of America's conflicts, one out of five recipients of the Medal of Honor are first-generation immigrants.

Immigration is vital to America's grand strategy because it maximizes the nation's military potential. But there is a deeper meaning that the traditional openness to immigration brings to the identity in the ranks of the US military, a universal sense of racial and ethnic equality that not only defines why Americans are inspired to fight against hateful tyrannies but also shapes the way all US troops fight: with a respect for the dignity of adversaries.

There's a reason President Truman ordered the racial integration of the armed forces long before that integration was accepted in the civilian society of all the states. It wasn't just because the army had to obey the president. It was because Truman had experienced ethnic integration himself as an American doughboy in World War I. It started in boot camp, when he befriended a fellow Kansan named Eddie Jacobson. The two men served together in Europe, and after the war went into business together. Jacobson was Jewish, and his parents had immigrated from Lithuania. Serving in combat together broke down the barrier between their ethnic divisions. Their story goes to show how immigration and the military are intertwined in reinforcing the American creed generation after generation.

And so, thirty years after his service as an artillery officer in World War I, Truman had the opportunity to enhance civil rights decisively, and he took it. On July 26, 1948, he abolished segregation in the armed forces by issuing Executive Order 9981. It stated that "there shall be equality of treatment and opportunity for all persons in the armed forces without regard to race, color, religion, or national origin." By the end of Truman's time in the White House, the military was almost totally integrated.

Although Truman and Jacobson weren't notably innovative in their business, or profitable, the entrepreneurial spirit they shared was something common among Americans relative to other peoples. The freedom to build, and to invent, attracted millions of risk-takers around the world and paid invaluable dividends in the technological race that came to define the American Century.

Chapter 11
Brains

If and when war comes, Hitler will realize the harm he has done Germany by driving out the Jewish scientists.

— **Albert Einstein**

If the dismissal of Jewish scientists means the annihilation of contemporary German science, then we shall do without science for a few years!

— **Adolf Hitler**[1]

The Hsu clan's escape from Maoism is a harrowing one. Christopher Hsu was born in the Sung village in Henan province, where the family could trace its roots back to the Yuan Dynasty during the 13th century. Despite losing his mother in childbirth and suffering through the Japanese occupation, Christopher (whose birth name is Ching Chung) and his cousin Chester escaped to Canton when Mao Zedong's communist revolutionaries swept across the country. A family relative, a general in Chiang Kai-shek's Nationalist Army, helped the two boys reach the southern coast. From there, they escaped by boat to Taiwan.

Christopher worked as an interpreter supporting US Air Force fighter jet squadrons that were deployed by President Eisenhower in 1955 as a show of force against mainland China's shelling of Kinmen (Quemoy) Island. "I loved seeing the U.S. military in action. What a bunch of dedicated airmen defending freedom against communism. I was very impressed with their speed and efficiency in dealing with the crises of the Cold War. America was the superpower small nations could count on to fight communist aggression."[2]

In 1963, Christopher was given a rare opportunity to study English at a US university as part of a program to help the FBI. He traveled by sea through the Panama Canal to arrive on the East Coast of the United States. Once on American soil, he decided to switch colleges to study at Kansas State University because that was the home state of Dwight Eisenhower. The only other state he considered was Louisiana, because, of course, that was the home state of General Claire Chenault. Chenault was the man who led the "Flying Tigers"—a mercenary force of fighter pilots who resisted the Japanese occupation of Asia long before the attack on Pearl Harbor. Christopher married an American woman and they decided to settle in Baton Rouge. Before his graduation from Kansas State, however, the newlyweds found time to visit the Eisenhower museum in Abilene three more times.

Christopher and Mary Hsu settled in Louisiana and had four children, Kathy, Susan, Chris Jr., and Joe. In the 1980s, both sons received nominations to the US Military Academy at West Point. Both graduated with honors. And both served overseas in the US Army. Joe served in Iraq doing trauma surgery for American soldiers, Iraqi civilians, and even enemy combatants. Chris deployed to Bosnia in 1995 with the 1st Armor Division. Today, Joe Hsu is a successful orthopedic trauma surgeon in Charlotte, North Carolina. Chris is a Silicon Valley innovator, most recently serving as the chief operating officer of Hewlett Packard Enterprise and then CEO of Micro Focus, a multinational tech company with tens of billions of dollars in revenue.

The Hsu family's story is a common one in which the second generation, counted officially as native born, thrives in the United States in no small part thanks to the support and encouragement of their immigrant parents. Many first-generation immigrants thrive as well, but the lesson here is the subtleness in the American creed that revolves around the word merit. Millions of immigrant families like the Hsus might not look talented when they first arrive. Time and again, refugees who seem needy and burdensome upon arrival end up flourishing. This should make us wonder if the idea favoring rich and educated foreigners with a so-called merit-based immigration system is wise. Rather, it is the American creed of equal opportunity that rewards merit that can only be revealed by hard work and brains, not sheepskins and bank accounts.

The US Constitution offers equal opportunity, not an ethnic or ideological utopia of equity in outcomes, and that stands in contrast to so many countries of origin where there are relentless barriers to individual achievement. Some barriers are raw poverty, weak education systems, and the like. But too often the barriers are religious and ethnic. So much human potential, unable to blossom abroad, takes root in America and generates tremendous value. I'll review in this chapter some evidence of the "brain gains" that the United

States receives from immigration but also warn readers to think carefully about skeptics who warn of a "brain drain" suffered by sending countries. In a zero-sum world, it might make sense to fret over the transfer of the brightest talents from Country X to the United States. But this is not a zero-sum world. Christopher Hsu exemplifies this, as he would most likely have been killed by the communists or at best been stunted in his personal development if he'd not escaped Maoism. Rather, the brain gain of American immigration likely is a source of gain for the whole world, and even a net benefit to sending countries.

There's a riddle I like to pose to students in my classes to make this point because so many immigrants become mainstream successes in the United States that even Americans don't know who is an immigrant and who is a native. I read a dozen names aloud, and you (the students) have to guess which six are immigrants. Ready?

Andrew Carnegie
Alexander Hamilton
Arianna Huffington
Eddie Van Halen
Elon Musk
Joseph Pulitzer
Knute Rockne
Madeleine Albright
Natalie Portman
Patrick Ewing
Salma Hayek
Werner von Braun

Which six were born abroad? You're too smart not to recognize this is a trick question. There are no wrong answers to the riddle because all twelve names belong to foreign-born American immigrants. And there are so many more, overflowing in every possible category. Athletics? Albert Pujols and Hakeem Olajuwon and Martina Navratilova. Artists? M. Night Shyamalan and Michael J. Fox and Charlize Theron. Innovators? Rupert Murdoch and Sergey Brin and the founder of Chobani, Hamdi Ulukaya. Most important for national security (if we are thinking merely in terms of hard power) there are the scientists. Nikolai Tesla and Enrico Fermi and the most famous of all immigrants, the physicist Albert Einstein.

Einstein

Known as the greatest physicist of the 20th century for the theory of relativity, Einstein developed the first of his groundbreaking theories while working as a clerk in a Swiss patent office in 1905. Although born in Germany, Einstein spent some time in Switzerland as a pacifist during the First World War, but he was back living and working in Germany as a German by 1918, after the close of the war. What drew him back to a nation raw with defeat was a matter of academia: Germany's universities were the finest in the world, rivaled only by Oxford and Cambridge.

You probably know what happens in this part of the story. Awarded the Nobel Prize in physics in 1921, Einstein had already achieved worldwide acclaim and begun touring the world, speaking to huge crowds in the United States, Britain, France, and Japan. His biographer, Walter Isaacson, described Einstein's two-month tour of the United States in 1921 as evoking "the sort of mass frenzy and press adulation that would thrill a touring rock star. The world had never before seen, and perhaps never will again, such a scientific celebrity superstar."[3]

Back home, however, in the wake of Germany's humiliating defeat in World War I, the German Jewish community was facing increasing pressure, and Jews were the scapegoats for the catastrophic war. Even before Einstein's recognition with the Nobel Prize, German cranks had been attacking the theory of relativity as a "big hoax" that reeked of "Jewish science." The very name "relativity" was easy to caricature as a rejection of solid, traditionalist German values. This hostility wasn't just for cranks but was soon joined by one of the most distinguished scientists in Germany, Philipp Lenard, who himself had received the Nobel Prize in physics in 1905. He became a leader of the "Deutsche Physik" movement in the 1930s that attempted to discredit Einstein's discoveries. "The Jew wants to create contradictions everywhere and to separate relations, so that preferably, the poor naïve German can no longer make any sense of it whatsoever," wrote Lenard in the foreword to a textbook.[4] This attitude toward Jewish intellectuals did not stop at theoretical physics. To be "Jewish" in the Weimar Republic was synonymous with an almost hysterical fear of the modern, the exotic, the diverse, the liberal, the challenging, and the different. Impressionism, surrealism, pacifism, open displays of homosexuality, women's independence, cabaret halls, cosmetics, and even women's slacks were all viewed as highly suspect by the conservative nationalists licking their wounds after a humiliating defeat. There became an increased effort to divorce German Jewish identity from German identity, with tropes that continue to this day within far right propaganda of the perfect, traditional Aryan family and the depraved immorality of "The Other."

The hostility toward Einstein and other German Jewish academics and creators would ultimately mutate into the Holocaust, a program of genocide that over time peeled away the privacy, freedom, and independence of all Jews within Germany, forcing them to give up their property and move into ghettoes, then work camps, then death camps. But the murder of 6 million Jewish people across Europe, a genocide so enormous that the global Jewish population has never recovered, was preceded by two decades of hostility. As early as 1922, right-wing extremists were murdering senior officials of Germany's democratically elected government, notably foreign minister Walther Rathenau who happened to be Jewish. Einstein was warned to stay out of the public eye as he was targeted for assassination, particularly with the added unpopularity regarding his decision not to fight for Germany in 1914.

Einstein realized that he had to leave his homeland. It was in December of 1932, a month before Adolf Hitler became chancellor, that Einstein made up his mind to emigrate to the United States. He left his home in Caputh with over a dozen boxes and suitcases, supposedly for a visit to CalTech, and told his wife as they left their home, "Take a very good look at it. You will never see it again." The Nazis raided his home in Berlin after he was gone, not once, but five times. That same spring, when the Nazi regime banned Jewish people from holding official positions anywhere in Germany, including at its famous universities, fourteen Nobel laureates were forced out. Isaacson put the impact in context: "Fittingly, such refugees from fascism who left Germany or the other countries it came to dominate—Einstein, Edward Teller, Victor Weisskopf, Hans Bethe, Lise Meitner, Niels Bohr, Enrico Fermi, Otto Stern, Eugene Wigner, Leo Szilard, and others—helped to assure that the Allies rather than the Nazis first developed the atom bomb."[5] Fermi came from Italy. Szilard from Hungary. Meitner from Austria.

In 1939, a year before he would pass the official test to become an American citizen, Einstein wrote a letter to President Franklin D. Roosevelt detailing the potential of the atom bomb, warning that Germany could be in the process of developing their own bombs, and urging the United States to adopt a nuclear program. This famous letter prompted the Manhattan Project. Had this effort not been undertaken, the destruction unleashed by Germany's nuclear program would most likely have been far more horrible than the manner in which the United States used the bomb—devastating attacks on the relatively small cities of Hiroshima and, three days later, Nagasaki as examples and warnings.

One recent research paper by economist Petra Moser and her colleagues found statistical evidence that the Einstein effect is not merely anecdotal. "Patenting by US inventors increased by 31 percent in émigré fields," they found.[6] Russian emigrés during the Cold War have been shown to have the same positive impact. And currently, 9 percent of US innovation can be attributed to Chinese and Chinese American scientists.[7]

As for the Manhattan Project, it was so named because the original work was done at Columbia University in New York, led by Fermi and other immigrants. Even the scientist who led the project, Robert Oppenheimer, was a second-generation immigrant. His father Julius had come from Germany in 1888, penniless and uneducated. He worked, as so many Jewish migrants did then, in textiles as his career. Nobody in Germany lamented the brain drain of Julius Oppenheimer.

The Jewish Diaspora

The economic strength of Nazi Germany can be easily overestimated by many casual historians, not realizing just how much of its industrial strength was based on the short-term capital returns from the nationalization of resources, including hundreds of billions confiscated from their Jewish citizens.[8] The Third Reich looked mighty with its blitzkrieg victories against France, Poland, and much of the continent, even the first round of battles against British forces. But in retrospect, its economic model was engineered for short-term production, not longevity, and one that was more a well-engineered public relations facade than a strong fiscal policy.

We should never forget that the "zi" in Nazi stands for "socialism," a predatory philosophy that has everywhere been associated with early nationalizations that hollow-out productive incentives. The move from the accountable private sector to an increasingly dictatorial, paranoid, and absolutist governmental authority served only to suffocate a healthy diversity within the economy and stunt the advancements of the industrial, medical, and technological fields that would have profited from less rigid restrictions, not least on whom they could hire, fund, or source ideas and supply chains from. Even if the moral ugliness of racism is ignored within the economic discussion, it is impossible not to acknowledge the profound lack of sense in limiting your workforce and ingenuity to one ethnicity, gender, and ideology.

The sociological impulse to scapegoat a minority was hardly original to *Mein Kampf,* and the particular abuse of the Jewish community as a people predates Christianity. The story of the Jewish diaspora is one of the great sagas of human suffering and perseverance. In the course of studying the brain gains of American diversity, I was surprised by the relationship between the strength of empires and nations across the centuries and their tolerance for diverse minorities, particularly tolerance for Jewish people. From this long experience, a peculiar lesson emerges: intolerant societies tend toward decline whereas those more tolerant societies tend toward strength.

Of the 15–25 million Jewish people alive in the year 2018, half are living in the United States, another third are in Israel, and the remainder are scattered, with significant minority clusters of around 1 to 2 percent of the national population across the countries of Europe, Latin America, and Asia. The wide range of estimates of the total population is due not to trouble counting heads but to categorizing them. For example, the Pew Research Center published *A Portrait of Jewish Americans* in 2013 that estimated the number of Jewish citizens to be between 4.2 and 5.3 million based on whether they included people whose religion is Jewish or a more expansive definition that counted the ethnicity via just one parent.[9] Other scholars place the number over 7 million.[10] The state of Israel maintains a slightly more refined and expansive set of definitions from the smallest "core" global population of religious and ethnic Jews to the broader population eligible for citizenship under its 1950 Law of Return. Under the narrowest definition, half of the core population lives in Israel, 40 percent in the United States, and 10 percent elsewhere. Under the more expansive definition, 51 percent of the world's Jews reside in the United States and 28 percent live in Israel.[11]

It would also be remiss not to mention that there has been a mass exodus through the increased persecution of Jewish civilians living in other Middle Eastern countries besides Israel. Egypt, a nation that had 80,000 Jewish civilians in 1948, began a process of expelling them and sequestering Jewish property. This caused a radical decline in the number of Jewish Egyptians to just five persons in 2019. Similar declines occurred across the latter half of the 20th century with the rise of anti-Semitic sentiment across the Middle East: Iran had 150,000 Jewish civilians in 1948, and now it has 8,756. Saudi Arabia had 800 Jewish people in 1950, but by the 1970s, foreigners wishing to work in the kingdom had to sign an affidavit stating that they were not Jewish. In Iraq, 121,633 Jews left between 1948 and 1951, leaving 15,000 behind, with numbers dropping to just ten persons in 2018. Despite the relative silence of the international community on this issue, it would be wholly irresponsible not to acknowledge the extensive upheaval that the Jewish people have faced over just the last sixty years, continued on from centuries of genocides, pogroms, and ethnic cleansing. In fact, America resembles something of an anomaly in being a relatively consistent and stable home for Jewish refugees and immigrants.

In its 244-year history, America has never legislated to separate our Jewish population in quarters or ghettos, deport them, nor to forcibly convert the Jewish people to Christianity. The authorities in the United States have never legislated against the right of Jewish Americans to build their own homes, temples, and synagogues on American soil, or sought to legislate against their right to worship freely. The American people have never legislated to tax Jewish citizens at a higher rate than American gentiles. Congress has never refused the rights to land, trade, education, or property to people of Jewish descent or faith, nor has it restricted the right of a Jewish person to marry into the majority Christian community. In fact, when the highly anti-Semitic businessman Austin Corbin sought to ban Jewish people from Coney Island in 1879, he inspired such national outrage that his "un-American" ban was condemned across the country as an infringement on the Constitution, forcing him to back down. It is unsurprising, therefore, that in facing so much legal and social persecution within Europe and the Middle East, many Jewish communities have sought to make America their home.

All this accumulates to one point: the Jewish population in America represents a profound shift across the last century. In the wake of growing religious diversity throughout the Reformation and Enlightenment, although not without sporadic anti-Semitic terrorism, Europe had become home to more than 80 percent of the world's Jewish population in 1700, 1800, and also in 1900. Yet the atrocities of the past century changed the locus entirely, such that fewer than 10 percent remain in Europe today. US census records indicate that there were around 500 Jews living in New York City in 1820, and 50,000 nationwide in 1848. Their national population increased to roughly half a million in 1900, and 5 million in 1950.

American Jews emerged as a major new ethnic population in New York and other eastern cities after fleeing persecution during the Russian pogroms of the 1880s. These were not shtetls and ghettos that the American government legally or systematically forced people to reside within but independent neighborhoods that formed naturally and acted like a gravitational force for the refugees of violent upheavals across Europe. This was followed by further mass migration from Europe from European Jewish communities in the 1940s following the Holocaust and further persecution in returning to their homes and villages, and further migration from Middle Eastern Jews fleeing persecution or pogroms and massacres in Iran, Iraq, Syria, Jordan, Lebanon, and Egypt and Tunisia in the 1950s and '60s.

Lessons of History

What Einstein's generation experienced is only the latest major peregrination. The Jewish diaspora began when the kingdom of Judah was conquered by the Babylonians in 597 BC. Thus began seventy years of suffering for the Jewish people, some held as captive slaves to their new rulers and many forced to wander after the Babylonian Exile, never to return to the Holy Land. Babylon was a city-state that existed south of present-day Baghdad, powerful for the blink of a historical eye, yet the exile of the Jews was permanent in effect. The destruction of Jerusalem by the Babylonian king Nebuchadnezzar II was total. In the words of Ephraim Stern, a modern archaeologist, "Many towns and villages were either completely or partly destroyed. The rest were barely functioning. International trade virtually ceased."[12]

Many of Judah's exiles fled east to Persia (an area now called Iran), the most open society of the era. As recently as 1979, on the eve of the Ayatollah's Shia revolution, there were 80,000 Jews living in Iran, descendants of the Exile.[13] When Persia's Cyrus the Great conquered Babylon in 539 BC, exiled Judeans were permitted to return. The Old Testament's book of Ezra describes the rebuilding of the Temple of Jerusalem two years after Babylon's fall. Sadly, though thousands of Jewish families lived in Persia for over two millennia, the Ayatollah's regime forced most to flee after 1979. Fewer than 9,000 remain as of a 2013 Iranian census. This should be remembered as nothing short of tragic rejection of the tolerance of Persia at its peak, when Cyrus proclaimed:

> I announce that I will respect the traditions, customs and religions of the nations of my empire, and never let any of my governors and subordinates look down on or insult them.[14]

The Roman Empire conquered most of the known world during the first two centuries after the reign of Augustus Caesar, an expanse that would have been impossible without tolerance for the many gods of its many lands. But multi-ethnicity did not allow for outright rebellion, and the people of Judea revolted against the high taxes of Rome starting in AD 66, a revolt that ultimately became an outright war. The Roman siege of Jerusalem in AD 70 killed an estimated 1.1 million people and destroyed its great Temple, which was the heart of Jewish life. This second forced exile of Jews from the Holy Land led to an unbroken history of movement, alienation, and persecution for the ensuing twenty centuries.

During the Dark Ages, Jews found protection in some parts of Europe where local kings, such as Charlemagne's son Louis, granted them protection in return for bondage as royal property. Jews were often barred from occupations but were usually free to operate as merchants and moneylenders (medieval Christian theology banned its believers from charging interest on loans). When the bubonic plague spread across Europe, killing perhaps a quarter of the population, the Jews were scapegoats.

> In that time of horror tens of thousands of Jews were burned, drowned, hanged or buried alive in retaliation. Massacre became endemic; 350 Jewish communities were decimated in German lands alone. The English were the first to expel the Jews entirely. The Jews of England belonged to the Crown, which had systematically extracted their wealth through a special Exchequer to the Jews. By 1290 it had bled them dry. Edward I thereupon confiscated what little they had left and threw them out. They crossed to France, but expulsion from that country followed in 1392; from Spain at the demand of the Inquisition in 1492; from Portugal in 1497.[15]

The survivors fled east, some to Holland and Germany, but many more to Poland and to the most powerful empire of that era: the Ottomans. Peace in those eastern regions lasted for many generations but ended abruptly. During the 1600s, Poland was broken into smaller and smaller pieces after losing successive wars against Sweden and Russia. Likewise, the Ukraine changed hands from the Turks to Russia as the once-mighty Ottoman receded into oblivion at the dawn of the 20th century.

In retrospect, the great powers that expelled their Jewish subjects tended to do so at the peak of their power, then declined soon after. Rome's power ebbed after Emperor Trajan's death in AD 117, some forty years after the destruction of the Temple in Jerusalem. Imperial Spain was the dominant power to emerge from the Middle Ages, until the forcible expulsion of Jews in the year 1492 (ironically the same year Christopher Columbus discovered America), then began its slow decline.

The Ottoman Empire's rise and fall, coincidental with the recruitment and later oppression and persecution of the Jewish people, is perhaps the most interesting. Though these judgments are somewhat subjective, most historians seem to believe that the Ottoman was the greatest empire in Eurasia during the 16th century. It was also the most relatively religiously tolerant of the many Islamic states in history. After Sultan Mehmed II conquered Constantinople in 1453, he ordered the resettlement of thousands of Muslims, Christians, and Jews from all over his empire to his new capital, renamed Istanbul. Jews came to make up one-tenth its population and were a commercial force.

Forty years later, the Sultan welcomed Sephardic Jews who were fleeing the Catholic inquisitions in Iberia and also the low-grade hostility to Judaism across Christendom. By some accounts, there was a twentyfold increase in the number of Jewish families living in Jerusalem and other Mediterranean cities where the Ottomans ruled.

Istanbul's reach extended from Austria to the north, east to the mouth of the Euphrates, and around the entire southern coast of the Mediterranean, encompassing all of Greece, Palestine, Egypt, and Libya. Its cities were glorious and its level of learning the most advanced in the world at that time, bringing most famously the Arabic numerals 0 through 9 to the West. Like the Romans, the Ottoman Turks allowed conquered peoples to keep their faiths and allowed unmatched religious and economic equality within its empire. Tolerance ebbs and flows, and like all great powers, the Ottomans hardened into a conservative hostility toward disruptive technologies from abroad and religious hierarchy that marginalized its minority religions, notably during the 1800s, the century of its demise.

None of this means that Jews are a magical people who bring the fortune of the one true God to the kings and queens who protect them, nor that they are unusually gifted in some way beyond other ethnicities or religious groups. Rather, the co-relationship of national tolerance and greatness stands on its own legs, obvious for those willing to see it. A society able to meet the promise of freedom in all its forms—religious, economic, political, and cultural— will reap many good things. Peace is one, innovation another. But the one uncontestable harvest of a freer society is a surge of migration by people oppressed elsewhere. The most intelligent and educated elites, not just the huddled masses, will clamor to the freest shores.

Great Minds Gravitate

Among the millions of victims of the Nazi regime, institutions were destroyed along with human beings. One of those was Germany's great university system. It was arguably the best in the world following the 19th-century reforms of Wilhelm von Humboldt, a giant of scholarship and statecraft whose vision of a liberal education is a cornerstone of liberalism worldwide (i.e., general principles of science, language, and the arts rather than vocational training and indoctrination). Although he was German and resided in Germany, he was invited to join the American Philosophical Society in 1822. Humboldt's University of Berlin and others "pioneered such hugely influential concepts as academic freedom and the combination of teaching and research in one institution."[16] Those practices spread far and wide to other countries but only after German schools became an intellectual center of gravity that attracted many of the brightest young minds from around the world.

The dominance of German universities might have lasted to this day if not for the rupture of Nazism with its book burnings and hostility to impure ideas. The genocides of the 1930s and 1940s were followed by social unrest and stifling bureaucracies in the 1960s. Foreign students stayed away, and a new center of gravity emerged. As recently as 1996, an article in *Science* magazine titled "The Decline of German Universities" lamented the extreme decline in international students seeking to attend college in Germany; foreign students in Germany at that time were fewer than one-sixth the number in the United States.[17]

Whether policymakers in Washington know it or not, college education is one of America's great export industries, reaping billions of dollars from foreign students with brands such as Harvard and the University of California that are as dominant in their field as Nike and Amazon are in theirs. There are more than 5.3 million international students globally, of which 19 percent are studying at US colleges and universities, according to the most current figures.[18] Those numbers arguably understate the students who travel between countries, given that adults can move freely within the nations of the European Union. Twenty years ago, one in four international students was in one of the nineteen countries in the European Monetary Union, but that has declined to one in five students in 2017, the same level as in the United States.

American schools are even more dominant in the competition for graduate students. Two-thirds of all foreign graduate students are in the United States, according to Ben Wildavsky, author of *The Great Brain Race: How Global Universities Are Reshaping the World*.[19] In STEM fields—science, technology, engineering, mathematics—foreigners account for 40 to 50 percent of PhD students at American universities.

Policymakers have periodically threatened to cut off this educational pipeline. Wildavsky pointed to the 9/11 reaction, after which there were "massive delays in [student] visa issuance and a drop in the number of international students at both the graduate and undergraduate level." This particularly affected young men and women from Pakistan, India, and China. Deans and provosts alerted Washington politicians to the harm being done, which led to those restrictions being streamlined. The number of international students in the United States set a record high in the 2018/19 academic year at 1,095,299, according to the Institute of International Education, a US non-profit organization.[20] The students added $44.7 billion directly to the

US economy. Their longer-term contributions are undoubtedly far larger, if difficult to quantify.

For an even more impressive example of how much foreign brainpower adds to US global leadership, consider the Nobel Prize. From 1901, when the first prizes were awarded, to 2019, there have been 597 awards. The prizes are given for advances in multiple fields: physics, chemistry, medicine, literature, peace, and (since 1968) economics. Given the post-war agglomeration of academic talent at US universities and corporations, it's no surprise that the United States has been dominating the science prizes for the past seven decades. One in three laureates since 1901 have been Americans, but the ratio is even higher for more recent years. That's not what made 2016 so strange.

As the recipients gathered in Stockholm from around the world in early December, many were not traveling from their country of birth. The Nobel committee takes care to note each recipient's current home as well as their birth country. In 2016, there were eleven recipients, seven of them working in the United States. But only one of them was born in America. That was Bob Dylan, awarded the literature prize for the poetic lyrics of his famous folk songs. The others were born abroad, and all had chosen to become naturalized American citizens. Fraser Stoddart, an immigrant from Scotland, was awarded the chemistry prize "for the design and synthesis of molecular machines." David Thouless and Michael Kosterlitz, also from Scotland, along with Duncan Haldane of England, earned the Nobel Prize in physics for discoveries about condensed matter. Oliver Hart of England and Bengt Holmstrom of Finland won the economics Nobel for their "contributions to contract theory," with insights on the idea of moral hazard, CEO pay, and group incentives that clarify what works and doesn't work in capitalism.

The fact that more than half the Nobel winners in 2016 were American immigrants was a story in itself, but not out of the ordinary. In 2014, four of the nine US recipients were immigrants. Again in 2019, four American laureates were immigrants, including Indian-born Abhijit Banerjee and his French-born wife Esther Duflo. The two economists are professors at the Massachusetts Institute of Technology who revolutionized the field of development economics. During many of their media interviews after receiving the Nobel Prize, the couple were asked about the irony of being immigrants and adding to America's scientific dominance when so much of the political debate was wondering if the level of migration had gone too far. In one interview, Banerjee noted how ironic it is that development economics has long found that there is too *little* immigration. "The idea that people don't actually migrate enough is a very old idea in development," he said, noting that the flow of people has been shown to help both sending and receiving regions.[21]

For the United States, the scientific brain gains of more openness to immigration are beyond debate. The pattern of Nobel Prizes before and after 1960 is too stark to deny. A recent analysis by the National Foundation for American Policy, a US-based think tank, found that "between 1901 and 1959, [American] immigrants won 21 Nobel Prizes in Chemistry, Medicine and Physics but won 84 prizes in these fields—four times as many—between 1960 and 2019."[22]

But what explains the dominance of American universities and scientists? In his book *The Gift of Global Talent*, William Kerr, a professor at Harvard Business School, explained the economic logic of high-skill agglomeration. Most types of economic activity such as dry-cleaning, dentistry, or gardening are performed proportionally to the scale of the population, and there are no benefits to having a concentration of producers in one place. Boston doesn't enjoy dentistry that is twice as good, for example, if it has twice as many dentists as New York. However, there are certain types of activity that become much more productive when key inputs are concentrated. Economists call this agglomeration.

The classic example is the agglomeration of auto production in the Detroit area, which involved a concentration of factories but also designers, engineers, marketers, and even factory managers. Unlike normal industries where an excess supply of producers causes lower wages, these peculiar industries generated increasing wages alongside increasing efficiency, profits, and innovation. Moreover, these peculiar industries are able to sell their products far beyond the region where production occurs. In other words, they are globalized industries. Historically, such industries made goods that were durable, cars being a perfect example. But that's not all. We see micro-agglomeration in places that aren't global. Car dealerships tend to cluster in the same areas. Shopping malls are a type of agglomeration of consumption. And don't you notice that a bank on one street corner is usually across the street from another?

The key differentiator that caught Kerr's attention is not consumption-driven agglomeration but the increasing returns of concentrated talent. Talent agglomeration is the key to economic success in the 21st century. As the world is shifting toward service industries such as software, health care, and digital content, the talent agglomeration is increasing. Unlike automobiles, there are no physical costs to shipping digital products 10,000 miles, over mountains and over oceans. Once a talent-cluster is established—think of the venture capital firms dotted along Sand Hill Road in Palo Alto—it becomes a self-reinforcing center of gravity that attracts talent from all over.

Silicon Valley has been the center of gravity for computer hardware (and now software) for half a century. Apple was founded there in the late 1970s, and that was decades after the actual silicon chip producers like Shockley, Hewlett-Packard, and Intel. Then in the 1990s, another generation of Internet companies was born there, thanks to clustered startup support infrastructure of investors, advisers, accountants, and lawyers, not to mention the mentors at Stanford and Berkeley. Google, Yahoo!, Facebook, Palantir, LinkedIn, Lyft, and literally hundreds more.

There's only one problem.

Talent agglomeration can be fragile.

China's War for Talent

The rest of the world isn't sitting still while American politicians constantly question the value of foreign students and scientists. The core of Wildavsky's 2010 book was to describe the increasing engagement of foreign governments in the war for talented students and talented professors, all being lured to universities, especially in Asia and the Middle East. Mainland China, for example, had a negligible number of international students at its universities in the year 2000, then 1.9 percent of the global total in 2010, rising to a full 3 percent today. That may only be one-sixth the US level, but unlike Germany's, the Chinese numbers are growing.

The ruling elites in Beijing are acutely aware of the central importance of brainpower to great power competition. Consider, for example, its Thousand Talents Plan, which was created in 2008 in response to what was perceived as a brain drain of the brightest young Chinese citizens, especially to America. At the end of the last century, Beijing recognized how far behind its economy was in terms of technology and science, and therefore encouraged its brightest citizens to study abroad. I personally befriended a young Chinese man during the summer of 1989, sent to America to study computer science, and watched the Tiananmen Square protests on television with him. His girlfriend was part of the protests, I recall, and he was very worried.

Twenty years ago, there were 39,000 Chinese students studying in the United States. As of 2017, there were over 600,000.[23] If not for the Covid-19 pandemic, the numbers would still be rising exponentially. By comparison, there are only around 10,000 American students at Chinese colleges. Beijing is increasingly worried about its prodigies who are leaving and not coming back. In the first two decades after the Cold War ended, only one of five

Chinese-born students returned to China after finishing college in the United States. Beijing moved aggressively to change that, so that now four of five students return to China.

The Thousand Talents Plan was designed to recruit 1,000 leading international experts in scientific research, innovation, and entrepreneurship to China, and it was expanded significantly in 2010 by the Central Committee of the Communist Party. The expanded plan has three tiers: one targeting 1,000 Chinese citizens who were educated in elite programs overseas, another targeting 1,000 elite foreign scholars, and a third targeting 1,000 elite younger scholars under the age of 40. On the surface, the plan has been a success many times over, but there are signs that the most elite Chinese scholars are either rejecting the program or participating nominally. A report in the *Chronicle of Higher Education* found that the PhD recipients willing to return to their homeland were rarely coming from American university positions, but from less prestigious institutions elsewhere. According to a US government agency, "92 percent of Chinese who received a science or technology Ph.D. in the U.S. in 2002 were still in the U.S. in 2007. For India the figure was 81 percent and for Canada 55 percent."[24] In other words, the Chinese scientists in America were *less* likely to return home than graduates from other countries. Another problem has been that returning scholars tend to take up part-time or temporary positions at Chinese institutions while retaining their tenured positions abroad.

Some US officials see a nefarious motive in the Thousand Talents Plan, particularly the lucrative grants awarded to lure away scientists working on advanced technology. In 2019, a Senate committee headed by Senator Rob Portman of Ohio, one of the most respected legislators in Congress, described hundreds of Beijing's talent recruitment programs as a security threat. "China unfairly uses the American research and expertise it obtains for its own economic and military gain," the report concluded.[25] Although most scholars who participate in the program are totally innocent—teaching at a college in France or Japan is no more a crime than teaching in Shanghai—there are concerns that the Chinese government is exploiting these programs to gain a strategic advantage in nuclear energy, nanotechnology, cryptography, and artificial intelligence (AI), among other areas. In early 2020, federal prosecutors charged and formally indicted a renowned Harvard chemist who pioneered nanoscience, Charles M. Lieber, concerning his participation in Thousand Talents. Lieber may prove to be innocent, but his case is just the latest and highest profile example of increasing tensions.

The US attorney leading the case against Professor Lieber explained in an NPR interview that China's talent recruitment programs are brilliantly simple.[26] They exploit the Western academic framework of open collaboration, "And that's not illegal, per se. You can do that." It's when Americans hide the money or lie about their participation that flags a more sinister technology transfer.

The instinctive response of security hawks is to sever ties. Doves, on the other hand, deny that espionage is happening at all. It is smart to fight the espionage, but draconian tactics will backfire. Whereas it is inevitable that foreign powers will spy, the greater threat faced by interaction is not the loss of ideas but the loss of brains. On that score, the United States is far ahead. The number of Chinese scientists migrating to work for American companies and research institutions is ten or a hundred times higher than the reverse.

Extraordinary

Don't mistake the talent race for "brains" in the simple sense of trying to lure academic geniuses alone. The United States has programs in place already that offer a priority welcome to foreigners with "extraordinary ability" in multiple fields, from the arts to business. One US program offers permanent legal residency—the (employment-based) EB1, 2, and 3 visas—to foreigners of extraordinary talent, a type of visa granted to John Lennon of the Beatles in 1972. Three to six thousand EB visas are granted annually. There is another category of visa for non-immigrant visitors. The O-1 and P-1 visas allow extraordinarily talented foreign scholars, artists, and athletes to stay in the United States for up to three years. More well-known is the H1-B visa, another three-year program open to 65,000 high-skill workers.

Here I am hand-waving, or rather, giving an official nod to good programs that serve a good purpose but which I am afraid miss the point. It would be a mistake to think that a country can design programs to screen potential immigrants in order to welcome only the most talented *after* their talents have emerged. There's nothing wrong with welcoming exceptional people, but it would be wrong to neglect everyone else. Exceptionalism is not something that can easily be addressed with a formula. There are many accounts of unremarkable youths or relatively average individuals experiencing an epiphany or breakthrough that transforms their lives and millions of others, in everything from indie folk music to the advanced study of brain activity in toddlers. Consider for example that most American entrepreneurs start their companies after the age of 40, not before. It is also obvious that ingenuity is linked to what you are exposed to: you don't become a fantastic mountain climber by living on the great plains, or a brilliant neurosurgeon working down in a mine in Uganda. The brainy immigrants who have cumulatively added the most value did not come to America on such special terms. Their brains were revealed after settling, often as refugee children.

Sergey Brin, co-founder of Google, was born in Moscow in 1973 and escaped to America with his family in 1979. He was six years old.

France Hoang, associate White House counsel and Army veteran whom I mentioned at the opening of this book, arrived in the United States as a refugee from war-torn Vietnam when he was less than two years old.

Carlos Santana, one of the greatest guitarists in the history of rock and roll, migrated from Mexico with his family in the 1960s when he was a teenager.

None of these three were recruited to the United States, and arguably neither they nor their parents would have been admitted under a merit-based immigration system. Instead, they, like so many others, simply flourished after arrival. The true genius of American innovation is the "American dream" aspect of wide-open opportunity that is most often expressed in the free market through entrepreneurship.

The Yoran brothers, Elad and Amit, are a good example. Born to foreign parents who expected to return to Israel, the two boys were raised in New York suburbs and went to public schools. Like Joe and Chris Hsu, the Yoran boys graduated from West Point in the early 1990s and served in the US military. Elad led a platoon in Mogadishu, Somalia, during Operation Restore Hope 1992–'93. Together they founded one of the first cybersecurity companies, Riptech, that was acquired for over $100 million in 2002. Amit was appointed cybersecurity czar by President George W. Bush and today is CEO of Tenable, a publicly traded cybersecurity company.

Keep in mind that immigrants make up 13 percent of the nation's citizens, but they create 30 percent of the new companies. In a random sample of 100,000 native-born Americans, 260 of them will start a new company this month. Twice as many immigrants to the United States, 520 out of 100,000, will start a new company this month.[27] Why so high? Surely a major reason is that entrepreneurship involves risk, meaning that the type of person willing to work in a job without job security, health insurance, or a pension plan tends to be more risk-loving. They believe in themselves and rely on themselves. This is exactly the type of personality that is willing to leave hearth and home for a new land.

A common misperception is that the high entrepreneurship rate of migrants is a simple correlation with the high percentage of foreign scientists and engineers among the pool of immigrants. The most-often quoted statistic about immigrant entrepreneurs comes from research done by Vivek Wadhwa that half of Silicon Valley startups were founded or co-founded by immigrants.[28]

That is stunning. Even more stunning, however, is this: refugees to the United States are more likely to start their own business than other immigrants. In 2015, refugee-owned businesses generated $4.6 billion in income.[29] Even today, if you visit Britain, France, Spain, or Italy, you can easily meet scores of bright young people desperate to start businesses and careers in the United States in the wake of high taxation, heavy market controls, and limited opportunities in their own countries. Many don't even attempt it, however, put off by what they see as "impossible" visa restrictions and an icy governmental attitude to outsiders.

Other cities and countries have tried for decades to create their own tech-clusters. America's rivals as well as her allies understand the importance and the logic of the race for technological leadership—a permanent feature of the modern world—coupled with the relentless "war" for talent. America may have lucked into the lead with a first-mover advantage, but isn't it curious that it has done so across nearly every industry? Films and music in Hollywood. Finance in Manhattan. Automobiles in Detroit. Technology in Silicon Valley. Entertainment in Las Vegas. There is something exceptional about the economic culture of the United States that differentiates it from other places, something that attracts talent.

The Land of Opportunity

Why come to America? This is a question we should ask about Einstein, about Banerjee, but also people with all kinds of talents. Actors. Artists. Athletes. Why is the United States the destination of choice for refugees when a foreign country falls into war or civil chaos? The answer, according to Bill Kerr, is that "global talent tends to flow to where great opportunities exist, and this often occurs side by side with increased involvement of talented natives."

American babies aren't more talented than babies in France or India or Egypt. Natural talent is distributed relatively evenly throughout the world, certainly if we grant that the average newborn of every country has equal potential and value. Opportunity, on the other hand, is not evenly distributed among countries.

Economic freedom is a decisive "pull" factor according to most economists. For a time, I served as the director of a Heritage Foundation project to measure economic freedom across all the countries of the earth, ratings that covered ten different categories from labor regulation to tax rates. The United States was ranked #17 out of 174 countries according to the Heritage Index of Economic Freedom in 2020. The World Bank created a similar program a few years after Heritage that has gained the attention of heads of state eve-rywhere, known as the Ease of Doing Business Index. It reveals how long it takes for a budding entrepreneur to get a license, and how many forms are required, among other things. In some countries, simply creating a legal busi-ness takes months, and reams of paperwork. The United States was ranked #6 overall in the latest Doing Business rankings.[30] What the scores don't tell you beyond a snapshot in time is how long the American economy has set the standard for economic freedom, literally decades of openness, relatively low taxes, and a regulatory environment that encourages entrepreneurship while whole swaths of Europe, Asia, Africa, and Latin America experimented with state-run socialist dictatorship.

The migration patterns of the talented elite tell the story. Consider Indra Nooyi, the CEO of PepsiCo from 2006 to 2018. Born in Madras in 1955, Nooyi traveled to the United States twenty-three years later for graduate edu-cation at Yale, then chose to stay. William Kerr points to diversity as a decisive pull factor, and not just cultural diversity. "The global migration of talented women has grown by 150 percent since 1990," he observes, "and women now represent more than half of skilled immigrants."

We would do well to think of American diversity as its own kind of meta-agglomeration. Most everyone on Earth feels a connection to the people of the United States because there is an ethnic cluster for nearly every ethnicity in the country. Chinatowns are ubiquitous, of course, and represent the kinds of enclaves that dot cities from coast to coast: Hmong Americans in Saint Paul, Pakistani Americans in Chicago, Peruvian Americans in Paterson, Kurdish Americans in Nashville. If you pick a random country in Africa, you can find a half dozen enclaves of immigrants in the United States. Consider refugees from Somalia, one of the most destitute countries in the world. Over 60,000 Somali Americans reside in Columbus, Ohio, and that's only the second lar-gest enclave in the country.

Yet America often takes its special position in the global talent race for granted. Not only has America done little in recent years to make itself an at-tractive place for talented immigrants, but some of its policies have actively dissuaded and blocked talented migrants. As emerging opportunities abroad continue to chip away at America's economic and cultural dominance, the country is likely to lose some of its gravitational power. America's ability today to attract the kinds of talented individuals who win the country Nobel Prizes is passive at best, and in order to stay competitive in the global talent race, it should do more than simply keep the doors open.

This isn't new. Winning the talent race on behalf of national security is something President Harry Truman understood in 1945.

From Passive to Active: Operation Paperclip

Nobody before or during the world wars thought of immigrants as a strategic advantage in foreign affairs. The US policy approach had actually turned sharply isolationist between the wars. Indeed, the immigration of Jewish scientists during the 1930s was an exception to the rule. That changed once Harry Truman walked into the Oval Office.

After World War II, Truman directed the executive branch to change the national attitude toward foreign brainpower, and he immediately began persuading legislators to do the same. The Nazis might easily have conquered all of Europe, and the key to their military prowess was a technological advantage. The V-2 rockets that rained down on London represented the kind of weaponry that no other country had. Nazi fighter aircraft were the first, indeed only, fighters with jet engines and were shredding the propeller-driven fighters such as British Spitfires and the American P-51 Mustangs.

Truman changed the American policy toward Third Reich scientists from passive to active, starting with a program conceived before Adolf Hitler was dead, a program code-named Operation Paperclip. The US Army tried to gather up German engineers before the Soviets could. That competition for brains was one of the first, and most consequential, battles for talent ever waged. It defined the great power dynamics of the Cold War era. And it was anything but innocent and bloodless.

Wernher von Braun is perhaps the most famous of the hundreds of scientists recruited to the United States under the operation, the "father of rocketry" who had led the German research program at Peenemunde. Von Braun wasn't just a member of the Nazi Party but a member of the SS, yet his defenders argue that his participation as a leading German scientist predated Hitler. However, Jewish prisoners at the concentration camps such as Buchenwald reported that he could be seen coming to the camps to choose slaves for labor on his projects. Prisoner Adam Cabala reported that "Not one single time did Prof. Wernher von Braun protest against this cruelty during his frequent stays . . . near the ambulance shed, inmates tortured to death by slave labor and the terror of the overseers were piling up daily. But, Prof. Wernher von Braun passed them so close that he was almost touching the corpses." Von Braun responded by saying that he had felt helpless in how to respond to the condition of the camps, arguing that his interest in rocket science was driven by an idealism for space travel and discovery rather than support for Nazism, and he used government money to further the science regardless of whether it was Hitler's or Truman's.

Operation Paperclip was initiated by the Joint Chiefs of Staff under a different name on July 20, 1945. Later that summer, the secret program was made permanent under the guidance of a new Joint Intelligence Objectives Agency that ultimately brought in 1,600 German scientists, engineers, and technicians over the following decade and a half.[31] Immigration authorities often refused to process the Germans, so the US Army found creative ways to grease the bureaucracy. Von Braun liked to tell the story of his being secreted into Mexico and then driven by streetcar across the southern border outside of El Paso, Texas, where local border officials granted him official entry into the country.

Though some of these men had worked side by side with Adolf Hitler, Heinrich Himmler, and Hermann Göring, who were responsible for murders, war crimes, and development of weapons of mass destruction for Nazi Germany, the United States knew that having the talent of these scientists working to support the national security of the United States towered above other concerns. The logic was straightforward: better to have these minds working for America than against it, particularly with Soviet repression more obvious and threatening as the iron curtain descended across the "liberated" countries of Eastern Europe.

Even though Allied intelligence had gathered literally tons of documents about the German rocket program as well as test models of cutting-edge engines and the weapons themselves, comprehensive documentation wasn't good enough. They needed the human capital to make sense of it. After an intense debate, the US government decided that the value of former Nazis' knowledge outweighed crimes, in most instances.

Officials realized that this operation would not be well received by the public, rattled by the war, many with families back in Europe who had seen their lives decimated through six years of relentless war crimes, racism, and hatred. As the first images of the concentration camps and mass graves flickered into movie halls up and down the states, many of those who had previously promoted American isolationism or even support for Hitler fell silent. The operation, along with the Joint Intelligence Objectives Agency, allowed a degree of privacy to avoid the potential scandal of hiring Nazi and Nazi-affiliated parties, quietly accepting Nazi scientists, chemists, and engineers to enter America at the same time that the Nuremberg trials were watched by a stunned world.

It is a question we, as a country, still have to answer today. Who merits entry into the United States? Who can add value? Sadly, the current policies governing entry into the United States do not set a standard but instead set numeric caps. Sixty thousand refugees per year has been the cap, but that was ratcheted down during the Trump presidency, and remains far below previous levels

There is no easy or permanent solution to this moral dilemma, but one thing is as bluntly apparent today as it was seventy years ago: brainpower wins wars. Truman was aware of the trade-off between future national security and forgiving the unforgivable. He was willing to fight hard against the stark racism in US immigration policy writ large while simultaneously recruiting members of the most racist regime of the century. Today, in contrast, American policy makes it increasingly difficult for foreign brainpower to come for a visit, for a job, or God forbid, to join the nation permanently.

PART IV

MICRO AND MACRO

I have come to a few realizations after my many years working in the political arena, and perhaps my greatest, in the sense that it changed my perspective more than any other, is that many of our great debates amount to a battle between foresight and myopia. As an example, the national debt and ever-widening annual budget deficit have become monstrous because the present trumps the future. Democracies are impatient. It is one of their only weaknesses, and sometimes a fatal one.

This final part of the book applies time analytically to the American immigration debate. The next two chapters (12 and 13) were originally one lengthy discussion of the economics of immigration, but I separated them to make two distinct points. The traditional immigration narratives could use some updating, which is the focus of chapter 12. There are some profound and neglected stories in US history that deserve our attention. Chapter 13 goes to the academic heart of the economic debate, featuring two economists who are our profession's version of celebrities. They disagree terribly, and I admire them both.

As compelling and endless as that economic argument is, the issue causing the deepest unease with mass immigration is culture and identity, the subject of chapter 14. In most countries, culture is a conservative affectation. Our town has always worshiped thus, farmed thus. Outsiders are anathema to culture. There is validity to that logic, particularly for a people with a lengthy heritage in place, but that validity is ambiguous in America: a nation with a culture that is fundamentally an egalitarian melting pot of outsiders.

The book then concludes with two chapters, one with the bite of policy prescriptions and public polling for the here and now. I make the case for incremental reforms, with genuine hope that President Biden and his successors seize on bipartisanship to craft a legislative agenda that will solidify the current era's immigration levels and strength. Chapter 16 closes with a longer-term view and a focus on core principles for successful reform.

It reminds future policymakers of the wisdom of so much of our current system, namely, the strength of family ties and assimilation, which is so unlike the crass merit-basis that underlies other nations' immigration institutions. Why would America change what has made it the strongest country of all time?

Chapter 12
Narratives

Love ye therefore the stranger: for ye were strangers in the land of Egypt.

— **Deuteronomy 10:19**

Three predominant narratives of American immigration form the nation's origin story: Pilgrims landing at Plymouth Rock in search of religious freedom, African slaves shipped and sold as cargo, and finally the Statue of Liberty welcoming millions of huddled masses from the Old World. We've dealt with some of those narratives earlier, shedding light on common oversimplifications such as the fact that many of the Pilgrims weren't Pilgrims but rather hired guns, and it was those "Strangers" who served as the first American rebels that demanded a written social contract and breathed life into democracy in the New World.

Nevertheless, the three narratives are indelible but have become tangential to the modern debate. There is a rising concern, perhaps a more vocalized concern, about immigrants as job thieves and cultural misfits. I'd like to suggest some new and updated narratives to illuminate these tensions in the modern context. This new century is one of dizzying technological and social change, an atomic blast of creative destruction.

On a personal level, my understanding of the vast diversity of America began when I arrived at the Air Force Academy for basic training in the summer of 1986—I and a thousand others, which amounted to about two per congressional district. There were kids of every skin color and religion, but the diversity that made the strongest impression on me was the crazy quilt of accents. Deep southern drawls mixed with California beach dudespeak, Tennessee twangs, Bronx yawps, and my own plain vanilla from the Midwest.

We didn't get out much that initial year, but my first taste of the world beyond the Ohio valley came during a spring break when the cadets were given leave for a week. I drove through the Mojave Desert in my classmate's brand-new red Acura with its ice-cold air conditioning blasting, heading from Colorado to California. Suddenly, out of nowhere, a bizarre city appeared on the horizon, shimmering in the heat.

That was my first sight of Las Vegas.

The city in the late 1980s wasn't very big up close, certainly not a metropolis. Scanning over the census records today, it seems the population of the surrounding area was 800,000 when I first saw the Strip's great casinos rippling from afar across the desert heat waves. At the time, I didn't know the city was in the midst of a population boom. And the population is still growing faster in the Mojave than just about any place in America, thanks to 50,000 migrants per year, foreign and domestic.[1]

Las Vegas is the ultimate boom town, a city that literally grew from nothing into a globally famous destination and a glittering monument to American excess, maybe to greed, but also to the extremes of liberty. It's the largest major city established in the 20th century, defying the laws of urban birth and growth. And it's 99.999% based on migration. Consider this: in 1900, there were twenty-two human beings in the negligible oasis in the Mojave Desert. Today there are 2.2 million.

The rap on Vegas is that it's tacky. Has no culture. Loud. The epitome of cowboy capitalism. Let's grant that those knocks and more are true, yet it remains a marvel that attracts millions of visitors every month, among them thousands who move permanently. How did it happen?

Vegas lies next to no great river or ocean as nearly all ancient cities do, such as Athens, London, or Tokyo. No one in 1920 decided to relocate to this forgotten strip of desert to monopolize trade routes or create a military outpost. It straddles no intersection of global commerce, like Istanbul, Singapore, or New York. It had no strategic value in military or geographical terms at all. The impressive weirdness of the city's growth is its total lack of natural resources— no forests or mines, no crops or grazing lands. There would be no gold rush, no oil boom, and no land grabs for grazing dairy farmers. Just heat and desert. And yet the city population more than doubled each decade.

I have thought about that strange city many times in the decades since, often daydreaming about it when I was a student during lectures about immigration. Economists tend to lecture about immigration in the context of labor markets and in the very short run. There's been some research about fiscal effects (whether migrants pay more in taxes than they cost in government welfare and benefits) and some about inequality effects (bottom line: the best tool to fight inequality is to disallow refugees, which makes me think inequality is a dumb thing to fix). But we economists almost never look at the impact on the economy overall. And that's why Las Vegas comes to mind.

Sex, Natural Resources, and Atom Bombs

Now that I tend to stand at the front of the room during classroom discussions, I use the example of Las Vegas because it illustrates a few interesting principles. First, migration is one of the pillars of economic growth, something we already learned about growth in which labor (L) is a core factor. And, second, natural resources aren't very important for growth at all, something most people simply don't understand.

Oil, diamonds, and mineral deposits are often a hindrance to a robust, modern economy. Economists call this the "Dutch Disease," a term coined in the 1970s to describe the sudden decline of manufacturing in the Netherlands after the largest natural gas field in Europe was discovered in the country's Groningen province in 1959.[2] There was so much gas underground that Dutch workers and capital shifted away from production industries into gas extraction. Discovery of the natural gas mother lode hurt the country's long-term development, without question, but it was a puzzle. Development economists also started to notice that some of the richest and fastest-growing nations in the modern era such as Japan and Singapore possess few natural resources. The lesson is that necessity fosters human capital formation and innovation.

A city such as Las Vegas, with truly no resources, could not have developed in any other century. Its growth has been 100 percent based on the service industry, and it exists to serve visitors who travel from far away. In its formative years, the city was little more than a water stop for travelers, valuable precisely because it was in the middle of nowhere. Let's not forget that brothels were legal in Nevada since the 19th century. Hundreds of miles separated the area from fertile soil in either direction along the trail. When construction on the Hoover Dam began in 1931, thirty miles to the southeast, Las Vegas had a population of barely more than 5,000, but it prospered for five years hosting construction workers and as a coordinating point for dam logistics. After the dam was completed in 1936, the city hosted the tourist traffic that came to ogle the wonder.

What really changed the city's fate was national security, a consequence of the arms race during the Cold War between the Soviet Union and the United States. Some government agency determined that the vast wasteland near Vegas was the most isolated part of the country and therefore the best place for nuclear weapons tests. In 1950, Nellis Air Force Base was established by President Harry Truman, situated in the remote landscape sixty-five miles north of Las Vegas, then a sparsely populated town of 25,000. Also known as the Nevada Proving Ground, it created expressly for live-fire tests of nuclear weapons.[3] Bombs were dropped from airplanes in "atmospheric" tests that produce the infamous mushroom clouds. With so little known about ra-diation poisoning and the extraordinary risks it posed to health, this wasn't considered unsafe at the time. Families would gather to watch the mushroom clouds that were set off once or twice a month, and tourists on the Strip were invited up to casino rooftops for watch parties.

Though the explosions could be seen up to 100 miles away, and nighttime skies were alight as far away as the California coasts, the government officially opened the tests to the public in April 1952 to celebrate US power. Journalists were invited by the Atomic Energy Commission to view a 31-kiloton atomic explosion nicknamed "Big Shot." From a perch ten miles from ground zero, a newspaperman named John Kerigan wrote this description:

> You put on the dark goggles, turn your head, and wait for the signal. Now—the bomb has been dropped. You wait the prescribed time, then turn your head and look. A fantastically bright cloud is climbing upward like a huge umbrella. The rest is anti-climax. You brace yourself against the shock wave that follows an atomic ex-plosion. A heat wave comes first, then the shock, strong enough to knock an un-prepared man down. Then, after what seems like hours, the man-made sunburst fades away.[4]

The broadcast and print reporting of Big Shot created a tourist industry over-night, way beyond the draw of casino gambling. Las Vegas began to advertise itself as "Atomic City" around the country. There were atomic cocktails in all the bars, a Miss Atomic Beauty Contest, and once every three weeks an explo-sion that could be seen day or night for the next eleven years.[5] In fact, calendars throughout the city advertised detonation times. Atmospheric nuclear tests would continue until 1963 when they were banned by international treaty. By then the city population had grown by nearly 200 percent, but the population in greater Las Vegas, including Henderson and other developments in Clark County, was much larger (Table 12.1).

There's a critical lesson for understanding the economic impact of immi-gration in all this—what I like to call the "moral of Las Vegas": did the 3,000 immigrants to Las Vegas during the decade of the 1920s steal all the jobs from the 2,000 residents already there in 1920? Of course not. These migrants added more jobs than they could ever take away. Consider any other decade and you'll find the same riddle. Did the 16,000 people who moved from other cities and states during the 1940s displace the 8,000 workers in Vegas at the start of the decade? Consider a longer time period and you stretch the ques-tion to absurdity: Did the 100,000 migrants who arrived from 1950 to 1970

Table 12.1 Population of Las Vegas

Year	City	County
1900	22	
1910	220	
1920	2304	
1930	5165	
1940	8422	
1950	24,600	48,300
1960	64,400	127,000
1970	125,800	273,300
1980	164,700	463,100
1990	286,600	805,500
2000	484,500	1,428,700
2010	583,800	1,951,300
2020	670,000 est.	2,300,000 est.

Source: US Census Bureau

steal jobs from the 25,000 residents there at the start? How can four migrants possibly steal one job?

The kicker is that the unemployment rate in the city was essentially unchanged over all these years. The workforce grew, but the unemployment rate hit the same 4.4 percent mark again and again in 1990, 1996, 2004, and 2009, varying up and down with the business cycle. The moral of Las Vegas may be the single most important lesson you get from this book: immigrants do not steal jobs.

Job Thieves

Sometimes a new person takes a job held by another person—as any professional athlete can attest. Sometimes jobs simply disappear. That's reality in a healthy, dynamic economy. Sometimes, however, the competition mutates beyond frustration into a rage that can be hard to fathom.

Cesar Chavez, the American civil rights activist who led the United Farm Workers (UFW) labor union in the 1960s, is a hero to leftists at home and abroad. Streets across the country have been renamed to honor his memory. And newly elected president Biden prominently placed a bust of Chavez on the table behind his desk in the Oval Office. Born in 1927, Chavez became a leading labor organizer for farmworkers in California. What is often neglected in the retelling of his story, however, is that he was convinced that Mexican immigrants were breaking his strikes, particularly illegal immigrants. In the mid-1970s, Chavez launched a program that sent union members to guard the Arizona border with Mexico. He also launched a campaign to identify and deport farmworkers who were undocumented. Those tactics alienated many liberal allies, which ultimately led to his demise, but they also remind us of the microcosm of lived competition between insiders and outsiders.

Lived experience often defies chalkboard theories and empirical social science data. The challenge all academics face is to move from anecdote to data. History affords us few natural experiments that can bridge the gap, and those that emerge are often highly influential. Sudden, unexpected, and large immigration shifts are especially rare. The most famous is perhaps the influx of 125,000 Cuban immigrants into Miami during the long summer of 1980.

The "Mariel boatlift," as it came to be known, followed dictator Fidel Castro's surprise declaration on April 20 that anyone could leave for the United States from the Cuban port of Mariel, including hundreds of jailed criminals and mental patients. America's long-standing "dry foot" policy granted residency to all Cubans who could find their way to its shores. Thus began Miami's conspicuous immigration experiment, a shock labor force increase of 7 percent. Did the new arrivals steal jobs? An influential research paper published in 1990 by economist David Card found that labor markets actually strengthened in Miami from 1979 to 1981, and not just in isolation. Unemployment rates declined in Miami, and did so more than in comparable cities such as Tampa, Atlanta, and elsewhere.[6]

Other natural experiments have had far less happy endings. Consider one from a century and a half ago when rather than an influx of labor, there was a sudden negative shock of job loss. The year was 1869, and the shock was not a recession. Jobs just vanished, faster than the automobile displaced the horse and buggy, but with one swing of a hammer.

On May 10, 1869, the transcontinental railroad was completed with a golden spike connecting the Central Pacific line with the Union Pacific line in Promontory, Utah. The cost of traveling across the United States dropped afterward by about 85 percent, expanding what was already a great westward migration. It also stranded tens of thousands of Chinese immigrants who had come to America to work on the railroad line.

Leland Stanford, who founded the university that pays my salary, was president of the Central Pacific Railroad in 1869 and declared in a letter to President Andrew Johnson in 1865 that without the Chinese workers, who ultimately comprised 90 percent of the workforce, "it would be impossible to complete the western portion of this great national enterprise, within the time required by the Acts of Congress."[7] The Chinese were willing to do more dangerous work than native workers, particularly in the heat and height of the Sierra Nevada mountains. The work was grueling. It is thought that one in ten immigrants who built the Central Pacific railroad died during its construction.[8]

My colleague Thomas Sowell brought the plight of Chinese Americans to my attention with his book *Ethnic America*, recounting the fate of the 67,000 Chinese living in the United States immediately after the transcontinental railroad was completed. The initial surge of Chinese migrants came to America following news of the gold rush in California in 1849. Through a quirk of fate, they were overwhelmingly from one province in southern China, Kwantung, and more specifically from one particularly mountainous district in that province, Toishan. They spoke their own dialect, and word spread quickly that one could earn ten times more per day in the United States than in Hong Kong. "They worked cheaply and lived frugally, saving money out of what would be considered a pittance by Americans," according to Sowell. "These very virtues, however, made the Chinese feared and hated as competitors by white workers."

Sadly, the Toishan men had little else to do but work, since they had come without their wives and families. Transported for free by the railroad companies, they were largely unable to afford passage home after the golden spike was struck. Denied citizenship and also occupations that were reserved for US citizens only, the Chinese migrants drifted to work wherever they could. For example, the percentage of farm laborers in California who were Chinese grew from 10 percent in 1870 to 50 percent in 1880. Consequently, Californians in that era were some of the most virulently racist people in the nation, agitating Congress for the 1882 laws barring further immigration from Asia.

"American employers who hired Chinese were subjected to harassment and threats, so the Chinese were left with little more than self-employment or work as domestic servants. For several decades, their principal occupation was as laundrymen," writes Sowell. "Even as late as 1920, more than half of all employed Chinese worked either in laundries or restaurants."[9] One particularly cruel example of regulatory harassment was a special fee levied by the city of San Francisco on laundries that delivered by hand instead of horse and buggy, and further made it a misdemeanor crime to "carry baskets suspended on a pole across the shoulder" because that was how the Chinese delivered clothing. Multiplying their misery, laws passed by Congress in the 1880s made it illegal for the migrants' wives, or most any Asian women, to immigrate legally. The 20-to-1 ratio of Chinese men to women in 1860, more imbalanced than any other ethnicity, actually worsened to 27-to-1 by the end of the century.

All across the western states, Chinese migrants were forced to live in ghettos known as Chinatowns, unassimilated because assimilation was made illegal, yet working tirelessly. So many remittances were sent to Toishan that it became one of the wealthiest districts in China, with paved and lighted streets long before other cities. Yet in America, hostility to the low-skilled workers intensified to the extreme. The Rock Springs massacre of 1885 is possibly the worst singular incident of violence against immigrants in American history.

Unrest began soon after dawn on September 2, 1885, in a coal mining town called Rock Springs in the southwest corner of the state of Wyoming. The Union Pacific Railroad owned the coal mine, using it as a constant supply of fuel for its trains. The Knights of Labor, a miners' union, had been quietly planning a strike against the company up and down all the Union Pacific mines in the Rockies. But members knew that the Chinese workers were unlikely to participate. Strikes had been repressed during the previous decade when ownership hired Chinese workers who were not interested in striking. So there were about 600 Chinese miners working Rock Springs that September compared to 300 non-Chinese miners.

The Knights were actually planning for the strike to begin a few days later at a different mine, but some of the Rock Springs unionists jumped the gun. It began with an alleged work assignment miscommunication that sent a pair of workers (possibly immigrants from Finland, ironically) to a certain coal pit number six where two Chinese miners were already at work. A disagreement escalated to a brawl, with the latecomers bashing the skull of one Chinese miner with a pick-axe, then beating the other.

By 10:00 AM, all the non-Chinese miners went on strike and retreated to the local saloons, where they began agitating one another with resentments toward the non-participating Chinese. A warning was sent to residents of the local "Chinatown" encampment, giving them a one-hour warning to leave. That afternoon, around 150 miners attacked the encampment in a well-orchestrated pincer, securing two key bridges to prevent escape, then systematically assaulting, robbing, and frequently gunning down the Chinese workers in cold blood. Some were robbed of their gold and cash before being bashed, others before being murdered. The massacre lasted late into the night, with the Chinese fleeing into the hills in every direction. Some of the immigrants were dismembered. More than few were burned alive when every tent and structure in Chinatown was afire.

The Wyoming governor arrived on the scene to restore order the very next day, condemning the violence and asking for federal troops. Officially, there were twenty-eight confirmed deaths, but the real number was likely far higher. The massacre created a diplomatic furor. Though it was condemned by editorials along the East Coast, papers throughout the American West were muted.

In the end, none of the rioters were convicted in the courts. Sixteen men were arrested, but no one was punished. No witnesses were willing to testify. Instead of justice, the lesson of the Rock Springs massacre that spread nationally was that murderous anti-Asian rioters were tolerated, a lesson heeded by American mobs across the western states. Copycat attacks in Oregon, California, Washington state, and even Georgia occurred in the following weeks.

Dynamo

How do we reconcile these tensions—the moral of Las Vegas and the Rock Springs massacre?

The moral of Las Vegas is the big picture, the objective truth, the long-term view. Immigrants take zero jobs in the long run. But there is another truth we cannot deny: the perspective of personal experience, the short-term view, the husband who comes home early on a Friday with a ghostly look in his eyes, muttering to his worried spouse, "I got laid off." The narrative of Rock Springs is identical to every town in every time that experiences an influx of outsiders: a certain rage of loss and futility and frustration, regardless of the macro statistics.

An honest look at the economic issues surrounding immigration must consider both perspectives: the personal (micro) and the aggregate (macro). The micro perspective has been the primary focus of academic research, exploring the impact on local workers' jobs and wages and asking whether any group gets hurt. However, economists have all but ignored the macro perspective because the answer is so obvious. Immigrants have a negligible impact on unemployment rates and a directly positive impact on output. Only the macro perspective matters when it comes to national security, particularly great power competition. The micro debate, however, matters to voters, and that's the narrative that recurs every election.

What can bridge the top-down view of steady employment aggregates and the bottom-up view of individual turmoil? We could call it an irresolvable tension between short-term and long-term perspectives. And it is fair to critique the academics, because time is the key dimension too often ignored in the micro debate. But time alone cannot explain how both viewpoints are true simultaneously. A relatively new area of empirical economic research called "economic dynamics" can.

Using detailed data on gross numbers of jobs created and gross numbers of jobs lost over a period of time, we can see dynamics of job churn that aggregate numbers miss altogether. This dynamic approach was pioneered by John Haltiwanger at the University of Maryland, Steve Davis at the University of Chicago, and Scott Schuh at the Federal Reserve in numerous scholarly papers that culminated in their 1996 book, *Job Creation and Destruction*.[10] Soon after its publication, the federal government began reporting a series called business dynamics statistics (BDS), data showing that even when the number of jobs and the unemployment rate were essentially unchanged, job destruction was constant and larger than anyone realized. "The annual job creation rate is about 18 percent (as a percent of employment), suggesting that, on average in any given year, about 18 percent of jobs are newly created," Haltiwanger concluded with his co-authors in the seminal study of the BDS in 2008. "The very high rate of gross job creation is balanced with a very high rate of gross job destruction [of] around 16 percent."[11]

Another part of the picture is the constant churn of companies and jobs. Old firms die and startups are born. Old jobs fade and new occupations emerge. In 2010, I published an analysis of the BDS employer data that revealed a surprising fact about startup companies. It confirmed the theoretical insights of Joseph Schumpeter, the great Harvard economist who was himself an immigrant from Austria, who coined the phrase "creative destruction."

I found that 3 million jobs are created every year in the United States by startup companies, four times as many gross jobs that are created by older cohorts of companies (where a cohort includes all companies created over ten years). In contrast, the net job creation of all cohorts except startups is negative.[12] For example, if we consider the companies created during the past decade (2011–2020), some are adding jobs on net this year while others are downsizing. Add the gross job changes from all this cohort's firms and it's always a net loss. Always, for every age group of companies. In short, there is no net job creation in America without entrepreneurs, a research finding that caught the attention of the Obama White House, which emphasized the importance of entrepreneurship in its policy efforts.[13]

Dynamism isn't all milk, honey, and progress. As a professor, I teach my students the virtues of Adam Smith's invisible hand, but I also remind them there is often an invisible backhand, too. A boomtown like Las Vegas can ignore the downsides of dynamism because new companies, new casinos, new restaurants are able to obscure the failing ones. The growth narrative will often dominate over the loss narrative in a culture like America's. Often, but not always.

13
Economies

A comprehensive accounting of the benefits and costs of immigration shows the benefits of immigration exceed the costs.
— **The 2005 Economic Report of the President**

The world's top expert on the economics of immigration reached into an icy tub full of soda cans at the same time I did, and we practically knocked skulls. We laughed about it, introduced ourselves, and got to talking. This was at Jim Hamilton and Marjorie Flavin's backyard barbecue party for incoming economics doctoral students at the University of California at San Diego (UCSD). I admitted being nervous about coming back to academia after so many years in the military. He assured me that I would be fine as long as I worked hard and maintained a sincere curiosity to discover new things.

"Look at me," he said, "born in Havana in 1950 and immigrated to the United States a few days before the Cuban Missile Crisis."

I saw a prototypical professor: tall, uncoordinated, gregarious, mostly bald, with big glasses that made his large, happy eyes look even larger. His introduced himself as George Borjas, and told me that he had been recruited from one college to another, each increasingly prestigious. He confided to me that afternoon that he was accepting a permanent professorship at Harvard the following autumn, where he works to this day.

I didn't study immigration in graduate school nor did I have a chance to take a class with Professor Borjas. My specialties were economic growth, development, labor dynamics, and also, to be honest, helping a friend start up a software company using this new invention called the Internet. Even so, Borjas's rising fame was a delight to me—he was constantly cited and often quoted directly in newspapers and magazines about the surge of migration happening across the country during the 1990s.

After leaving for Harvard, Borjas authored the widely used textbook *Labor Economics*, now in its eighth edition, and a handful of books focusing exclusively on the topic of immigration. His latest book is *We Wanted Workers: Unraveling the Immigration Narrative*, published in 2016. That same year, Donald Trump cited Borjas by name when accepting the Republican Party's presidential nomination. POLITICO named him as #17 on its list of the top fifty policy thinkers with this description: "The real message he has been delivering since his pioneering 1994 study is that both political parties are far too simplistic when they talk about immigration's harms and benefits."[1]

The most simplistic view, ironically, is one espoused by restrictionists who cite Borjas most often. It must be said that his rhetoric makes this association all too easy. At issue is whether he has exaggerated the negative effect. Consider the title of his latest book, *We Wanted Workers*, a phrase made famous by the Swiss intellectual Max Frisch who said of the millions of non-European guest workers in the late 20th century: "Wir riefen arbeitskräfte und es kamen menschen." Translated, that is a witty, "We wanted workers, and people came."

Yet the *most* simplistic view of immigration is that foreign workers steal jobs and do nothing more. Restrictionists invariably invoke Econ 101: more workers for the same number of jobs means lower wages and real disemployment, right? Wrong. In the text of his book, Borjas says that politicians and pundits need to move beyond simple assumptions, but his book title fails that test. The phrase "We wanted workers" is loaded with false assumptions. First, who is "We"? Many natives want migrants to join the nation permanently, to assimilate and diversify in the best ways. Second, the assumption that "workers" operate only on the supply half of the equation is just bad economics.

Consider Figure 13.1. The first supply and demand chart represents the original labor market, where the equilibrium defines the wage level (W_0) and the number of jobs (Q_0) in the national economy. The second chart shows the naïve interpretation of immigration: labor supply grows, pushing the LS curve to the right. By looking at only part of the impact of immigration (the supply shift) the result is partial equilibrium analysis. This new partial equilibrium assumes everything else stays the same (such as demand for goods and thus demand for labor), yielding lower wages (W_p) and higher net jobs (Q_p).

The correct analysis using general equilibrium recognizes that immigrants also consume goods, rent homes, and more. This is shown in the third chart in which immigrants cause an increase in the aggregate demand for labor as well. Here the size of the supply shift is matched by a demand shift, and an overall increase in net new jobs, implying no net displacement effect.

And there we have it: the starting point in any serious consideration of immigration on the domestic economy is that there is no negative effect on

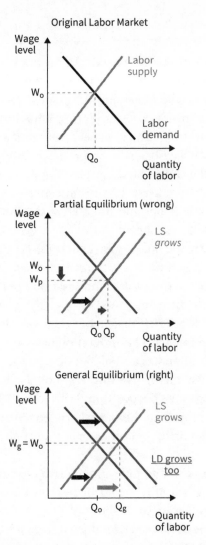

Figure 13.1 The immigration impact on labor supply and demand.

average. But there's the rub. Nobody is average. Even if most Americans gain, there are some who don't. At least not in the short run.

The Devil in the Details

George Borjas has consistently warned that not all native workers benefit from immigration. Some may benefit, indeed most may, but not everyone, specifically the cohort of low-skilled Americans who faced the main surge of competition from low-skilled immigrants from Latin America in the 1980s and '90s.

Immigration wasn't always so skewed. In his book *Heaven's Door*, Borjas contrasts the immigrants of 1960—who were better educated on average than natives and earned incomes just 13 percent less—to 1998 when the "newest arrivals had almost two fewer years of schooling" and earned 34 percent less than natives.[2] In dozens of papers, he found a cohort that got hurt. "Immigration seems to have been an important contributor to the rise in economic inequality in the United States, depressing the economic opportunities faced by the least skilled workers," he concluded in *Heaven's Door*.[3] He granted the gains benefiting the upper and middle classes, but argued that fairness demanded an honest accounting.

That nuanced view made Borjas subject to some hostility in left-leaning academia, but it also made him a hero to restrictionists and anti-immigration policy groups such as the Center for Immigration Studies.[4] Was his work so out of line with the mainstream? David Card's 2007 comparison of immigration across US cities concluded that "more than two decades of research on the local labor market impacts of immigration have reached a near consensus that increased immigration has a small but discernible negative effect on the relative wages of low-skilled native workers" but also a small, positive effect on wages for native workers overall.[5] Similarly, in his 2013 book *Exodus*, the eminent British economist Paul Collier excoriated the timidity of many social scientists who "have strained every muscle to show that migration is good for everyone."

Borjas ultimately decided to take aim at Card's seminal 1990 research on the Mariel boatlift, which after two decades had become a kind of gospel truth. As you will recall, the supply shock of 125,000 Cuban "Marielitos" was unbalanced—only one in three had graduated from high school, roughly half as many as other Cuban Americans. Looking carefully at a cross-section of native Miami citizens, Card found that "the influx of Mariel immigrants had virtually no effect on the wage rates of less-skilled non-Cuban workers." Nor did he find any increase in unemployment among comparable cohorts of low-skill workers of any ethnicity.

It's important to understand exactly what evidence Card was analyzing, described by him as "individual micro-data for 1979–1985 from the merged outgoing rotation group samples of the Current Population Survey (CPS)." Using CPS data as well, Borjas's reappraisal study was issued as a working paper in late 2015 that was peer reviewed and published in the *ILR Review* two years later.[6] He argued that the four comparison cities selected by Card were ad hoc, and also that the poorest workers hadn't been examined specifically—both worthwhile points. He concluded quite strongly:

> The examination of wage trends among high school dropouts quickly overturns the stylized fact that the supply shock did not affect Miami's wage structure. In fact, the absolute wage of high school dropouts dropped dramatically, as did their wage relative to that of either high school graduates or college graduates. The drop in the average wage of the least-skilled Miamians between 1977–1979 and 1981–1986 was substantial, between 10 and 30%.[7]

The reappraisal was not well received in some quarters. A Bloomberg writer went so far as to call the study "fishy" and questioned whether Borjas suffered from confirmation bias.[8] Despite the overheated response, the real problem was that the Borjas microdata were extraordinarily micro. In order to identify the native-born workers in Miami who faced labor market competition from the Marielitos, he restricted the subsample to males. He further restricted it to high school dropouts. That left just roughly twenty observations for the years 1979–1982. A number so small has a wide margin of error, especially in the context of 6 million residents of the Miami metro area.

The Borjas paper was countered by Giovanni Peri, a highly respected professor of economics at the University of California at Davis. One very comprehensive analysis was written by Peri and his co-author Vasil Yasenov. By exploring a wider set of CPS microdata and developing a bulletproof "synthetic" city to compare against Miami's trends, the scholars concluded, "Neither wages (annual, weekly, or hourly) nor unemployment rates of high school dropouts differ significantly between Miami and its control group during the 1981–1983 period."[9] A fair reading of the Borjas approach versus the Peri approach—accepting that both findings are true—leaves one with a recognition that wage data for a small number of people over relatively short time frames are inevitably noisy.

During a 2016 POLITICO interview, Borjas summarized his argument for the political class:

> Clinton ignores the hard truth that not everyone benefits when immigrants arrive. For many Americans, the influx of immigrants hurts their prospects significantly.... When the supply of workers goes up, the price that firms have to pay to hire workers goes down. Wage trends over the past half-century suggest that a 10 percent increase in the number of workers with a particular set of skills probably lowers the wage of that group by at least 3 percent.[10]

That 10-to-3 ratio sounds believable, but restrictionists will run with it as their gospel whereas more careful thinkers would ask a follow-on question. What's the time frame? How long does the wage depression last? The answer is that the small negative wage shock mostly fades within a year or two. Dynamism matters.

The Borjas-Peri debate sparked renewed interest among academics, leading the *Journal of Economic Perspectives* to feature four separate papers on immigration in its Fall 2016 issue. One of the papers showcased the stalemate with its very title: "The Impact of Immigration: Why Do Studies Reach Such Different Results?"[11] Its authors observed that the same method applied to the same microdata can yield different results simply based on how the data are divvied up. For example, should we use three education categories or five when comparing subgroups? Four skill levels or one? A five-year time frame or ten? You can get whatever result you want, within reason.

Step back from the squabble and realize how small it is. None of the scholars argue that immigration hurts the *average* worker's wages. They barely mention employment rates. Nobody is saying there is permanent harm done to economywide incomes or poverty. If we are guilty of anything, it is ignoring the net positive effect immigration has on most natives in the labor market, and more important, the overwhelming positive contribution to overall national strength.

The States of Growth

Reading paper after paper with microdata, one cannot help but wonder if the stalemate can be resolved by looking at the forest instead of the trees. Why not contrast fifty forests: the fifty states? Microdata involve individual-level observations, in contrast to macro data, which look at regional averages. Microdata tell us details about a sampling individual, whereas macrodata tell us an overview of everyone. As an example, macrodata for the US unemployment rate was 3.8% in the winter before the Covid-19 pandemic, then shot up to 13.0% three months later. The most important macrodata for great power comparisons isn't the unemployment rate; it is GDP.

To my surprise, when I began the background research for this book, nobody had published a paper comparing the immigration effect on GDP across the fifty states, so I asked a graduate student named Zach Rutledge to help me conduct such a study. We did what is known as a spatial-correlation approach, and it comes with an asterisk: exploring geographical variation over long periods of time is complicated by dynamics. People are mobile, right? So if boatloads of refugees arrive in a given Florida city, it is inevitable that some of the local workers will find better opportunities elsewhere. That dynamic will obscure the effect we want to measure. Nonetheless, we can deploy sophisticated techniques to control for such dynamics, and besides, the big picture is essential for policymakers.

Zach and I compared state performance decade-by-decade from 1980 to 2015. We assembled data on immigration shares, GDP, population, economic growth, and a handful of employment indicators. We even calculated a new variable for the employment-to-population ratio (E/POP) of native-born workers in each state.

The bottom line is that the states with the fastest immigration growth also experienced the fastest GDP growth. For every 10 percentage point increase in a state's immigration share, it had an economic growth bonus of about 1 percentage point. State GDP growth averaged 5 percent annually in fast-growth states and one-third that pace in a handful of slower states.

Immigration levels have tripled since 1980 in raw numbers and doubled relative to the national population,. The increase during the 1990s was particularly extraordinary. Today, California has the highest share of foreign-born among its population, a share that includes Holocaust survivors as well as tourists who overstayed their visas. Some of these immigrants became citizens half a century ago, and some will never become citizens.

In 1980, the average state had an immigrant share of 4 percent of its total population. California's was 15 percent. By 2015, the average state's immigration share rose to 9 percent, whereas California's jumped to 27 percent.

Growth in immigration was initially concentrated in a few states— California, Nevada, New York, New Jersey, Florida, and Texas—but it became more evenly spread after 2000 (Figure 13.2). For example, during the 1980s there were only eleven states that saw immigration shares rise by more than 1 percentage point. In fact, seventeen states had an immigrant share of less than 2 percent to begin with in 1980. It is this variation across states that enables us to explore whether the high and varied growth of immigration in the 1990s is related to strong income growth during that same time (Figure 13.3).

Let me emphasize that we looked at these data in two ways, first comparing *levels* and then by comparing *growth* rates. Because we had observations from each decade, we could also compare Ohio in 1980 against Ohio in 2010. That gave us a total of 250 data points. What we found is that states with higher levels of immigrant shares tend to have higher levels of GDP per capita. This relationship persists after taking the first difference to compare changes (i.e., growth), indicating that states that experienced an increase in the share of

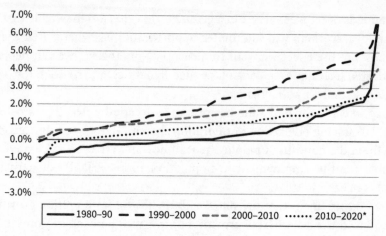

Figure 13.2 Change in foreign-born share of the labor force across fifty states, ranked. Data from US Department of Homeland Security.

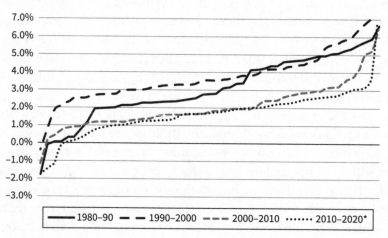

Figure 13.3 Economic growth rates across fifty states, ranked. Data from Bureau of Economic Analysis.

immigrants also experienced larger increases in GDP. Economists have reported a similar relationship globally: member countries of the Organization for Economic Co-operation and Development (OECD) with a higher ratio of immigrants are richer. Full stop. They are also growing faster.

Three charts capture the basic relationships vividly. Figure 13.4 shows a negative relationship between the level of the foreign-born in the workforce and native employment. More immigrants, less native employment. This surprised me, but let's not jump to conclusions. One interpretation is that

Figure 13.4 Native employment to population ratio vs. immigrant share (by state, 1980, 1990, 2000, 2010, 2015). Data from US Department of Labor and Department of Homeland Security.

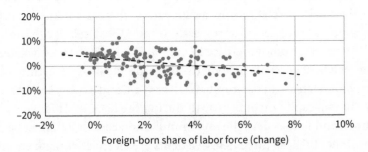

Figure 13.5 Change in jobs per capita vs. change in immigrant share of labor force (by state 1980, 1990, 2000, 2010, 2015). Data from US Department of Labor and Department of Homeland Security.

immigrants cause fewer job opportunities for local folks. Alternatively, the relationship could mean that places with older native populations tend to draw in larger numbers of young migrants to take up jobs. Figure 13.5 looks at changes in the total jobs per capita, which declines as the share of immigrants in the statewide labor force increases.

In contrast, Figure 13.6 reveals a positive relationship between states' GDP growth and the changing immigrant shares of the workforce. Just like the explanation above, this doesn't say whether one thing is causing the other, but it confirms that high growth states tend to be high immigration states.

Zach and I also did a lot of statistical modeling and ran thousands of econometric regressions to look for causal effects. The longest-term relationship we could test with our data was thirty-five years, and that showed an unambiguous positive correlation between GDP and immigration. And once the

Figure 13.6 GDP per capita growth (annual) vs. change in immigration share of labor force (by state, 1990, 2000, 2010, 2015). Data from US Bureau of Economic Analysis and Department of Homeland Security.

data are cut into decades—allowing us to control for both time and state effects—the positive relationship disappeared whereas a short-term transition negative was revealed. Our regressions found that, relative to the average state, a 1 percentage point increase in the foreign-born share of a state's labor force causes a 0.32 percentage point decrease in state GDP growth, a 0.28 percentage point decrease in per-capita GDP growth, and a 0.30 percentage point decrease in per-capita income growth during the decade. This seems like an indictment, and it does dent the pro-immigration case, but it must be understood in context. These three negative dents are all short-run effects within a ten-year period.

We also know that those negative effects dissolve over time, because the effect of a higher *level* of immigration has no significant effect on the levels of GDP per capita or even personal income. For example, the negative short-term pressure on average incomes is likely driven by the relative poverty of new immigrants when they first arrive. They still add to aggregate demand and the overall size of the local economy, but the total GDP *per person* looks smaller. It's a transitory mirage.

Another wrinkle in all of these figures is that immigrants during this time period were much less educated than the native-born US population. Furthermore, there were two very different concentrations: one of highly educated migrants and a larger group of far-less-educated migrants. Since then, the immigrant education gap has shifted dramatically. According to the US census, the average years of schooling for native-born Americans was 11.8 years in 1980, compared to 10.6 years for the foreign-born and 8.9 years for the subset of foreign-born Hispanics. Well, in the decades since, the proportion of Latin Americans has been shrinking while the education levels for all groups have been rising. In 2010, foreign-born Hispanics had an additional year and a half of schooling, whereas foreign-born Asians averaged 14.2 years of education, and Europeans 13.9. Among the Mexican-born population in the United States, the average amount of schooling has risen by three years.

The changing educational attainment of recent immigrants has implications for long-term GDP growth. Recall our growth model $Y = f(A, K, L, H)$. Every immigrant regardless of education adds to the "L" labor pool. The bonus is that when the average immigrant comes with more education, they adds directly to the "H" human capital. That translates directly into more innovation and even faster economic growth.

An exclamation point of sorts was put on this new outlook in 2016 when the National Academies of Sciences, Engineering, and Medicine (NAS)—a congressionally supported nonprofit—published a 600-plus-page report titled "The Economic and Fiscal Consequences of Immigration." That study was overseen by a panel of a dozen scholars, including Borjas, that comprehensively reviewed the research and, importantly, included an analysis of overall economic activity (GDP). It also included a special look at long-run economic growth. Referencing the new human-capital-centric models, the NAS report concluded that the, "long-term dynamic immigration surplus could far exceed its estimates based on static models."

Let's take a breath here and think about what this mountain of evidence means. Borjas and Peri have been fighting a proxy battle for skeptics and advocates of immigration for many, many years, continuing a disagreement that has been ongoing for almost all of American history. It is a timeless debate, but what I hope we've been able to confirm is that it is a lot of sound and fury, signifying nothing (in the long run). Besides, it's a micro debate, which is simply irrelevant to the issue of national power on the world stage. Moreover, the demographic transition in the educational makeup of recent agreements means that entire micro-data economic literature—Borjas, Card, Peri included—should be taken with a grain of salt. Turning to the macro impact of immigration on GDP, these last three chapters show an overwhelming positive effect of immigration. It shows up when we consider fifty states, and it is confirmed when we break down the data into state-decade observations.

It's time to make total GDP growth the main point in the national debate on immigration. And with it front and center, we should ask no more about the short-term pressure of a few pennies of hourly wages but about the billions of dollars in total economic output. And just maybe, we should about the long-term existential economic threat facing the nation.

Debt Threat

At a June 2010 breakfast organized in Washington, DC, the chairman of the Joint Chiefs was invited to speak. The audience expected to hear remarks from Admiral Mike Mullen about geopolitical strategy perhaps, or an update on the wars in Iraq and Afghanistan. Instead, Mullen spoke about a rising new threat alarming him as well as Secretary of Defense Robert M. Gates.

"The interest on our [national] debt is $571 billion," Mullen said. "That is, noticeably, about the size of the defense budget. It is not sustainable."[12] The chairman found a receptive, bipartisan audience to his warning. Economists of both parties had found their warnings about debt ignored, but Mullen's perspective was new, and he spoke with more intensity over that summer. "The most significant threat to our national security is our debt," he said in August.[13]

During the following years, even after Mullen had retired, defense wonks echoed the sentiment. "A bipartisan group of prominent national security figures on Tuesday will call on U.S. leaders to reduce the country's long-term debt, which they consider the greatest threat to the nation's security," reported *The Hill* in 2016.[14] Michael O'Hanlon, the well-respected national security expert at the Brookings Institution, wrote in 2012 that "much less money will be left for other things" when the cost of debt crowds out the federal budget.[15] O'Hanlon's warnings of trillion-dollar deficits that were novel in the Obama years became normalized during the Trump years.

Why is this relevant to immigration? A common perception is that immigrants are a drag on the federal budget. Decades ago, the great libertarian Milton Friedman said that open immigration was incompatible with a welfare state. His most succinct statement comes in a letter he wrote to a fellow economist: "There is no doubt that free and open immigration is the right policy in a libertarian state, but in a welfare state it is a different story: the supply of immigrants will become infinite."[16]

For a long time, I took Friedman's words as a salvo against the welfare state, not immigrants, but my friend and famous libertarian, Bryan Caplan, opened my eyes. Our hero Milton Friedman truly was a skeptic. Friedman's concern is one voiced often by Americans who worry that poor migrants (particularly the "illegal immigrants" from Mexico) come here to sponge off of American welfare. Let's admit, if forced to choose, most voters would prefer to keep social security instead of an open immigration policy. But what if Friedman's dilemma is a false choice?

While teaching economics at George Mason University, Caplan also made time to write *Open Borders*, a graphic novel calling for unlimited immigration. As narrator, cartoon Caplan takes on cartoon Friedman directly. Rather than adding to the national debt, he explains that immigration is mathematically like the reverse of secession (e.g., when the Confederacy rebelled against the Union). Secessionists don't take an equal proportion of the nation's debt load when they break away, but immigrants actually do accept a portion of their new nation's debt when they arrive, implicitly agreeing to pay taxes here and here only. Compared to the native population, migrants are far less likely to be school age or retirement age.[17]

When talking about immigration work habits, critics of immigration often want to have their cake and eat it, too. If Caplan or I point out that immigrants tend to have a higher labor force participation rate, critics will say that means they are stealing jobs. But if the average immigrant was less likely to be employed, that same critic would complain that he is getting unemployment benefits.

The NAS report in 2016 calculated the long-run fiscal effect of immigration. They calculated the net tax revenues of immigrants and their offspring who would otherwise not be Americans, and also the potential costs of extra government expenditures. The numbers are large, and the lesson even larger. The average *existing* immigrant who is currently living in the United States adds a net present value of $58,000 to the country, meaning that over their lifetime the typical immigrant will pay that much more in taxes than they cost in revenues. But NAS also reported the net present value of is $259,000 for the typical new immigrant arriving today, which is five times larger. In other words, the best weapon against the Pentagon's top national security threat is more immigration.

There may be a welfare system so poorly designed that migrants are a net cost, but that is not the system America has in place now. Legal immigrants are barred from drawing the most expensive programs such as food stamps and Medicaid for a full five years, and they cannot qualify for Social Security until they work for ten years. Sure, their US-born children attend public schools, but that's a cost that is outweighed by the benefit of literate, productive future workers, the same as it is for educating native-born children. The reality is that 50 to 75 percent of undocumented immigrants pay taxes into Social Security and other welfare programs, yielding billions of dollars we otherwise would miss dearly.[18]

The Problem with People

For all of his excellent research and numerous books, and for all of the attention given to him by restrictionists, Borjas has never written that immigrants hurt the US economy. Rather, he emphasizes that immigrants in recent decades have been primarily less-educated and low-skilled. Consider how he described his own work in the weeks before the 2016 election:

> Here's the problem with the current immigration debate: Neither side is revealing the whole picture. Trump might cite my work, but he overlooks my findings that the influx of immigrants can potentially be a net good for the nation, increasing the total wealth of the population.[19]

In the final analysis, the real problem with immigrants is not economics. We wanted workers, and people came. People are social animals, with religions, cultures, tribal loyalties. The pogroms against Jews and the Catholic-Protestant wars that haunted nearly every European nation in the past 500 years should remind us that governing a diverse population was never easy. Cultural tensions do not appear in mathematical models of labor markets, but they are no figment of the imagination.

Those skeptics, even the ones with economics bona fides, eventually come around to the same point, as did Borjas: "What would happen to the institutions and social norms that govern economic exchanges in specific countries after the entry or exit of perhaps hundreds of millions of people? . . . [W]ould these institutions be overwhelmed by the inefficiencies that hampered growth in the poorer countries?"[20]

These are important questions. But again, let's be honest. They are not economic questions. They are cultural, and hardly new. What's new under the sun is that the United States emerged from the wilderness of the New World and not only created institutions that resolved the tensions of cultural diversity that hobbled great powers of old but also nurtured that greatness with immigration, not in spite of it. It has worked for over two centuries, which begs the question: how long is the long run?

Chapter 14
Cultures

immigrant *noun* /ˈɪm.ə.grənt/ a person who has come to a different country in order to live there permanently. *syn* migrant, emigré, refugee, nomad, settler, traveler, colonist, alien *ant* native

native *noun* /ˈneɪ.tɪv/ a person who was born in a particular place, or a plant or animal that lives or grows naturally in a place and has not been brought from somewhere else. *syn* aboriginal, ancient, citizen, dweller, local, national *ant* immigrant, foreigner, stranger

citizen *noun* /ˈsɪt.ə.zən/ a person who is a member of a particular country and who has rights because of being born there or because of being given rights, or a person who lives in a particular town or city. *syn* inhabitant, resident, taxpayer, national, voter, occupant *ant* alien

alien *noun* /ˈeɪ.li.ən/ someone who lives in a country of which they are not a legal citizen. *syn* immigrant, outsider, foreigner, invader, stranger *ant* citizen

culture *noun* /ˈkʌl.tʃər/ the way of life, especially the general customs and beliefs, of a particular group of people at a particular time.

The phrase "melting pot" entered the American lexicon in the year 1908, when a stage play of the same name was performed in Washington, DC. Written by Israel Zangwill—and cheered by President Teddy Roosevelt on opening night—the play celebrated the assimilation of many cultures into one, a fusion of foreign peoples and foreign cultures into a stronger new people and new culture. Unfortunately, the phrase has been turned on its head by woke activists. Training materials issued by the University of Minnesota list "America is a melting pot" as an example of a macroaggression that denies a person of color identity and demands they assimilate to the "dominant culture." What a shame that modern progressives are willing to erase the actual progressive history of the phrase: Zangwill and others were celebrating diversity at a time when eugenics was popular and a virulent populist nativism was fueling a revival of the anti-Black, anti-Jewish, anti-Catholic, anti-immigrant Ku Klux Klan.

There is something wrong in the current American conversation about race, something ahistorical and fantastical that aims to displace the creed of equality with tribalist euphemisms and seemingly unquenchable grievances. The problem is with people who believe in white supremacy on the right (racists) as well as those on the left (racialists). Both extremes are obsessed with whiteness as an identity, but it is the left's pseudoscientific belief in "white fragility" and critical race theory that represent the gravest threat to a common culture of equality, color blindness, and assimilation to shared principles of the American constitutional democracy. That rotten tribalism will never be comfortable with a nation of immigrants. The new culture war is not left versus right; it is identity politics versus egalitarianism. My case is that America's culture of openness to immigrants is, was, and will always be fusionist, and moreover that new immigrants will invariably be a source of constant change.

Many Americans have a specific image in their memories of the melting pot, a cartoon showing people of different hues being mixed together in a stew of some kind that was broadcast on Saturday morning as part of the *Schoolhouse Rock* public service commercials. That was in the 1970s, when the idea of assimilation was understood as a strength of the American system and a positive concept in its own right. It is inaccurate to think of American assimilation as a subjugation of minority cultures to the mainstream culture, though that sense may be the prevalent experience elsewhere. American assimilation— the melting pot—is literally a fusion metaphor, hence the national motto, *e pluribus unum*.

Melting pot is a metallurgical term, from smelting pot or crucible: a pot in which metals or other substances are melted together into a new metal known as an alloy. For example, bronze is produced by melting together copper with some tin, yielding a stronger substance than either metal alone, one that resists corrosion, is relatively frictionless, and doesn't spark. Another alloy is steel, the martial metal—iron mixed with carbon—perfected in the smelting and hammering of swords.

The etymology traces back to J. Hector St. John de Crevecoeur's 1782 *Letters from an American Farmer*: "Here individuals of all nations are melted into a new race of men, whose labors and posterity will one day cause great changes in the world." Ralph Waldo Emerson echoed the sentiment in a private journal entry in 1845, praising the "smelting pot" of a new people mixed culturally and racially. And the famous historian Frederick Jackson Turner described the American people as a product of the frontier where "immigrants were Americanized, liberated and fused into a mixed race, English in neither nationality nor characteristics." The explicit non-Englishness of the new alloyed American people is a vital corrective to the modern debate about race.

The Illusion of Whiteness

So what are we to make of the "national conversation" about race, which in our era has become distorted by the idea of white supremacy and the illusion of a coherent white majority? Identity politics seeks to organize and emphasize group identity of minorities on racial or religious boundaries that frame collective grievance against systemic oppression by a dominant majority. It collapses in the absence of a dominant majority, of course, which motivates the narrative of a white oppressor and the obsession on the left with white/nonwhite divisions. But the coherence of both whites and nonwhites literally melts away in an egalitarian society in which intermarriage and assimilation are normalized.

The vanguard of tribal ideology is a group of academic proponents of critical race theory (CRT) whose self-described organizing principle is that "a regime of white supremacy and its subordination of people of color have been created and maintained in America" as promulgated by Kimberlé Crenshaw and her co-authors of the seminal 1995 CRT text.[1] Not so long ago, the dominant culture was understood to be WASPs (White Anglo-Saxon Protestants), not whites, but skin color became the essential frame for CRT. Historically, to be sure, there were popular beliefs in a European master race (remember "Nordics" and "Anglo-Saxons"), but scant support for that view can be found today. Not only does CRT prop it up, but proponents carry the narrative to an extreme rejection of core American values:

> CRT recognizes that racism is engrained in the fabric and system of the American society. The individual racist need not exist to note that institutional racism is pervasive in the dominant culture. . . . CRT identifies that these power structures are based on white privilege and white supremacy, which perpetuates the marginalization of people of color. CRT also rejects the traditions of liberalism and meritocracy.[2]

The problem is that whiteness as a dominant ethnicity falls apart on inspection. Arabs, Egyptians, Iraqis, and Persians are all categorized as "White" in the 2020 US census.[3] That raises an interesting question about why some census groups are broad and others extremely narrow. Why does the census account for Europeans, North Africans, and Middle Easterners as a monolithic white group but treats other continental ethnicities as distinct? One could argue that Asian ethnicities are distinct in US law because they represent long-standing nationalities that, as an organizing principle, fought wars. For example, the Japanese and Chinese people fought many wars over many centuries. But so did the French and English. So did the Greeks and Persians. So did the Russians and Swedes. Does anyone think there was ever in history some grand "white tribe" of Eurasia where folks got along just fine and never killed, pillaged, raped, or enslaved one another?

The absurdity of a coherent white majority has become apparent as the diversity of immigration widens. Children with dark skin are awkwardly forced to declare they have a white ethnicity on school forms, teased by classmates, challenged by teachers, and made to feel alienated. "Growing up, whenever I told people about my Middle Eastern heritage, they almost always accused me of lying," explained a New York University (NYU) student when she found out the 2020 Census wouldn't include a category for ethnicity.[4] This is a group of millions of Americans whose status is twisted in knots. Consider the current "Student Ethnicity Collection and Reporting" guidelines for identifying white students at the University of California, reprinted in Box 14.1.

When Frederick Jackson Turner spoke of a new "mixed race," he meant something subtler than the ahistorical debate that codifies racial categories by skin color. Consider, for example, that the US census has included separate categories for a variety of Asian ethnicities for over a century, starting with Chinese in 1870 and for Vietnamese, Korean, Filipino, Japanese, Samoan, Asian Indian, and Chamorro in 2020. The sum total of all citizens checking one of these Asian ethnicities is 6 percent of the US population. Yet the census has never offered distinct categories for people of European heritage such as German, Irish, or Polish, each one of which alone would account for more than 6 percent of the population.

The census, taken every decade, has never used the same set of racial categories twice in a row. A question about citizenship, however, has been included in some form or fashion since 1820. In that year, households were asked how many foreign-born people in the home were "not naturalized." Imagine the confusion that would cause then. Imagine it now. In 1870, the question was

Box 14.1 Ethnicities counted as white

European	Israeli
Caucasian	Jordanian
Middle Eastern	Kurdish
North African	Kuwaiti
Afghan	Lebanese
Algerian	Libyan
Armenian	Mauritanian
Assyrian / Chaldean	Moroccan
Azerbaijani	Omani
Bahraini	Palestinian
Berber	Qatari
Circassian	Saudi Arabian
Djiboutian	Somali
Egyptian	Sudanese
Emirati	Syrian
Georgian	Tunisian
Iranian	Turkish
Iraqi	Yemeni

Source: Guidelines issued by the University of California in accordance with federal regulations.

framed in terms of whether each person in the household was a "male citizen." From 1890 to 1910, census workers asked about the naturalization status of foreign-born men age 21 or older.

Some form of citizenship question was asked on the census of all households for 150 years. It was dropped in 1960, then re-introduced in 1970 for a random sampling of households. Roughly one in six homes were randomly given a "long form" until 2010 with a question about citizenship along with an array of other detailed economic queries. As the government prepared for the 2020 census, the Trump administration sought to re-introduce the citizenship question for all households, but the move became mired in political controversy and was ultimately blocked by the Supreme Court. Opponents of the change argued that asking about citizenship would have a chilling effect on immigrant response rates. That's a speculative argument, yet it represents a disturbing erosion of the importance and validity of citizenship (Box 14.2).

Nor does social science substantiate the salience of a white identity in a psychological context. A recent Pew survey found that one in four American

---

Box 14.2 How the US census asked about citizenship

1790
All households were asked the number of "Free white males, Free white females, Other free persons, and Slaves"

1820
All households were asked about "foreigners not naturalized"—*the first appearance of a citizenship question.*

1890
All households were asked about the naturalization status of foreign-born *men* age 21 or older.

1920
All households were asked about the naturalization status of foreign-born *people* age 21 or older.

1940
All households were asked about the *citizenship* status of foreign-born people age 21 or older.

1960
No households were asked about citizenship.

1970
A sample of households (given the long-form) were asked, "Is this person naturalized?"

1990
A sample of households were asked, "Is this person a citizen of the United States?"

2010
The long-form census is eliminated. No households were asked about citizenship.

Source: National Vital Statistics Summary, Centers of Disease Control, the Global Terrorism Database, and the *New York Times.*

---

adults who identify as black consider their race or ethnicity unimportant to their self-identity. Four in ten Asian Americans felt race was also unimportant to their self-identity, the same proportion as Hispanics. Among Americans categorized as white, only a quarter think race is important to their identity.[5]

Ironically, Pew excluded people of mixed racial identity in the survey, even though that group is growing faster than any other. Nine million individuals were counted as "multiracial" in the 2010 census. This is a categorization not allowed in the last century. Not even in 1990. I can still remember when my son was born at Andrews Air Force Base Hospital. As I held Sean in my arms, a nurse came into the room and told his mother, an ethnically Japanese woman, and me that we had to select "one and only one" race—hers or mine—when registering his birth. We declined to select any, and, threatened with disciplinary action, I added a box for "human race" and checked it.

No doubt, some readers will object to my argument that whiteness is an illusion, as if I am suggesting that blackness is as well. So let's be clear: nobody can deny the African American experience, nor should there be any erasure of societal memories of slavery, lynching, and Jim Crow laws. From

1500 to 1860, tens of millions of Africans were enslaved and forced to migrate, mostly to Caribbean sugar plantations. Six hundred thousand were taken to North America and sold there. After the Constitution was adopted and the United States was formed, there was progress made in the abolition of slavery in all northern states by 1805, and outlawing the import of slaves nationally in 1808. Even so, there were very few free blacks in 1860, no more than one-tenth the number of enslaved. Despite the ban on the international slave trade, the children of slaves were themselves enslaved, so the population grew. In many southern states, it was illegal for blacks to be taught to read or to own a firearm. Finally, on June 19, 1865, federal troops were able to enforce the emancipation of all slaves in the South.

An honest history will also face the fact that the scale of black slavery was far larger than the enslavement of Native Americans and indentured servitude of Europeans, though those numbers were sizable as well. The treatment of black people was especially cruel, and ill-treatment persisted in the South for a century after emancipation. That cruel history cannot be denied, but neither can we deny the lived experiences of anti-Semitism, the Rock Springs massacre, the lynching of Italian Americans, or the persecution and alienation of Muslim Americans. Even now in 2021, there have been vicious street attacks on elderly Asians in Oakland, California. The point is that one can understand the hardships of any individual or group with an ethnic identity in America without needing to believe in a homogenous oppressor.

Race and Language

Historians of immigration are fond of remembering Benjamin Franklin's query, written fifteen years before the Declaration of Independence: "Why should Pennsylvania, founded by the English, become a Colony of Aliens, who will shortly be so numerous as to Germanize us instead of our Anglifying them, and will never adopt our Language or Customs, any more than they can acquire our complexion?"[6] He changed his mind after 1776 when he observed successful assimilation in the new civil society. But, in a very specific sense, Franklin's prediction came true. The most common ethnic roots of Americans at the dawn of the 21st century are German, African, Irish, and Mexican, in order, according to a 2014 study. There are fewer English Americans today than German Americans, and quite a few other ethnicities as well.

Intermarriage rates among people of different ethnicities have risen worldwide, not just in the exceptionally fusionist United States. Fifty years after the 1967 *Loving v. Virginia* Supreme Court case that ruled marriage across racial lines was legal, the percentage of such marriages in the United States has risen from 3 to 17 percent,[7] and the trajectory is unlikely to stop before multiracial American children are the majority.

Intermarriage is relevant to assimilation because it often leads to what is known as *ethnic attrition*, when the descendants of immigrants from a particular country such as France cease to identify as French ethnically when surveyed. They simply identify as Americans. This is why so few people categorized as white consider themselves that way. They simply identify as Americans. Ethnic attrition skews survey data that looks for differences within the population, thus overstating gaps in income, education, and other social indicators. A 2007 academic conference, organized by George Borjas, brought this issue to light, thanks to research by Brian Duncan and Stephen Trejo:

> Virtually all (99 percent) first-generation immigrants born in a Spanish-speaking country identified as Hispanic in the census, but the rate of Hispanic identification dropped to 83 percent for the second generation, 73 percent for the third generation, 44 percent for the fourth generation, and all the way down to 6 percent for higher generations of Hispanics.[8]

Modern usage here of ethnic hyphens (e.g., Irish-Americans) is a harmless turn of phrase nowadays that was extremely controversial a century ago. The concentration of naturalized eastern Europeans in the sprawling cities of the 1900s was a source of unease. Massachusetts Institute of Technology (MIT) president Francis Amasa Walker was calling those who arrived through the Ellis Island screenings "beaten men from beaten races." In contrast, Teddy Roosevelt was celebrating the diversity of fellow Rough Riders and the assimilation of migrants from Ireland and Germany into the police forces of his native New York, while also shouting that there was "no room in this country for hyphenated Americanism."[9] Roosevelt, whose surname was Dutch, believed passionately in the melting pot, dismissed Anglo-Saxon as an "utterly unscientific word," and even objected to conflating nationality and race.

The irony is that the language used to discuss and debate immigration policy is constantly evolving. For most of American history, the foreign-born were not called "immigrants" but rather "aliens." If we look further back into the etymology of words and their meaning in the English language, *race* originally referred to speakers of a common tongue (e.g., the Celtic race), then evolved to signify national affiliations (the French race), still later became a description of people with similar physical traits (the Yellow race). This current usage of race is all but meaningless biologically: there is as much genetic variation between two people of the same census racial category as between people categorized in different races.

The word *nation* comes from the Old French word for "place of origin" with deeper Latin roots as "birthplace." The Bible uses nation to describe a people with a distinct culture, and the 19th-century federal government used the term to describe native tribes (the Indian nations), not foreign polities. In the 1700s, a polity was called a state, not a nation, which is why the Constitution refers to a "United States" and does not contain the word nation even once.

In earlier eras, leaving your town, let alone county or state, would have been unusual. Marrying someone from a different congregation in the same town would have made you the subject of gossip. Dutch Methodist neighborhoods were wary of English Methodist ones, and German Protestants were paranoid about Italian Catholic communities. Accusations of lechery, drunkenness, immorality, and criminality abounded, often to the extent that to employ or support a slightly divergent person was controversial. "Irish Need Not Apply" was a common appendage to Help Wanted signs.

Students are told that the noose is a uniquely painful symbol of white oppression, even though lynchings were used against European Americans and African Americans both. The lynching of Italians in New Orleans in 1891 was particularly disturbing, and should not be forgotten. Nine Italian men were put on trial for various charges surrounding the murder of the city's police chief. None were convicted, but the judge ordered the men returned to prison anyway, where a mob gathered, threatening to kill every "dagoe" that could be found, including men who weren't even on trial. Eleven Italian Americans were lynched, some left hanging for days.

The melting pot had bubbled over. But it didn't crack—quite the contrary. Italians and Jews assimilated over time, not into a white mainstream but into an American egalitarianism. We would be wise to celebrate those advances—breaking down barriers rather than building up racial divisions.

Cultural Challenges Today

Although caricatures of ape-like Irish drunks and hook-nosed Jewish bankers abounded a century ago, the substance behind those xenophobic symbols was that democracy would be undermined by unassimilable aliens. Similarly, Thomas Jefferson once expressed concern that immigrants from alien parts of Europe would not understand the principles of self-government. The concern haunted many of the founders. Yet over the centuries, American assimilation was so effective in democratizing people from non-democracies that today we take it for granted.

In the early 1990s, Nathan Glazer famously asked if assimilation was dead, highlighting how his Harvard students disliked the concept. "Neither liberals nor neoliberals, conservatives nor neo-conservatives, have much good to say about assimilation," he wrote.[10] More recently, Peter Beinart wrote a lengthy analysis of hyperpartisanship for *The Atlantic* that warns of a sudden, hardening orthodoxy among Democrats that favors unlimited immigration while opposing any kind of assimilation. Identity politics has turned against the American creed.

Let's clarify what exactly it is that immigrants are assimilating into. Francis Fukuyama argues in his book *Identity* that the "de facto diversity of the United States made it impossible to define American peoplehood in either religious or ethnic terms" from the beginning. Two other characteristics can define a *people*: a shared language and a shared commitment to common principles of government. Those have been the core channels of American assimilation, but both are under assault from the critical race theory left.

To be sure, religion was once a source of xenophobia. John F. Kennedy's 1960 campaign for the presidency had to contend with this anxiety directly. Weeks before that November election, 150 Protestant ministers met in Washington, DC, to warn that if Kennedy did not repudiate the teachings of the Catholic Church, then he could not be trusted to keep America free of the Vatican's control. That sentiment is all but gone.

A common tongue, however, remains popular, especially among immigrant parents. More than 80 percent of Americans favor making English the official language, not as a racial barrier but as a unifying force that breaks down racial barriers. Although a multiculturalism movement opposed English-language assimilation in the 1990s, immigrant parents pushed back. They did not want their children to be balkanized in public schools.

Meanwhile, the question voiced by some on the right is that assimilation itself has changed. It's not language that concerns modern-day restrictionists. It's the concern that assimilation toward "common principles of government" has been ruptured.

Mark Krikorian, leader of the Center for Immigration Studies, argues that low-skill immigrants haven't changed but the American economy has. His theory is that with more jobs requiring higher education in the knowledge economy, immigrants in this new century are more likely to remain stuck outside of the mainstream, literally alienated. Reihan Salam, leader of the Manhattan Institute, whose parents are Bangladeshi immigrants, warns that there are two kinds of assimilation happening today, one into the mainstream and one into an alienated underclass. Given that labor markets are worsening and the middle class is shrinking, high levels of low-skill immigration will "make a middle class melting pot impossible," concludes his 2018 book *Melting Pot or Civil War.*[11]

Salam paints a picture of millions who migrated for the American dream and then found themselves, even after multiple generations, permanently poorer than everyone. As he eloquently puts it, "In a country as diverse and unequal as ours, not everyone is assimilating into the same America." This line of argument is the Yin to the progressive Yang: *if Democrats are giving up on assimilating immigrants, then Republicans should give up on immigrants who won't be able to assimilate.*

Let's inspect the assumptions in this critique. Do the foreign-born have significantly higher poverty rates? In 2009, just under 14 percent of the native-born population had incomes below the poverty line, compared to 18 percent of the foreign-born.[12] That is hardly a radicalizing gap, especially when closer examination reveals no poverty gap whatsoever among urbanized immigrants and natives. Among more recent immigrants, yes, their incomes are lower than the average naturalized citizen. Government data indicate, for example, that one in four low-income children in the United States are children of immigrants. But that's a function of the particular demography of recent surges of Central Americans, not evidence of assimilation failing.

This narrative of unwashed masses has been embraced by some policymakers on the left as well as the right. When Democratic leaders tell voters that inequality is the "defining challenge of our time" (as Barack Obama said in 2013), it feeds the anxiety among all voters who see caravans heading north. Let's admit that the gap between rich and poor in America would be narrowing, not widening, but for immigration—which leads to one or the other logical conclusion: either low-skill immigrants are undesirable or inequality is a frivolous concern. I tend to find it frivolous, but Democrats in Congress do not, which explains why they maintain tight limits on the number of work visas granted to low-skill foreign workers.

Where skeptics of immigration get traction is looking not at the immigrants or the citizenry but at the American political system, because that's where race-based identity politics have intensified. The Democratic Party, like left-leaning parties globally, is increasingly focused on stoking racial grievances to increase the vote share of minorities. As Francis Fukuyama observes, the European left in recent decades "downplayed the importance of integrating immigrants into the national culture."[13] And in the United States, "identity politics has fractured the left into a series of identity groups that are home to its most energetic political activists." Eschewing assimilation as a goal means the left is unwilling to celebrate the exceptionalism of American institutions. The left embraces hostility not only to the melting pot but also to constitutional principles including free speech (which it calls hate speech), gun rights, elections (i.e., the electoral college), and more. Do immigrants buy into the left's anti-American message?

Ultimately, the only card in the restrictionist deck is the supposed cultural erosion of the "norms and institutions" of American democracy. But there isn't much empirical evidence that the 21st century is as different as Krikorian claims.

Immigration Does Tip the Political Scales

Can immigrants hurt a democracy? The one person who made me think twice about that question is Garett Jones. We shared a graduate student office in the UCSD economics department in the 1990s, with a view of the Pacific Ocean just outside our door. A few years after graduation, Garett began writing interesting papers on economic growth, particularly on the root causes of institutional change. Too many scholars have a black box view of institutions. Garett asked: If property rights are so important, shouldn't we study the places where they have abruptly collapsed?

The reality is that immigrants do change democracies, but not the way conventional wisdom imagines. Usually the impact is slow, usually it is positive, but sometimes not. Consider Argentina if you want to understand how immigration can change institutions, says Professor Jones. A century ago, Argentinians had higher average incomes than the French, and their country was considered one of the richest in the world. Buenos Aires was a more attractive destination for many than New York City. By 1913, roughly one-third of the people of Argentina were foreign-born.

Suddenly, in the middle of the 20th century, Argentine politics turned against free markets in favor of an authoritarian style of socialism. Industries were nationalized by the state, bank assets of everyday people were seized, and the national growth rate stagnated. There is no denying that an immigrant-fueled democratic revolution overthrew capitalism in Argentina. The country has been in a terrible cycle of debt and collapse ever since, even while neighboring countries have passed it by. Is it ridiculous to blame immigrants for Argentina's institutional devolution? Not for the *Penguin History of Latin America*:

The Argentine trade unions were led by anarchists and syndicalists; many of these were Spanish or Italian immigrants who had brought with them from Europe a belief in direct action and the revolutionary general strike as the instruments with which to overthrow the bourgeois state.[14]

That's not the opinion of conservative romantics but rather a common refrain in histories and academic studies of Argentina. Peronists actually celebrate immigrants for helping break down the old oligarchy. Meanwhile, incomes in Argentina are half of those in France today. The lesson seems crystal clear, but Argentina is actually an anomaly. The political effect of immigrants generally tends to favor libertarian parties not autocratic ones.

Consider the political shifts driven by immigration into US cities and states. Whereas most states are considered safely red (Republican) or blue (Democratic) in the electoral college, have you ever noticed how the swing states change every four years? The shift is driven by internal immigration. The Covid-19 pandemic is likely to make the electoral map far different in 2024.

Table 14.1 highlights my analysis of the US states with the fastest and slowest population growth after 1970 (the modern era of foreign immigration) and a handful of other interesting states. Five southern states doubled their populations (Texas was close), while five midwestern states were flat. I also calculated the contribution of foreign migration, and in none of the top

Table 14.1 Population growth in selected states, 1970–2015

State	Net increase	Percentage increase	Immigrant contribution
Nevada	2,083,265	260%	66%
Arizona	4,099,350	151%	29%
Florida	10,498,590	108%	34%
Utah	1,529,595	105%	14%
Texas	13,200,448	93%	30%
California	15,326,038	65%	36%
New Jersey	1,570,598	21%	18%
New York	2,189,111	12%	14%
Illinois	1,412,529	12%	10%
Pennsylvania	928,009	8%	3%
Ohio	807,460	7%	2%
Iowa	208,189	7%	4%
Michigan	655,637	7%	2%
West Virginia	−108,591	−6%	1%

states did it add more than a third of a net increase. In New Jersey, meanwhile, the population increased by 21 percent from its level in 1970, though all but 3 percent of that was due to foreigners. And New York would have literally shrunk during the past half century but for foreign migrants. To be fair, the change in population was due partly to births and deaths, not just moves, but it's stunning to think that something like one in nine New Yorkers left the state since 1970, each one replenished by a migrant from overseas.

California was safely in the Republican column for decades. It went blue in 1992 during the quirky election between Ross Perot, Bill Clinton, and George H. W. Bush. But it didn't flip back. The political class was surprised in 1996 when the states didn't resort to their old alignment. To be sure, the realignment of southern states from Democrat to Republican was counterbalanced by the realignment of Northeast states in the opposite direction, but the underlying migration of native-born Americans from North to South was like a tidal wave that changed the partisan balance almost everywhere.

Indeed, the most compelling evidence about domestic migration reshaping a state's politics comes from the Pacific states. California was radically changed by migration twice: the gold rush in and the red rush out. When Mexico achieved its independence in 1821, it encompassed most of the Pacific Coast of North America. The area was sparsely populated and ceded to the United States in 1848. With the discovery of gold immediately afterward, the territory experienced an oversupply of new citizens and an undersupply of housing. Despite the gold rush, the state's population did not rise above 2 million until early in the 20th century.

The second great migration to California was what we should think of as the red rush of the 1980s: foreigners migrating into the state were matched by an exodus of middle-income Republican voters. James Gimpel, a political demographer at the University of Maryland, called California's experience of population change "unique in American history and perhaps even in the world."[15]

Ronald Reagan was elected governor in 1967, a time when California was considered a conservative bulwark. During the two decades before Reagan's governorship, the state's population doubled from 10 million to 20 million, almost entirely because of interstate movement of Republican-leaning Americans. This is just one of the case studies that affirms Gimpel's hypothesis that "areas with large migrant populations will be more likely to support Republican than Democratic candidates."[16] In a 2001 paper, he and Jason Schuknecht found empirical support for their hypothesis in the most recent internal US migrations, particularly when the migration streams are large. A likely explanation is the economic bias of migration, meaning that there is a higher propensity for migrants to be wealthier and more sensitive to differential tax rates, and those characteristics are more commonly found among Republicans. The psychology of immigrants has always been entrepreneurial, which is what also surely contributes to the political orientation of newcomers.

Californian voter registration leaned so heavily in favor of the GOP that Democratic candidates for president didn't bother to campaign there in the 1960s and '70s. Then, during the 1980s and '90s, a surge of foreign migrants reshaped the demography just as domestic migration reversed. Millions of native Californians moved out. That dual surge coincided with a political realignment, though it's not clear what caused what. Regardless, the Democratic Party now has held veto-proof supermajorities in both houses of the state legislature. There are three Democrats for every one Republican in the California Assembly and the Senate.

Realignment as a consequence of poorer immigrant voters is an obvious explanation. A bit too obvious. A more powerful cause of the realignment is the outmigration of conservative Californians. On net, 900,000 California citizens have departed in the past decade. And it turns out that Republicans are far more likely to migrate than Democrats. They always have been. A study in 1960 found that 71 percent of Democrats raised in an urban area still live in the same area as adults, but only 46 percent of Republicans do.

So many Californians are leaving for Texas—60,000 or more per year—that some worry the coastal diaspora might flip the Lone Star State to the left, or at least make it competitive in the electoral college. And that was a concern before the Covid-19 pandemic. The extended lockdown of economic activity in 2020 forced companies in Silicon Valley to shift to online work, and some have made it a permanent transition. Google and Facebook, for example, announced that all work would be done remotely until at least the summer of 2021, allowing employees to relocate out of the expensive San Francisco Bay area. According to a report in the *Wall Street Journal*, 15 percent of tech workers have already left, and a majority of those who remain will go if their firms permit the move.

Flipping Texas is unlikely, regardless. According to some studies, recent transplants voted more heavily for Republicans in the 2020 election than did native-born Texans. And as Gimpel found, Democrats tend to stay in place, while Republicans are much more likely to move to new cities and states.

What's really interesting is understanding the migration motivation as a result of institutional competition between governments. Let's not forget that the right of movement is one of the most fundamental to a free people, arguably more vital than rights to free speech and more effective than the right to vote in keeping a government respectful and efficient. There's no stopping a citizen of Philadelphia from uprooting herself for a better life in Pittsburgh, or Miami for that matter. Taxes are lower in Texas and Florida, and the roads are better, too. The cost of rent in California's big cities is another motivation, to be sure, but it doesn't take an Einstein to figure out that high rents are caused by strict zoning laws that limit housing supply—meaning it really is institutions all the way down.

Think about tax sensitivity today. California has the highest state income taxes in the country, whereas neither Florida nor Texas have any state income tax at all. Those states raise revenue through sales taxes. But even their sales tax rates—6.0 percent in Florida and 6.25 percent in Texas—are a full percentage point lower than California's statewide 7.25 percent sales tax, not to mention big-city surtaxes.

What these migrations represent is not cultural erosion but a phenomenon I call *cultural confirmation*. People are voting with their feet in favor of "better" institutions. When California was booming with free markets and ample opportunity after World War II, the population boomed as well: a red rush of conservative voters. After California politics gradually shifted and adopted high taxes and spending programs, they once again voted "no confidence" with their feet.

This is the brilliance of federalism. With fifty states, America has a built-in structure for policy experimentation. If a policy (i.e., institution) is created and works well in one state, the resulting growth will attract people to move in. And vice versa. Illinois may adopt a tiny wealth tax or business regulation that doesn't seem radical, but the consequences slowly squeeze the profitability of small companies, and entrepreneurs at the margin find it easier to set up in other states. Or maybe the attraction is education policy. Minnesota was the first state to pass a charter school law in 1991. Colorado and Washington legalized recreational marijuana in 2012. Despite the creeping size of the federal government, state diversity remains a powerful force. Federalism works best when coupled with unrestricted insterstate immigration.

So what did the Golden State do that led to the red rush exodus? One possible explanation is that the "peace dividend" in the 1990s came at the expense of millions of jobs in the defense industries in southern California, creating a state budget gap that could only be balanced with higher tax rates. Perhaps that began the vicious cycle of outmigration, higher taxes, more outmigration, and so on. The theory that a surge of undocumented Mexicans came into California and voted overwhelmingly for Democratic candidates is not only fantastical but doesn't square with the facts. The econometric relationship between the share of migrants at the state level and the growth of total state expenditures is negative, not positive, according to a 2020 study by Alex Nowrasteh and Andrew Forrester. Whatever the cause of California's red rush exodus, it was not an erosion at the hands of foreign immigrants.

The Surprising Threat to Institutions

If immigrating foreigners aren't a threat to democratic institutions, what is?

Since 9/11, many Americans have worried about the non-assimilation of Muslim immigrants in particular. More than a few politicians have exploited that concern, emboldened by thoughtful public intellectuals such as Ross Douthat and David Frum. In contrast, my instinct to trust Muslim Americans is based my own personal experience as an intelligence officer in the military. Trained as a combat interrogator, I found that nearly every one of my fellow HUMINT (human intelligence) officers was fluent in multiple languages. My fellow officers had Thai, Korean, Egyptian, Jordanian, German, and Japanese parents. I truly came to understand that what unites American troops overwhelms what differentiates them.

There may be no story in this vein more touching than that of Humayun Khan, a captain in the US Army whose family immigrated from Pakistan when he was a young boy. Humayun's parents, Khizr and Ghazala Khan, gave up a life of great prestige in exchange for a simple life as ordinary American citizens, and you cannot read Mr. Khan's book about his son's death in Iraq without coming to tears:

> "Yes," I said. "That's my son." Because it was. It is a cliché, but he looked peaceful, as if he was sleeping, perhaps even dreaming of something pleasant. There were no marks or blemishes on his smooth brown skin. The dimple in his chin was unmarred. The only unusual detail was the bandage, a bright white strip of gauze stretched across his forehead, covering the wound where a piece of shrapnel had hit him above his left eye.[17]

Humayun was killed trying to protect his troops and the locals on a Tuesday in early June in 2004. It was twenty-six years after his father had completed his journey and taken an oath to defend the US Constitution. "I meant every word of it," he remembers.

As a scholar, I have to set such emotions aside. Maybe the Khans were a rarity. What does the evidence tell us about modern assimilation?

Fifteen years ago, John Fonte and Althea Nagai (scholars at the Hudson Institute, where I later worked), claimed that the American patriotic assimilation system was broken. They cited responses to a 2007 survey about Americanism, and even though the immigrant responses were heavily patriotic, they appeared less so than the norm. Fonte and Nagai had split the respondents into naturalized-native subsamples in order to assess any gaps. For example, seventy percent of immigrant citizens agreed that the United States is "better than other nations" compared to 92 percent of native-born citizens. Another question that stood out was about "Pride in being American" to which a slightly higher proportion of native-born citizens felt "very proud."[18] Their source data come from the *2008 Bradley Project on America's National Identity*, a highly publicized report about the weakness of civics education in the United States, which has been slowly replaced by a multicultural curriculum that emphasized separate identities. "To inform its work, the Bradley Project asked Harris Interactive to conduct a study on Americans' views on national identity. The good news is that 84 percent of the respondents still believe in a unique American identity. The bad news is that 63 percent believe this identity is weakening, and 72 percent are concerned about ethnic, cultural, and political divisions. Almost a quarter—24 percent—believe we are already so divided that a common national identity is impossible."[19] After a lot of digging, I found that the project mentions immigration five times and education thirty-three times; it concludes that the erosion of the creedal identity is not an issue of non-assimilation but of younger Americans being educated poorly in civics and history. Fonte and Nagai's repurposing of the underlying data was clever, but also cherry-picked. They neglected to highlight that only 1 percent of immigrant citizens felt "Not very proud" of America, compared to five times as many native-born citizens.

The Fonte-Nagai study circulated without much pushback until CATO scholars Nowrasteh and Forrester conducted a more in-depth study in 2019. They looked into a split sample of responses to the nationwide biennial General Social Survey (GSS) going all the way back to 2006. These results were based on a much larger sample, and in question after question affirmed *greater* patriotism among immigrant citizens than natives.[20]

Is America better than most other countries? Seventy-nine percent of immigrant citizens think so, but only 73 percent of natives do. Proud of being American?—75 for immigrants and 69 for natives. Ashamed of some aspects of America?—43 and 69. Think about that. Native-born Americans are 25 percentage points more likely to feel ashamed of their country. Nowrasteh and Forrester asked three questions about confidence in federal

Table 14.2 Immigrant patriotism in contrast with patriotism of natives and youths (percentage of respondents who agree with the following statements)

	Native-born citizens	Naturalized citizens	Respondents ages 18–29	Immigrant vs. Youth Patriotism
US Constitution is the best form of government	80	84	67	+ 17
The US is an exceptional country	79	84	70	+ 14
Prefer US citizenship more than any country	81	82	68	+ 14
All men are created equal: No person advantaged over others by race or religion	85	89	75	+ 14
English should be the official language	79	80	73	+ 7
Support for free speech	50	58	57	+ 1

Source: These results are from Kane-Brady's YouGov Survey, January 2020.

institutions—Congress, the presidency, and the Supreme Court—and in each case immigrants expressed more confidence than natives.[21]

To understand the root causes of the fraying respect for civic norms in America, we need a survey that not only contrasts citizens by birth origin but by age as well. Dave Brady and I did just that with our 2020 YouGov survey. We found very strong support for American institutions. Almost all respondents (80%) believed that the US Constitution was the best form of government and that the United States should be committed to the proposition that all men are created equal (86%). Most respondents (79%) would rather be a citizen of the United States than any other country in the world and believed that America is better than most other countries (78%). However, in every patriotic question, we found slightly more support among immigrants than among native-born Americans. In contrast, we found less support in double-digit gaps by younger Americans, as shown in Table 14.2.

The problem today is not that immigrants aren't assimilating to American values but that young Americans aren't assimilating to American values.

Citizenship or Tribalism?

"America was founded on white supremacy," Beto O'Rourke declared at a rally near the southern border. It was the summer of 2019, and the young Democratic candidate for president was struggling to find a message that would catapult him back into the race. O'Rourke's speech was motivated by nearby detention centers where unaccompanied migrant children were being held. Authorities had apprehended a record-high number of such children in 2019, double from the year prior, and arrested four times the number of children traveling with family members. Half a million human beings.

After the Democrats won the 2020 presidential election, the Biden administration maintained and even expanded the children's detention facilities. The crisis continued, and yet no one accused Biden or Vice President Kamala Harris of white supremacy. So why did O'Rourke say it when a Republican was in the Oval Office?

The Democratic Party is increasingly invested in a culture war led by CRT activists. Its "identity politics" go beyond organizing ethnic voting blocs to promulgating a harshly negative narrative of the United States as irredeemably racist. In their worldview, the roots of American culture are forever tainted by slavery on the continent (centuries before 1776), the three-fifths clause in the Constitution that denied full personhood to slaves, and the persistent nativist thread exemplified by the Know Nothings of the mid-1800s. CRT requires one to believe in binary things: white and black, bad and good, racist and anti-racist. It is puritan and unforgiving. It condemns Thomas Jefferson because he was a slave-owner, Woodrow Wilson because he was a racist, Lyndon Johnson because he used derogatory language in describing black citizens. The fact that these three men were progressive pioneers during their time and leaders of the Democratic Party matters not. Wilson's name has been struck from Princeton. Jefferson's statues are targets for toppling. Do they even care that LBJ singlehandedly upended the anti-immigrant laws with his 1965 legislative reforms?

The irony of modern debates is that racial fault lines are emphasized to the extreme by the CRT left whereas citizenship lines are blurred. This is backward. They would point to the three-fifths clause as the trump card in denying full citizenship or even full humanity to nonwhites. This reading of history implies that southerners preferred to count slaves as zero. Yet the records of the 1787 convention are undeniable: it was Charles Pinckney of South Carolina who called for apportioning seats in Congress according to state populations that fully counted slaves because that way would have given slave states more power in Congress. If slaves were counted as zero, slave states would have gotten 6 percent fewer seats in the House of Representatives. Never mind that, says CRT.

For a historically accurate understanding of US citizenship, Francis Fukuyama reminds us that Founders explicitly rejected the global standard of nation-ethnicity, writing that the "creedal understanding of American identity emerged as the result of a long struggle stretching over nearly two centuries and represented a decisive break" with monocultural European norms. And he warns that the virulent form of identity politics on the fringes of the right and the left today "is deeply problematic because it returns to understandings of identity based on fixed characteristics such as race, ethnicity, and religion, which had earlier been defeated at great cost."[22]

If the CRT narrative of an irredeemably racist system did represent the dominant US culture today, then millions of Africans wouldn't want to immigrate here. Census figures show that in 1980, there were a mere 130,000 immigrants from sub-Saharan African countries living in the United States. This population doubled in 1990 and rocketed to 691,000 in 2000. Since the 9/11 attacks, a million more sub-Saharan Africans have immigrated to America, bringing the total population to 2 million today. This is a profound testament to the American creed.

The nuanced reality is that the United States is not a country with a dominant culture, and it never was. American culture has forever been polyglot, mixed, and dynamic. Original while never aboriginal. This isn't to deny the existence of bigotry and racism in the nation's history but rather to deny its centrality. What is central is not racial division but the melting pot and the yearning of refugees to join it.

The paradox for the American left is that it wants to deny American exceptionalism while also welcoming unlimited foreign refugees. Its internal debate has become so twisted that any enforcement of immigrant limits is condemned as racist, while any celebration of American citizenship is considered nativist. The 2020 chant to "Abolish ICE" enthralled political rallies but alarmed centrist Democrats. At a deeper level, the abolition of border enforcement and granting of full rights to foreign migrants calls into question whether national citizenship has any meaning or value at all to the fringe left.

Citizenship is an automatic birthright for anyone born on US soil, a principle known as *jus soli* that descends from English common law. It is nearly universal in the New World, in contrast to the Old World principle of *jus sanguinis*, where the nationality or ethnicity of the parents is passed along to children regardless of birthplace. The United States codified *jus soli* with the adoption of the Fourteenth Amendment in 1868, which states: "All persons born or naturalized in the United States, and subject to the jurisdiction thereof, are citizens of the United States and of the State wherein they reside." Critics on the right have called for the principle to be overturned, which is disturbing, but no more disturbing than extremists on the left who want to abolish citizenship in all practicality.

If the borders were open and there were no limits on foreigners who could come to live in America, that might be okay. But what if they had no obligations of citizenship? What happens to civil society then? The warning of George Borjas—that democratic institutions might erode at the hands of unassimilated immigrants—has newfound importance. It is perhaps the only legitimate concern about large-scale immigration, even though it has, to date, no empirical support.

In the American experience, patriotic assimilation has proven to be a success based on the best evidence of three surveys presented here. The American dream is known and embraced by millions of foreign-born people who are drawn to this culture, culminating in an oath to defend the Constitution. Immigration is cultural confirmation.

Chapter 15
Americans

Now, this country is a constant work in progress. We were born with instructions: to form a more perfect union. Explicit in those words is the idea that we are imperfect; that what gives each new generation purpose is to take up the unfinished work of the last and carry it further than anyone might have thought possible.

— **Barack Obama**

The Ugly American started as a novel and ended as a catchphrase. It's used off-hand today to describe callous superpower tourists who don't speak the languages of the places they travel. Ugly Americans aren't there to conquer, that's so last century. It's an imperialism by credit card, an ignorance of culture beyond what Hollywood appropriates. The title entered the vernacular of global elites and never left. New money, no class.

The eponymous novel was more sophisticated and a surprise sensation on its publication in 1958. The book was a non-fiction analysis about diplomacy in Southeast Asia, converted to fiction at the urging of its publisher. John Kennedy was so impressed that he sent a copy of *The Ugly American* to each of his fellow senators. He was inspired by its message to shake up American foreign policy with the Peace Corps, the Green Berets, and the strategy of counterinsurgency in the bubbling Vietnam conflict. LBJ mentioned it during speeches in 1964, remembering its core message that Soviet diplomats in the fictional country of Sarkhan were culturally sensitive in treating the local people with respect whereas Americans were loud, obnoxious, and haughty. One of the main foreign characters visits the United States and finds its immigration officers are "cold almost to the point of insult."

The catchphrase lives on, even though the underlying reality has changed entirely. LBJ's revolution of America's immigration laws in 1965 marked the first abrupt and permanent change, driven by a desire to change America's perception in the world and of the world. Then in 1990, George H. W. Bush doubled down on that exceptional openness. As a result, today there is no nation more welcoming of foreigners than the United States.

The misperception that Americans are hostile to immigration is a figment of the media's imagination. Politicians are often portrayed as strongly hostile to immigration, which is another media exaggeration, but one thing is certain: the American public in the 2020s is more united and supportive of legal immigration than ever before. That disconnect between media portrayal and reality motivated me to dig into decades of public polling and even conduct a few polls myself.

The most startling finding in polling data is that the American people are more positive about immigration and ethnic diversity than the people of Europe. In a 2015 cross-country study, the Pew Research Center showed some striking anti-immigrant sentiment in the southern, eastern, and northern countries of Europe. The percentage who said that immigrants are a benefit versus those who said they are a burden split 51–41 in the United States, about the same as in the United Kingdom and a far more positive ratio than every European country. As you will recall from earlier in the book, Gallup has found that support among Americans for increasing immigration has gone up dramatically in the past twenty years.

In a separate 2016 cross-country study, Pew asked this question: "Do you think having an increasing number of people of many different races, ethnic groups and nationalities in our country makes this country a better or worse place to live?" Not a single European country had a majority favoring more diversity, but America did. Only 7 percent of Americans said that diversity made the country worse, but in Europe, the "worse" response rate ranged from a low of 22 percent in Spain to a high of 63 percent in Greece. France, England, Italy, Sweden, and every other country studied were far less welcoming than the United States. In Germany, the ratio of better/worse respondents was 1 to 1, compared to the ratio in the United States, where it was over 8 to 1.

All this goes to show that something changed in the United States after the *Ugly American* was published. In the wake of the postwar order when the nation took up the mantle of global leadership, maintained a Cold Peace with the Soviets, and fostered dozens of international organizations to promote economic development on every continent, it also made good on its creedal ideal. One might even say that the ugly American is a bit like the ugly duckling. He grew up into something exceptional.

What the American People Really Think

Dave Brady is famously cantankerous and hilarious, a distinguished political scientist at Stanford University and a colleague of mine at the Hoover Institution. A few years ago, we talked about how thin most public survey questions are on the topic of immigration. Dave agreed to work with me to develop a new survey of American public attitudes focused entirely on immigration. It turned out our timing was perfect, with Donald Trump elected and immigration being his signature issue. After a year of preparation, we had a lengthy and careful set of nearly thirty questions that we fielded early in the summer of 2017. We repeated the survey for this book with some new and modified questions in January 2020, bits of which I highlighted in previous chapters.

Our main objective was to go into greater depth than traditional public opinion polls. For example, Gallup typically asks whether immigrants are perceived as more of a benefit or a burden, then dig no deeper. Dave and I asked what specific aspects of immigration are considered beneficial or burdensome. Do economic concerns about jobs and wages matter more or less than cultural concerns? We also investigated whether there are different types of immigrants who are viewed as more/less favorable. Finally, our survey assessed the strength of support for a wide array of specific policy reforms.

We asked a question about general attitudes toward immigration in 2017 and 2020, offering respondents a scale from 1 to 7 to indicate whether they "lean closer to helping integrate immigrants into society (1) or closer to encouraging immigrants to leave the country (7)." In 2017, 44 percent of all respondents leaned toward "helping integrate" compared to 35 percent leaning toward "encouraging to leave." The 2020 results were unchanged. A majority of Democrats checked the two most welcoming responses, whereas Republicans and Independents were more evenly spread over the seven options. In fact, Democrats skewed more toward welcoming than any age, income, or even any ethnic cohort. Neither Republican nor Democratic attitudes shifted significantly from 2017 to 2020.

For more than twenty years, Pew has been asking whether "immigrants today (a) strengthen our country because of their hard work and talents," or "(b) are a burden on our country because they take our jobs, housing and health care." In 1994, when the question was first asked, the public chose burden over benefit by a 2-to-1 ratio, but opinions swung dramatically in the ensuing years and by 2016 were at the other extreme, 1-to-2. Asking this question verbatim, Dave and I added a third response "equally a benefit and a burden," a response favored by 2 in 5 respondents. However, we also confirmed that Americans' attitudes today are more supportive than in decades past.

What aspects of legal immigration are considered beneficial or burdensome? We described six "negative things" including crime, welfare, jobs, culture, voting, and neighborhoods. It turns out, there was a tendency for a person who thinks of immigration in a negative light to rank all of the issues as problematic with little variation. There was one exception. The most negatively rated burden was "using welfare benefits," a concern of a majority of Americans. Ten percent fewer people were concerned about crime and taking jobs from US workers, and 15 percent fewer were concerned about voting or eroding American culture. The least concerning issue was that immigrants would lower property values. Democrats tended to be less negative, but they worry about one issue more than Republicans and Independents: immigrants taking jobs.

On the positive side, Americans tended to rate specific benefits higher across the board compared to burdens by an average of 10 percentage points. Sixty percent of respondents agreed immigration brings valuable scientists to America and also workers who take on tough jobs that native-born citizens don't want to do. Sixty percent also agreed that immigrants add to cultural and religious diversity. Just under 60 percent agreed that immigrants affirm America's national heritage. A bare majority agreed that an important benefit is the population boost immigrants bring.

The takeaway from these data is that putting limits on access to welfare will make American voters more comfortable with expanding immigration. Maybe that means a longer waiting period before green card holders can become citizens. Likewise, the raw political calculus is that Democrats are likely to be less welcoming to work-based migrants because they are more susceptible to the lump-of-labor fallacy. That casts a rather dark cloud over proposals to adopt "merit-based" reform because it may well dull Democratic enthusiasm for immigration in the long term.

Refugees

How did our respondents feel about the thousands of refugees from Honduras, Guatemala, and El Salvador who overwhelmed the US-Mexico border before the Covid-19 lockdown? A majority felt the United States "has a responsibility to accept immigrants who are fleeing violent conditions in their home country," but only 44 percent agreed that anyone claiming asylum should be automatically accepted. There has to be a screening process.

The reality is that most people are not aware of the nuances of civil strife in faraway places. They expect their own government officials to apply fair rules to foreigners seeking entry. And when it comes to claiming asylum, a fair rule is that political violence is grounds for seeking international refuge whereas criminal and domestic violence are not. Seventy percent of our respondents think that US policy "should define refugees as people from a country where the government is repressive, not just a place with gang violence and poverty." As for the asylum process, 62 percent feel that potential asylees should have to wait in their home country or in Mexico for their cases to be decided.

Let us recognize that there is a critical difference between a refugee and a person seeking asylum. The refugee is someone who asks permission to come to your country at the local embassy or through some other intermediary while residing in their homeland. The asylee is someone who arrives at your border, port, airport, or checkpoint unannounced. Journalists and scholars often mix the terms and use "refugee" as a blanket to describe both. However, international law treats asylum-seekers separately.

Refugee rights and state obligations have evolved rapidly since they were first articulated in the United Nations 1951 Refugee Convention, a treaty offering universal recognition to refugees as those with a "well-founded fear of being persecuted for reasons of race, religion, nationality, membership of a particular social group or political opinion" in their homeland. The 1951 agreement was aimed specifically at communist repression in Europe, but the definition was extended to include all persons outside of Europe in 1967. The right to seek asylum is guaranteed in international law, but there is no guarantee it will be granted to all applicants, and states generally deny asylum to applicants who are arriving from a "safe third country."

The idea that refugees should have to wait in Mexico for entry into the United States is a bone of contention for refugee advocates but one that makes sense to average Americans. When a state falls into civil war or tyranny— think of Venezuela's sad collapse into socialism under Hugo Chavez and Nicolas Maduro—its citizens should flee and deserve every right to be welcome in neighboring countries. That is not a right to walk through countries A, B, and C to get to their preferred destination in country D. And to argue that Mexico isn't safe for refugees is an insult to Mexico, which is a prosperous democracy and longtime ally of the United States.

Nevertheless, legal advocates have argued that "safe third countries" must be agreed on by treaty. A precedent was set between Canada and the United States in 2002, though common sense suggests that Canada is safe for asylum even without that legalism in place. Nevertheless, the Obama and Trump administrations found themselves tied up in legal challenges when trying to block a surge of unqualified asylum applicants at the Mexican border. President Trump successfully negotiated "safe third country" agreements with a few Central American countries and instituted Migrant Protection Protocols (MPP) to deny admission to asylum seekers while their cases are considered. For the past two decades, asylum has been denied to about 60 percent of applicants. The Supreme Court overturned a challenge to the MPP program in early 2020, and its ultimate determination will hinge on whether making applicants wait in Mexico or Canada is the same as returning them to their homeland.

Reforms

Despite what seems to be the prevailing sentiment in the media, only one-third of Americans think that "open borders" would be good for immigration policy, making it by far the least popular of the immigration policies that we asked about in our survey. Table 15.1 shows American policy preferences on a 4-point scale, and it lists them in order of support (a combination of people marking "Strongly agree" and "Agree"). This series of questions considered

Table 15.1 Public policy preferences for immigration reform in 2020, ranked from most to least popular

	Strongly agree	Agree	Disagree	Strongly disagree
E-verify mandatory in all states	42%	37%	16%	5%
English the official language of the United States	47%	31%	13%	9%
Birthright citizenship for any child born on US soil	32%	37%	19%	13%
Prison terms for criminal illegal immigrants who re-enter after deportation	34%	34%	21%	10%
End catch-and-release	38%	30%	20%	12%
Green cards for STEM graduates of US colleges	18%	49%	26%	7%
Shift to merit-based green cards	17%	47%	29%	7%
Presidential discretion to ban foreign travelers	34%	28%	25%	13%
Legal status, not pathway, for illegal immigrants	13%	45%	26%	16%
Penalties for US sanctuary cities	32%	24%	22%	22%
Completion of the US-Mexico border wall	34%	22%	19%	25%
Auction H1-Bs (high skill work visas)	11%	42%	33%	14%
Increase refugee quotas	16%	30%	34%	20%
Open borders	10%	22%	30%	39%

fourteen distinct policies, though we could easily have asked about 300. We chose these to suggest a diverse set of policies that could serve as building blocks for incremental reform.

The most popular policy is use of E-verify, a program that electronically verifies the citizenship and legal work status of employees. It is required by some states but not mandated by the federal government. Four of five people agree that it would be good for US immigration policy to require employers in all 50 states to electronically verify the work status of everyone they employ. Recall that our survey oversampled foreign-born citizens in order to make statistically valid contrasts between them and native-born citizens as well as to compare the attitudes within the sample of non-citizen residents. Our main reason for this was to assess patriotic feelings and to show that fears of institutional erosion were misplaced, but it also meant that we could find whether there are contrasting views of different policies. Perhaps foreign-born Americans would find some programs offensive while others had no objections to them. Interestingly, support for nearly every one of the policy reforms we suggested was higher among foreign-born citizens than among US-born citizens, and in many cases, support was just as high among non-citizens. For E-verify, 79 percent of native-born Americans agreed that the program should be mandated federally and 82 percent of foreign-born citizens felt the same way. Table 15.2 highlights some of these contrasts.

Should English be the official language of the United States? An identical 49 percent of native and naturalized citizens agreed strongly with this idea, and an additional 31 percent agreed (not strongly). Another popular policy

Table 15.2 Attitudes of native-born and naturalized citizens (percentage who agree with the following statements)

	Native-born US citizens	Naturalized US citizens
The United States is an exceptional country	79%	84%
English should be the official language of the U.S.	79%	80%
Americans benefit from a more ethnically diverse population	70%	72%
Prison terms for criminal illegal immigrants who re-enter after deportation	68%	76%
Grant legal status for illegal immigrants	56%	63%
Complete the U.S.-Mexico border wall	55%	65%
Fully support freedom of speech, including "hate speech"	50%	58%

in our survey is not a reform but a continuation of the policy of birthright citizenship, or *jus soli*. That policy could not be changed without a constitutional amendment given that it is currently enshrined in the Fourteenth Amendment. However, rolling it back is a popular topic of discussion among some conservative activists. Yet in our polling, those who identify as conservatives are split evenly on the idea.

There is majority support for many of the policies that we tested, but "strong" agreement for two additional issues stood out. Keep in mind that these two policies are supported by a solid majority of Democratic voters, as well as Republicans. The first was harsher penalties for criminal migrants who cross the border illegally multiple times. We found 68 percent agreement for "Prison terms of 10–25 years for illegal immigrants who re-enter the US after being convicted of certain crimes here and deported" and half of that was "strong" support. Although we did not name Kate Steinle (the young woman who was shot in San Francisco in 2015), this policy has already been introduced in Congress. Only 10 percent of Americans strongly disagree with it. The second policy with such strong support is related to tightening asylum procedures. Again, 68 percent favored a policy to "Immediately return immigrants caught illegally crossing over the border with Mexico, instead of releasing them to live freely inside the U.S. pending a trial." The de facto policy is known as catch-and-release, and Americans do not like it. With such a policy in place, migrants have every incentive to come to a port of entry, not jump the wall, and promise to show up for a court hearing which will occur months in the future. Many fail to show up, and if they do, many refuse to comply with removal orders.

A more likely candidate for bipartisan action is "Offer permanent U.S. residence to science and engineering graduates of U.S. universities who are foreign-born." It's a top priority for tech companies around the country, one that Steve Jobs famously harangued President Obama about during a private dinner. Seventy-five percent of Democrats favor it. Sixty-one percent of Republicans favor it. There truly is no demographic opposed to this reform, with the exception of Washington politicians holding it hostage to all-or-nothing comprehensive negotiations without end.

Disagreement still exists regarding the issue of amnesty and its extension to those who have lived as illegal immigrants in the United States for many years. One-third of participants (34%) supported giving amnesty to all immigrants. A third supported amnesty only for children or immigrants who were brought here as children (34%), and a third opposed amnesty altogether (32%). In another question, we found bare majority support for providing a pathway to citizenship for illegal immigrants who spoke English, paid a fine, and passed a background check. Our findings were in sharp disagreement with a similar survey performed by the Pew Research Center, showing that 67% of their respondents wanted to establish a way for immigrants illegally in the United States to legally remain in the United States. Pew's respondents were divided on whether illegal immigrants should be deported, with 54% wanting to increase the deportation of illegal immigrants.

We all know, of course, that the way survey questions are phrased has a powerful effect on the results. But sometimes a single word is understood differently by different ears. Part of the confusion surrounding amnesty for illegal immigrants is the definition. Our survey confirmed this is exactly what's happening. Dave Brady and I included a question that teased out whether different treatments of illegal immigrants amounted to "amnesty" in the minds of the American people. What if instead of citizenship, they were offered a permanent legal status? Forty-six percent of our respondents call it an amnesty, but 29 percent say it isn't. Ironically, more Republicans thought permanent legal status was an amnesty than thought granting a pathway to citizenship (if it included paying a fine) was an amnesty.

This tension and confusion are why Congress should put the issue last on its reform list. Figuring out a consensus reform on illegal immigrants residing in the United States is the hardest reform of all, and it will only be solved once a working coalition has been established between centrists in Congress. Barring that, it would be pointless for policymakers and elected officials to attempt to negotiate potential amnesty paths to citizenship for the nation's undocumented residents.

Democrats Lost

The Democratic Party is losing its balance on immigration. The Pew Research Center found that the ratio of people who favor increased versus decreased legal immigration was 1-to-2 among Democrats fifteen years ago, but has flipped 3-to-1 as recently as 2018. Republican voters have also become more favorable to increased immigration, but the policy shift has become increasingly hardline among progressives. In 2017, Peter Beinart, the former editor of the *New Republic*, wrote, "A decade ago, liberals publicly questioned immigration in ways that would shock many progressives today."

Look no further than the party platforms adopted every four years by Democrats in contrast with Republicans. Somewhat symbolic of Trump's effect on the GOP, the Republican Party did not adopt a new platform in 2020, opting instead to reaffirm the 2016 version. The president did, however, issue his own statement of principles that included a multi-point emphasis on immigration under the headline, "End Illegal Immigration and Protect American Workers." Truth be told, all of his points are in line with policies that a majority of voters support. There was no mention of legal immigration.

Democrats were different. As Peter Beinart explained, the Democratic platform shifted dramatically on the immigration issue from 2008 to 2012 and even further in 2016. Gone are the "To be sure" caveats that enforcement of the law matters, replaced with full-throated embrace of immigrant rights, legal and illegal, over every moderating concern. Worse, any opposition to immigration is now viewed through the lens of racism, even though the numbers of immigrants from Latin America (especially Mexico) are flat, or even negative while immigration from East and South Asia is on the rise. Concerns of established constituencies on the left, particularly the unions that Bernie Sanders voiced until he was roundly chastised in 2015, have been totally displaced by neo-progressives who embrace what amounts to open borders. Sanders mocked open borders as a "Koch brothers" scheme to hurt workers at the time, and quickly "evolved" after a backlash in the presidential primary. These are not beliefs of the middle class or independent voters; they are beliefs of leftist activists who have transformed the Democratic Party and pushed it to the fringe.

During the 1990s, Democratic and Republican voters had nearly identical favorability toward immigrants according to the Pew Research Center, whose polls showed a mere 5-percentage-point gap between voters of both parties. In fact, during a debate in 1980 between Ronald Reagan and George H. W. Bush, both men called for a more open border with Mexico.

What changed? After conservative pundits rallied against President George W. Bush's 2006 comprehensive reform proposals, opinions diverged sharply among Democratic and Republican voters. Then in 2012, Republican nominee Mitt Romney repositioned himself as an immigration hardliner. By the time of the 2016 debates, moderates like John Kasich, Jeb Bush, and Marco Rubio simply had no appeal to the base voters. I wrote about the GOP debates at the time and noted that the one overriding sentiment was that there should be no amnesty for illegal immigrants. Democrats meanwhile have become increasingly focused on identity politics and have abandoned any hint of nationalism.

The 2020 Democratic platform blamed "exclusionary immigration" for racial injustice. The main emphasis of the platform's multiple pages concerning immigration took aim at Trump's policies and "xenophobia." Much of the language affirmed the vitality of immigration, but it constantly veered toward policy specifics that are not supported by the public, such as legislation to rescind the presidential authority over visas and screening at ports of entry and removing discretion over asylum applications: "We will reverse Trump Administration policies that prevent victims of gang and domestic violence, as well as LGBTQ+ people who are unsafe in their home countries, from being eligible to apply for asylum."

Perhaps the most tone-deaf policy of the Democratic National Committee (DNC) is complete opposition to the "unnecessary, wasteful, and ineffective wall on the southern border." When Dave Brady and I surveyed the American public, we found healthy support for completing and strengthening the wall. Fifty-six percent agreed, yet of the level of "strong" disagreement was higher than any other policy. When we dug into the details, we found more support for the wall among foreign-born citizens than native-born by a 10 percent margin. There is some variation by ethnicity, but even Hispanics are split evenly on support for the wall. The only demographic group that disagrees with the wall is registered Democratic voters, with 74 percent opposed to the policy. That is double the opposition that exists among Independent voters, and nearly triple the opposition expressed by foreign-born citizens. Democrats can go a lot further in attracting centrist voters if they pair support for higher legal immigration with a genuine concern about stopping illegal immigration.

Dreams and a New Diversity

The national population has always been profoundly diverse compared to other countries—ethnically, religiously, culturally. There's arguably more diversity among the major cities along the Mississippi River (Minneapolis, St. Louis, and New Orleans) than along any other major river in the world. The Danube runs through Vienna, Bratislava, and Belgrade, and the similarities among its peoples seem far stronger than those in the central American states. Minnesotans are famously nicknamed "Vikings" in recognition of the heavy concentration of Swedes and Norwegians who settled there in the 1800s, and today 10 percent of the state's population is foreign-born. Meanwhile, the thriving metropolis of St. Louis remains the great crossing point at the heart of the continent and today has one of the largest African American populations of any city. New Orleans is world famous for its eclectic mix of French and Creole culture, a vital port that has evolved into a global tourist hub. The great diversity within each of these cities is possible because of America's comfort with racial and class equality. But the diversity among American cities also affirms the national motto: *e pluribus unum*.

Unlike any other country in the world, the United States actually dedicates thousands of visas to a category for diversity, hosting a global lottery every year which gives billions of people around the world a chance to legally move and join the American people. There's never been a country in the world that did such a thing.

I met an Uber driver a few years ago, a delightfully joyous and talkative man with a thick accent and deep voice, who had immigrated and was thankful, so very thankful, because America had saved him, his wife, and their two daughters. When I asked where he was from, he said, "Persia!" and I chuckled. "You mean Iran, yes, my friend?" And he laughed. He told me that he had been putting his name in for the lottery visa every year for sixteen years, ever since the day his wife gave birth to their first child. "You do not want to have a daughter in a country such as Iran, where she can have no freedom. No dreams." And for sixteen years he could not find his name on this list of US diversity visa winners. Until finally, when his eldest daughter turned sixteen, "Allah answered my prayers and we won the lottery to come to America." I have never met a prouder man. Of course, his education qualified him for better things than being an Uber driver, but he was thankful, eternally thankful.

In 1990, President George H. W. Bush implemented the Diversity Visa (DV) program to welcome immigrants from countries that had historically been underrepresented. Because most legal immigrants have been selected via family connections since 1965, there has been a path dependency that in a sense rewarded countries that got the ball rolling earlier. This pattern occurs often in immigration histories, with enclaves forming in a host country that act as a gravitational pull to people from the same region and even town in the sending country. Those enclaves actually help new arrivals to ease their transition and, ironically, to assimilate to the new country's laws, procedures, and norms. With an uncle or sister to guide a recent immigrant, the newcomer learns far more quickly how to drive, where to bank, how to rent a home, and where to get groceries.

President Bush saw the strength of the existing family-based system: The Immigration Act of 1990 doubled the numbers of family-based green cards. But he wanted to supplement it as well with this new program that would welcome immigrants from neglected places. It makes 50,000 immigrant visas available every year, drawn from a random selection of individuals who apply; it is available only for applicants in countries with low numbers of immigrants in the previous five years. Yet the applicant pool is immense. Ten to twenty million people apply every year.

The diversity lottery has been criticized for its randomness, and as an open door for foreign terrorists and criminals, which is laughable. A foreign terrorist would much more likely obtain a temporary visa to vacation at the Grand Canyon than to try for the 1-in-400 odds of winning the green card lottery. Besides, applicants must pass an education and criminal background check. Nearly 200 million foreign visitors come to the United States annually, thousands of times more than those who are selected for the diversity visa.

And last, the data show that green card holders are massively less likely than US citizens to commit crimes, with diversity visa winners the least likely of all.

From a diplomatic perspective, the diversity lottery is a tremendous success. It represents a sharp turnabout from the Ugly American diplomacy of the past century. Can you imagine the Soviets offering a lottery to the people of the world? Beijing? Instead, the United States diversity visa is a tangible beacon of hope to oppressed people everywhere. It will be remembered as a highlight of American culture a thousand years from now.

Chapter 16
Futures

All dreaded it, all sought to avert it. . . . Both parties deprecated war, but one of them would make war rather than let the nation survive, and the other would accept war rather than let it perish. And the war came.
Abraham Lincoln

There are reasonable leaders in China who hope to avoid a war with the United States, mirroring those in the United States working to lower tensions and avoid open conflict. And there are nationalists and provocateurs on both sides who stoke grievances and nudge the superpowers toward greater hostility.

Nothing is inevitable, and though it is hard to imagine total war in the nuclear age, it is not hard to imagine new forms of violence that might be deployed in the coming century if tempers flare. Weaponizing a virus comes to mind. Cyber-attacks on financial databases. Political subterfuge and advanced algorithms that undermine civil trust on social networks. Nothing is certain today either, just as the past century's leaders could not know with certainty that Japan would feel compelled to attack Pearl Harbor in 1941 or that Khrushchev would pull back from the Cuban Missile Crisis in 1962. Perhaps the best we can say is that the odds are 50–50 that this new Sino-American superpower rivalry avoids outright conflict.

If the war comes, should not every possible action be taken to maximize American strength now? If your answer is yes, then consider immigration in a new light. A larger, younger, more patriotic population will be achieved with more immigration, not less. The questions is, What reforms could strengthen the country, militarily, economically, culturally, technologically?

On the other hand, we should also ask, What actions can policymakers take to prevent conflict? Here, too, the wiser policy orientation is to increase immigration levels. More Chinese immigrants today mean deeper familial ties and a deeper, more sympathetic understanding between countries. Prevention and power both demand a fresh look at immigration from a strategic perspective. As I said in the first chapter, ultimately the United States needs an immigration system that preserves American exceptionalism well into the 22nd century.

China has a bigger population and proportionally lower productivity, yielding an economy roughly the same size as the United States. Beijing's government oversees a nation that has grown miraculously and is rightfully proud of the great material and social progress made since the deft leadership of Deng Xiaoping. Yet the Communist Party is fundamentally anti-democratic. And the country has a prideful national identity based on thousands of years of ethno-cultural unity compared to the wide-open egalitarian creedal national identity of the United States.

A recent Georgetown University study of science and engineering graduate students across the United States found that the vast majority intend to stay in the United States rather than return to their home countries. "Graduates from China, India, and Iran have the highest intention-to-stay rates (around or above 90 percent), while graduates from the European Union, Canada, Turkey, and elsewhere are lower (historically at around 65 to 75 percent). Over time, intention-to-stay rates have increased or held steady for most countries."[1] Furthermore, half of all leading AI researchers study at US graduate schools (five times more than China), and 53 percent worked in the United States (also five times more than China).[2] These AI researchers are working for American tech companies like Google, often doing work to enhance America's national security. This is a war for talent, and the United States is winning, for now.

The Covid-19 pandemic, which originated in Wuhan, China, will be a source of antagonism for decades, not just with the relatively wealthy nations of North America and Europe but with the developing world as well. The year 2020 represented a sea change in world affairs, and the post-2020 landscape will be profoundly different from what will in retrospect be seen as the glowing three decades of techno-globalization that started in 1989 with the collapse of the Soviet side of the Cold War. Not knowing the contours of the new era, we should take stock of the global balance of power and major trendlines.

This could be the beginning of the end of mass immigration flows if Covid-19 mutates into something more than a historically mild pandemic. Surely, some countries will erect barriers to physical travel and trade that would have been unimaginable if, or when, new viruses are unleashed on the world. But many countries won't. Most countries will adopt smart, balanced policies that optimize economic vitality with biological security. And the demographic pressures that are the ultimate drivers of migration will remain just as powerful, though perhaps constrained to a smaller set of receiving countries. In other words, the post-2020 world may be a greater opportunity for the United States to enhance the brains, brawn, and bravery of foreign-born people who hope to join the American tribe.

A global survey by Gallup taken a few years before the pandemic found that nearly 150 million people would migrate to the United States if they were allowed. That makes it the most popular destination, larger than the next four most popular countries combined. Those potential migrants represent one out of every twenty-five people in the world, and would increase the population of the United States by half. They want to come, but will America let them in?

A Richer, Older World

America could maintain the same immigration system that it's had for the past fifty years, welcoming 1 million immigrants per year, but straightaway we will experience a very different immigrant. That's because the world itself is transforming. First, the world is richer, both overall and on a per capita basis. Second, the demography of every country is shifting radically as people are healthier, live longer, and have fewer children. The net result is that the character of mass migrations will shift to a richer, older, and better educated mix. Despite the prosperity boom, income inequality continues to dominate US political debates.

A few years ago, a French economist named Thomas Piketty became famous worldwide on the publication of his book cheekily named after Karl Marx's famous book: *Capital.* Piketty caused a sensation by highlighting rising income and wealth inequality in the United States and Europe, especially his claim that inequality is just as severe today as it was a hundred years ago. For those who have lived long enough to have witnessed dozens of life-improving innovations, from the microwave oven to the Internet, Piketty's argument seems hard to square with reality. Nor can those who read the book avoid more strident language, such as the part where Piketty wrote: "The poorer half of the population are as poor today as they were in the past, with barely 5 percent of total wealth in 2010, just as in 1910. Basically, all the middle class managed to get its hands on was a few crumbs."

This is simply wrong. The ratio of incomes of the poorest group relative to the richest group may be unchanged. That's inequality for you. But if everyone's income has doubled, or tripled, or grown by a factor of ten (as has actually happened), then it's scholarly malpractice to claim that people are just as "poor" (his words) and have only experienced "crumbs" (his words). Set aside a discussion of average incomes in the United States for a moment, and let's consider the whole world. According to data from the United Nations and the World Bank, the total value of the world economy was $11.8 trillion in 1961. That's $11,832,723,884,098 inflation-adjusted dollars using purchasing power to compare the GDP of different countries. That amounts to $3,800 per person. That may seem meager, and goes to show how much poorer the world was in 1961. Yet the most recent data for 2017 show the world economy is producing almost eight times as much, or $80.2 trillion, which amounts to over $10,600 per person.

The surging prosperity is not caused by rich countries getting richer. Poorer countries have grown far faster. China is arguably the most miraculous of the East Asian miracles, as the typical Chinese peasant was far poorer than the average African not so long ago. Likewise, measures of human development such as literacy, health, and civil rights show astounding progress. Scan the World Bank's Human Development Index (HDI) 2020 report, and you cannot find a single country—not even Libya—whose 1990 HDI measure was better than 2020. Our era is a story of relentless, universal progress. Children living longer, young girls learning to read, diseases beaten back. Just to take one example, the wifi bandwidth that was available to the richest countries in 2007 when the iPhone was launched was a tenth of the average bandwidth available in the poorest countries in 2020.

If material progress is difficult to measure, immaterial progress is impossible to measure. Although the most common fatal conditions of 1910 have been cured, try to imagine getting a cancer diagnosis a century ago. The five-year survival rate for breast cancer today is 91 percent in the United States, much better than the 75 percent rate in 1975. But in 1910, the survival rate was zero. You survived breast cancer only if you were misdiagnosed.

And consider the dangers of birth in 1910. Of every 100 births, one mother died. According to the Centers of Disease Control, 10 percent of newborns died before their first birthday. In the century since, infant mortality has declined by over 90 percent, while maternal mortality declined by 99 percent.

Piketty could hardly have picked a worse year for his comparison. Most homes did not have electricity in 1910 and few had indoor plumbing. Refrigerators wouldn't be invented for years and wouldn't become common in American homes until the 1950s. Today, refrigerators are in almost 100 percent of US homes, rich and poor, just like microwave ovens and vacuum cleaners. Even poorer, developing countries such as Thailand, China, and Brazil have refrigerator ownership rates of 70 to 95 percent.

Social scientists learned long ago that societies with higher incomes tend to have fewer children. As we discussed earlier in the book, the global economic boom of the past fifty years has caused a global drought of newborns, the "demographic transition" of fertility rates that are below replacement. Central American countries, the poorest in the Western hemisphere, are suddenly population stable. That means the so-called immigration problem of yesteryear (too many) is shortly going to transition to a new problem for advanced economies (too few). Cheap farm labor is likely a thing of the past.

There are famously 11 million illegal immigrants hiding in the shadows of the US economy. Yet that number has not risen in over a decade. If anything, there are fewer illegal immigrants in this country than there were a decade ago, and that stability was caused more by demographic push factors than by increased border security during the past twenty years. Outmigration from the United States to Mexico is the new normal. But this is bigger than Mexico. With birth rates per woman throughout Latin American countries falling from seven to two, the supply of migrant labor is drying up. It may well be that the immigration crisis America will face after 2020 is a drought, not a wave, of foreigners willing to come and do the hard work in fields and factories.

Make no mistake, a dwindling supply of workers to do labor-intensive jobs has a silver lining: the poorest workers globally are going to get a raise. Incomes are rising, or galloping in historical context. That just accelerates the demographic process. It may be a virtuous cycle, but it's a cycle with strategic global consequences.

American Families Versus Foreign Merit

Unlike any other country, the United States prioritizes family reunification when considering applicants for permanent residency. Canada, for example, introduced a point-based system in 1967 in which a person qualifies for immigration into the country only with a score of 67 points or higher, with points awarded for higher education, younger age, work experience, literacy, and a five-point bonus for familial relations. Every country in Europe has a similar merit-bias toward education and skills. The United States is the exception.

Many scholars, on the right and left, think that the states should consider a similar "merit-based" immigration system. I used to agree, thinking only about how to maximize the economy. Now, after looking at immigration as an element of geopolitical strategy and national security, I'm not so sure.

There are four pathways for legal migration to the United States: family, employer, refugee status, and the unique diversity lottery. Each pathway is independent, meaning a foreigner could qualify for two or more types of permanent visas. Family visas count for 70 percent of immigration to the United States, and there is a tremendous upside to that for patriotic assimilation.

There are actually two categories for family-based immigrants. The top priority is given to immediate family members of a US citizen—spouse, young children, and parents—with no limits on the number of green cards that can be awarded annually to this category. Between 250,000 and 300,000 spouses have been welcomed annually in recent years. Parents and children combined made up around 200,000 per year. The second category is "Family Preference" and is capped annually, which means there is a prioritized waiting list. This includes older children and siblings of citizens as well as immediate relatives of legal US residents who aren't yet citizens. Over 200,000 green cards of this kind are granted annually.

There are hard ceilings, or quotas, for the other pathways: 50,000 diversity visas; 140,000 employment-based visas (EBs); and a legislated target for refugees (not asylees) that has varied between 60,000 and 100,000 per year, though presidents exercise much more discretion. Also, no sending country can account for more than 7 percent of the total annual number of family-sponsored and employment-based visas, resulting in a lengthy backlog for some countries. The processing time for people from some countries has been more than twenty years.

The employment-based (EB) visa green cards are the most similar to a Canadian-style points system, though the employment categories are actually quite rigid. For example, there is a numerical limit of 40,000 for EB-1 priority workers, including people with demonstrated "extraordinary ability" in the arts, sciences, and a few other categories. Imagine demonstrating your ability with a Pulitzer Prize, Olympic medal, or patent for a life-saving medical device. You don't need those achievements if you have a PhD in engineering, but you will need to be sponsored by an American company. That makes sense, but one wonders: why is there a numerical limit in the first place? What about that 40,001st applicant, Rani the computer scientist from Mumbai with a sponsorship by Lockheed who has the misfortune of not making the bureaucratic cut? Why cut her at all? A lot of politicians have asked that question, which has been translated into a bipartisan push to massively expand the allotments of employer-sponsored green cards.

Merit is well and good conceptually, but it's vulnerable to legislative gamesmanship. One recent proposal under the guise of merit-based reform is more of a wolf in sheep's clothing. It would have reduced the numbers of future legal immigrants, all but eliminating family-based entry of adult children and siblings. That plan also scrapped the core of the current EB visa approach that requires a sponsoring employer in favor of a points system for education and English proficiency. President Trump's merit-based reform proposal, led inside the White House by Jared Kushner and chief economist Kevin Hassett, was much more admirable in that it maintained current levels of legal immigration.

Merit-based systems, for both host and emigré, foster a transactional nature of citizenship that devalues the importance of cultural assimilation. The challenge this book raises is whether assimilation matters at all. Because if it does, we should recognize that the current family-based and employer-sponsored system has performed superbly.

Many countries with merit-based immigration systems, notably those in Western Europe, have struggled with weak assimilation, resentment, and alienation. There are far more serious risks of crime and terrorism festering in European immigrant enclaves. Meanwhile, crime rates are far lower among American immigrants and patriotism measurably higher than among the native-born population. Maybe the unique American system is worth preserving, not getting tossed just because it's "old."

Five Strategies

What makes the American people uniquely dangerous is that they complain more than anyone else in the world. They imagine how something could be better and then are impatient to make it so. And they have no limits on their imagination, no historical experience with the nationwide hardships, castes, and stagnation that curb the dreams of non-Americans. They see oppression or genocide in a country on the other side of the planet and refuse to mind their own business. Presidents represent that urgent confidence to make peace in the Middle East, solving tensions that are thousands of years older than the Constitution. The danger, of course, is that Americans are apt to fix things that aren't broken, and worse, see things as utterly broken when really all that's needed is nudge, a repair, maybe an oil change or a pep talk.

After working on immigration policy for over a decade, I've come to the realization that the conventional wisdom that the system is "broken" is something like that ominous music in a horror movie that comes on whenever the monster is about to strike. Washington politicians are united in the belief that immigration is broken, and many of the reforms would end what has in retrospect been a pillar of American power and prestige for half a century. I hope this book has made an effective case for the strategic advantages of immigration—brains, brawn, and bravery—in addition to its centrality to the national creed. Here in closing, I'd like to focus not so much on policies but on policy strategies. After a lot of thinking, I've narrowed them down to five.

1. **Utilize immigration as a foreign policy tool.** Economics is often described as a way of thinking, and that's the main message I hope readers take away from this book: thinking of immigration in the context of national security, where it properly belongs. Americans should think big about what policies will maximize American power, and not just hard power. The diversity visa is a good example of a program that radiates soft power in a way that is unmatched by rivals, indeed, cannot be matched by authoritarian regimes. It is an ace card in the soft power deck. Don't throw it away.

2. **Develop immigration alliance agreements.** America should be looking for new programs that will leverage our immigration advantage over rivals, but also as a way to bolster alliances. First, when it comes to alliances, it would be wise to question why there are so many limits and restrictions on movement between two friendly countries. Britain and France, for starters, have fought side by side with the United States in two world wars, and three if you count the Cold War. Japan and South Korea have been unflinching allies, along with Germany and Italy, for seventy-five years. Perhaps the next version of economic agreements should be anchored not in the free flow of goods and services but in the unlimited flow of people. This need not mean an open border for citizenship but instead an answer to the question, "Why can an allied citizen visit for no longer than 90 days at a time?"

The United States has a visa waiver program with over thirty countries, meaning that citizens from those countries can fly in and be welcomed with nothing more than a passport. Countries that have been granted this status are wide ranging, including Chile, Norway, Poland, Taiwan, and Australia. Travelers are required to be certified with a background check for criminality, but there are no limits on when they can arrive, so long as they leave within ninety days. The question is why? We're not talking here about migration per se—the granting of citizenship with all it entails—but about free movement. Let's give a serious thought to alliance agreements that allow unlimited two-way travel, with the freedom to work and pay taxes, rent apartments, do research, and study together. Allied citizens would be granted the freedom to live and work permanently, and without needing permission, in America. Bizarrely, Mexico is not one of the countries that has been granted visa waiver status. That should change. A visa waiver will make the whole issue of illegal immigration moot, while providing more labor market flexibility, more tracking of temporary workers, and more security.

3. **Redefine the refugee program to promote human rights**. Historically, refugee policy has focused on individual people seeking refuge. That should not change, but the scope should be reset. My colleague Ayaan Hirsi Ali and others recognize that refugee programs have watered down the definition of refugee and are ripe for abuse. Consequently, the perverse incentives draw foreigners to seek asylum who are by any reasonable understanding economic migrants, not refugees. This is not a criticism. It's no crime to seek a better life. Yet the sad consequence is that America's ability to process asylum claimants has become overwhelmed (as has Europe's).

During the dozen years of Nazi rule in Germany, between 180,000 and 220,000 European refugees were admitted to the United States, according to various estimates (and the United States admitted more than any other country). Compare that to current levels of 300,000 to 500,000 people claiming asylum from Guatemala, Honduras, and El Salvador. It makes no sense. Germany's population then was twice the size of Central America's population today. Are we really to believe that Honduras in 2020 is more repressive than the Holocaust? I draw the analogy not to make the case that we shouldn't have sympathy for Honduran refugees. Rather, I want you to think about the $100 million disbursed to Honduras every year this century in direct US foreign aid. It would be unconscionable to give taxpayer dollars to a country that the federal governments knows is repressive, no?

Real tyranny is alive and well, and we shouldn't confuse it with poverty. The communist government in Beijing is creating a state of surveillance, replete with re-education camps for hundreds of thousands of Uyghurs in Xinjiang province. The once free city-state of Hong Kong is under siege. The people of Venezuela are starving to death in the rubble of a failed state. And all but one person in North Korea deserves to be recognized as enslaved by a police state—and a refugee. Something like 10 million Syrians are displaced in a brutal civil war. It's not as if genuine refugees are hard to find.

So why not call a spade a spade? That is, why not call a dictatorship a dictatorship? Common sense suggests that the State Department should determine whether a country should be listed as "failing" through civil strife or autocracy and that such a designation would then qualify its people as potential refugees. That doesn't guarantee they would receive asylum here, but it would put the world on notice. It would also clear the dockets. If a country is not a designated dictatorship, then its people should not be considered refugees by US officials. Such sharp lines require moral courage at the State Department, and it could help put some teeth in foreign aid policies to discourage repression, corruption, and outright tyranny.

It seems only logical that a nation that has become a failed, corrupt tyranny should not qualify for foreign aid or generous loan programs. FDR did not send foreign aid to Nazi Germany, and the United States should reconsider sending aid to any country that is the source of hundreds of thousands of political refugees.

4. **Set standards, not ceilings.** There is an alternative to the current practice of setting numerical caps on various green card categories. Why not establish standards instead? America already uses standards for non-immigrant travelers, scholars, tourists, and students from abroad: no criminals, drug dealers, or potential terrorists are permitted. Visitors are screened, as they should be. Likewise, there are standards rather than numerical limit on the international flights allowed into Miami, Chicago, and Los Angeles. Using standards for immigration would be a profound transformation in policy, and a win for all politically.

If immigrants come at a cost to the receiving country, then numerical limits makes sense. Paul Collier believes that an accelerating, worldwide exodus from poor countries to rich ones is imminent, arguing that the exodus risk justifies a "sound case from both self-interest and compassion for ceilings on migration" because of the potential erosion of wages and public goods. But what if he's just wrong? Both the cultural and economic concerns were addressed in earlier chapters and found wanting. In fairness, my focus has been on the American scene while Collier, an Oxford professor, was focused on Europe. Even so, policymakers should not become prisoner to a false binary choice between open borders or quotas.

If the median voter thinks that educated immigrants are good for the nation but the low-skill immigrants are not, fine. Congress could set the standard that any foreign-born person with a valid college degree can have a green card. The fear that America would be "flooded" with educated, literate, non-criminal foreigners is a threat to no one but the nation's geopolitical rivals.

But is America at capacity? With 331 million residents, won't another 50 million make the roads and cities overcrowded? Not at all, says John Cochrane, an economist and colleague at the Hoover Institution. When I asked John what the optimal number of immigrants per year might be, he suggested that the smart way to think about population density is actual population density.

There are fewer than 100 people per square mile in the United States but over 600 people per square mile in the United Kingdom, and over 1,200 in the Netherlands. "However you cut it, the US still looks severely underpopulated relative to many other pleasant advanced countries," says Cochrane.

5. **Executive action: overhaul work visas** to allow unlimited foreign guests who can work in the United States. Temporary guest workers are already working and living in America, and they are not second-class citizens any more than tourists are. They work and pay taxes but get no welfare benefits (unemployment insurance, stimulus expenditures, food stamps). Guest workers should have flexibility to change employers after a short term with an initial sponsor. Although many legal scholars believe Obama's executive actions were unconstitutional breaches of legislative authority, the guest worker programs are not in the same domestic policy sphere. The Constitution grants Congress authority over naturalization and citizenship. Visitors are a different matter, and there is a legal argument that the president's authority on this front is total. Guest workers are defined under existing law as non-immigrants. That is a foreign policy power of the executive branch.

It's time for a different approach. Congress should forget comprehensive reform and aim instead for pragmatic and incremental change. The president should be thinking creatively about how to engage allies, rivals, and aspirational foreigners. Instead of starting with the controversial topic of illegal immigration, begin with issues overflowing with consensus across party lines about legal immigration.

In the final analysis, we can see in retrospect that the American experiment designed 250 years ago has succeeded in the way the founders dared to hope. A new nation dedicated to a proposition of equality was able to fulfill its ambitions thanks in large part to the foreigners who flocked to her shores. Nearly one in six Americans alive today were born overseas. It's high time they received the recognition and respect they deserve as a pillar of America's power and the lifeblood of its national identity.

Sadly, the country's political media seem committed to emphasizing divisive stories of partisanship, populism, and a strangely un-American identity tribalism. Despite the sad state of mass media, there is reason to be hopeful. A partisan press is nothing new in American history. The nation experienced a far worse mix of yellow journalism, populism, and puritanism 100 years ago. The fear of foreigners, war, and a global pandemic in the early 1920s led directly to "emergency" immigration quota acts in 1921 and 1924 that lasted half a century. It took a long time to correct that mistake. Maybe this time we can avoid it altogether.

It is tempting to imagine that America stands at a crossroads, with paths the republic can take: a new isolationist century as Fortress America or a second American Century of global leadership. It's not so simple as that. There are many paths the nation might take, many ways new technologies and trends might pressure the ship of state. No doubt, this century's leaders will make a crosscurrent of choices, thoughtful and thoughtless, dynamic and reactionary. And like so many times before, they will create and reform laws with tremendous unintended consequences. Perhaps the shift toward free movement of citizens among many countries will be realized, as I suspect is inevitable. Perhaps a thousand Brexits of smaller sovereignties amid ever larger trade unions will unfold. One thing we can be sure of is that the unending debate over American immigration, despite the thread of nativism, will always be dominated by the stronger thread of radical human equality so long as the Constitution holds.

Remember the facts I have shared with you in this book. The United States welcomes more immigrants to its land than any other country in the world, and this openness has made the nation richer than any in history. The American people have become increasingly more, not less, welcoming to greater immigration during the past fifty years. And of all the places that foreign immigrants would move if allowed, the United States is the top destination by far. All of these facts paint a picture of a fantastic strategic advantage for the United States at the dawn of this new era. And, best of all, the advantage could be even greater.

With a pandemic in 2020, with race riots burning across the land, and with a terrible assault on the United States Capitol on January 6, anxiety about the future is understandable. It is also misplaced. President Biden will try comprehensive immigration legislation once again—a Sisyphean effort that will fail to pass but succeed as a necessary political symbol—and is already signaling a willingness to take incremental steps. If you despair, remember Abraham Lincoln and the bitterness his generation overcame, a triumph that would have been impossible without immigrants willing to fight for the Union cause. Mobs will rise and fall, presidents will come and go, but the American creed is more resilient than what the fear-mongers say. Progress comes in waves.

Notes

Chapter 1

1. Washington (1788).
2. Reagan (1989).
3. Klein (2019).
4. Kelly (2017).
5. Barone (2013), 3.
6. O'Toole (2018).
7. Gates (2019), A13.
8. Lazear, *Wall Street Journal* (2017).

Chapter 2

1. Nagel (2002), 972.
2. Bush (2001).
3. Woods (2011), 214.
4. Rosenblum (2011).
5. Ewing, Martínez, and Rumbaut (2015).
6. Nichols (2019).
7. Nowrasteh (2019).
8. Forrester, Weiser, and Forrester (2018).
9. Friedersdorf (2013).
10. Easterly and Gletzer (2017).
11. Mueller and Stewart (2018), 7.
12. Shen (2020).
13. Department of Homeland Security (2016).
14. Kochanek, Murphy, Xu, and Arias (2016).
15. Hetter and Pearson (2016).
16. Rossiter and Dresner (2004).
17. Blalock, Kadiyali, and Simon (2009).
18. Alia Wong (2019).
19. Johnson (2016).
20. Jansen (2016).
21. Byman (2019).

Chapter 3

1. Sonmez (2018).
2. *The Daily Beast* (2018).
3. Shane (2018).
4. Nelson (2020).
5. Sorkin (2017).
6. Frizell (2016).
7. Beckwith (2016).
8. Bove and Böhmelt (2016), 584.
9. Bove and Böhmelt (2016), 583.
10. Trump (2017).
11. Padgett (2003).
12. US Department of Homeland Security (2017).
13. Seville, Rappleye, and Lehren (2019).
14. US Customs and Border Protection (2019).
15. Chang (2018).
16. Ali (2018).
17. Shepard and Morin (2018).
18. Gould (2019).
19. Laporta, Touchberry, and Da Silva (2019).
20. Trump (2017), 9.
21. Gambetta and Hertog (2016).

Chapter 4

1. Noble (1907), 197.
2. Noble (1907), 181.
3. Swygart (2018).
4. Lincoln (1863).
5. Hanc (2016).
6. Smith (1776), 590.
7. Whitman (2005).
8. Gjelten (2016), 6.
9. Koch et al. (2019).
10. Daniels (1991), 3–29.
11. Easterlin (1972), Table 6.1.
12. Frum (2019).
13. Dickerson (2019).
14. Gibson and Lennon (1999).
15. Anbinder (2016), 116.
16. Centers for Disease Control (2017).
17. Ravenstein (1885).
18. Library of Congress (2020).
19. Roser (2018).

Chapter 5

1. Kennedy (2019).
2. Lester (1998).
3. Bailey (1966), 25.
4. Murray and Blessing (1989), 60.
5. Murray and Blessing (1989), 23.
6. Merry (2012), 15.
7. C-SPAN (2017).

Chapter 6

1. Bowen (1986), 206–8.
2. Washington (1783).
3. Washington (1788).
4. Daniels (1991), 114.
5. Anbinder (2015), 113.
6. Daniels (1991), 267.
7. Adams (2015).
8. Boeller (1985).
9. Boeller (1985), 61.
10. Arthur (1882).
11. Silverman (2015), 8.
12. Silverman (2015), 113–14.
13. Arthur (1882).
14. Library of Congress (2020).
15. Somin (2017).
16. Daniels (1991), 276–77.
17. Vought (2004), 30.
18. Daniels (1991), 280.
19. US State Department History Online (2020).
20. Shlaes (2016).
21. Campbell and Lennon (1999).
22. Wang (1974).
23. Daniels (1991), 296.
24. Daniels (1991), 300.
25. Lee (2019), 145.
26. Daniels (1991), 330.
27. Daniels (1991), 330.
28. Gerber (2011), 45.
29. Daniels (1991), 329.
30. Tichenor (2016).

Chapter 7

1. Putnam (2013).
2. Kennedy (1963).
3. Robinson (2003).
4. Frye (2019), 139.
5. Treadgold (1997).
6. Branic and Kubrin (2018).
7. Robbins (2006).
8. White House (2006).

Chapter 8

1. Poole (2005). The bifurcation of partisan voting is discussed extensively in Hubbard and Kane (2013).
2. Report of the National Commission on Social Security Reform (1983).
3. Fiorina (2017), xiii.
4. Dubner (2018).
5. Gehl and Porter (2017), 33.
6. Tapper (2014).
7. McGurn (2017).
8. Shear (2014).
9. Gallup (2020).

Chapter 9

1. Jones (2020).
1. British Broadcasting Company (BBC) (2013).
2. Schneider (2011), 113.
3. *Korea Times* (2011).
4. Nye (1990), 178.
5. Nye (2004), 4.
6. Lu (2017), 2.
7. Nichiporuk (2000), 8.
8. Reagan (1989).
9. Chishti and Kamasaki (2014).
10. Rytina (2002).
11. Elis (2017).
12. Kane (2017).
13. Johnson (2020).
14. US Census, 1870 (1874).
15. Kirby (2017).
16. Walker (1896).
17. Hodgson (1992).

18. United Nations (2019).
19. World Bank (2019).

Chapter 10

1. Frank Soboleski Obituary (2017).
2. Guarnere et al. (2008), 89.
3. Daniels (1991), 270.
4. Doyle (2015).
5. Anbinder (2016), 207.
6. York (2018).
7. Laskin (2011), 334.
8. Kane (2005).
9. Chishti et al. (2019).
10. Daniels (1999), 278.
11. Ambrose (1997), 281.
12. Ambrose (1997), 490.
13. Ambrose (1997), 490–91.

Chapter 11

1. Isaacson (2008), 408, 447.
2. Hsu (2012), 89.
3. Isaacson (2008), 289.
4. Lenard (1936).
5. Isaacson (2008), 407.
6. Moser et al. (2014).
7. Widener (2019).
8. Gralla (2007).
9. Lugo and Cooperman (2013).
10. Sheskin and Dashefsky (2018), 251–348.
11. DellaPergola, in Sheskin and Dashefsky (2018), 361–449.
12. Stern (2000).
13. Mahdi and Daniel (2006), 60.
14. Greenberger (2006).
15. Rhodes (1986), 177–78.
16. Wildavsky (2010), 89.
17. Kahn (1996).
18. UNESCO (2020).
19. Wildavsky (2010), 15.
20. IIE (2019).
21. Matthews (2019).
22. National Foundation for American Policy (2019).
23. Zhou (2018).

24. Sharma (2013).
25. US Senate Committee on Homeland Security and Governmental Affairs (2019).
26. Brumfiel (2020).
27. Kosten (2018).
28. Wadhwa (2012).
29. Kosten (2018).
30. Doingbusiness (2020).
31. Jacobsen (2014).

Chapter 12

1. Davidson (2019).
2. Corden (1984).
3. Fehner and Gosling (2000).
4. US Department of Energy (2013).
5. Public Broadcasting Service (2020).
6. Card (1990).
7. Kennedy (2020).
8. Rea (2014).
9. Sowell (1996), 139.
10. Davis, Haltiwanger, and Schuh (1996).
11. Haltiwanger, Jarmin, and Miranda (2008).
12. Kane (2010).
13. Economic Report of the President (2011).

Chapter 13

1. Tedesjo (2016).
2. Borjas (1999), 8.
3. Borjas (1999), 11.
4. Higgins (2017).
5. Card (2007).
6. Borjas (2017).
7. Borjas (2017).
8. Smith (2015).
9. Peri and Yasenov (2017).
10. Tedesjo (2016).
11. Dustmann et al. (2016).
12. Zenko (2011).
13. Tiron (2010).
14. Wong (2016).
15. Lieberthal and O'Hanlon (2012).
16. Friedman (2006).
17. Caplan and Weinersmith (2019).

18. US Congressional Budget Office (2007).
19. Tedesjo (2016)
20. Borjas (1999), 34.

Chapter 14

1. Crenshaw, Gotanda, Peller, and Thomas (1995).
2. UCLA School of Public Affairs (2021).
3. Parvini and Simani (2019).
4. Measher (2020).
5. Barroso (2020).
6. Franklin (1751).
7. Bialik (2017).
8. Duncan and Trejo (2007).
9. Vought (2004), 36.
10. Nathan Glazer (1993).
11. Salam (2018), 28.
12. Suro et al. (2011).
13. Fukuyama (2018), 166.
14. Williamson (2003).
15. Gimpel (1999), 33.
16. Gimpel and Schuknecht (2001).
17. Khan (2017), 216.
18. Fonte and Nagai (2013).
19. Bradley Project (2008), 8.
20. Nowrasteh and Forrester (2019).
21. Nowrasteh and Forrester (2019).
22. Fukuyama (2018), 158–59.

Chapter 16

1. Zwetsloot, Feldgoise, and Dunham (2020).
2. Metz and Mozur (2020).

Bibliography

Adams, John Quincy. 2015. "Notable & Quotable: John Quincy Adams." *Wall Street Journal*, October 7, 2015. Ali, Ayaan Hirsi. 2018. "We Need a Better Definition of 'Refugee.'" *Washington Post*, December 18, 2018.

Altonji, J. G., and David Card. 1991. "The Effects of Immigration on the Labor Market Outcomes of Less-Skilled Natives." In *Immigration, Trade, and the Labor Market*, edited by J. M. Abowd and R. B. Freeman. Chicago: University of Chicago Press.

Ambrose, Stephen E. 1992. *Band of Brothers: E Company, 506th Regiment, 101st Airborne from Normandy to Hitler's Eagle's Nest*. New York: Simon & Schuster.

Ambrose, Stephen E. 1997. *Citizen Soldiers*. New York: Simon & Schuster.

Anbinder, Tyler. 2016. *City of Dreams: The 400-Year Epic History of Immigrant New York*. New York: Houghton Mifflin.

Anderson, Kenneth. 2019. "The Bathtub Fallacy and Risks of Terrorism." *Lawfare*, October 31, 2019. Accessed February 23, 2020. https://www.lawfareblog.com/bathtub-fallacy-and-risks-terrorism.

Arias, Elizabeth, and Jiaquan Xu. 2019. *United States Life Tables, 2017*. National Center for Health Statistics. Accessed September 17, 2020. https://www.cdc.gov/nchs/data/nvsr/nvsr68/nvsr68_07-508.pdf.

Arnold, Zachary, and Remco Zwetsloot. 2020. "Foreign Brains Help America Compete." *Wall Street Journal*, January 30, 2020, 15.

Arthur, Chester. 1882. Speech on the Veto of the Chinese Exclusion Act. April 4. 1882. Accessed March 15, 2020. https://millercenter.org/the-presidency/presidential-speeches/april-4-1882-veto-chinese-exclusion-act.

Aviation Safety Network. n.d. "Aviation Safety Network Statistics." Aviation Safety Foundation. Accessed July 16, 2020. Accessed February 23, 2020. https://aviation-safety.net/statistics/period/stats.php.

Bailey, Thomas Andrew. 1966. *Presidential Greatness*. New York: Appleton-Century.

Bank, Justin. 2008. "World Trade Center Victims." FactCheck.org, March 2, 2008. Accessed February 23, 2020. https://www.factcheck.org/2008/03/world-trade-center-victims/.

Barnes, Alexander F., and Peter L. Belmonte. 2018. *Forgotten Soldiers of World War I*. Altgen, PA: Schiffer.

Barone, Michael. 2013. *Shaping Our Nation: How Surges of Migration Transformed America and Its Politics*. New York: Crown Forum.

Barroso, Amanda. 2020. *Most Black Adults Say Race Is Central to Their Identity and Feel Connected to a Broader Black Community*. Washington, DC: Pew Research Center, February 5, 2020.

Bartik, Timothy J. 1991. "The Effects of Metropolitan Job Growth on the Size Distribution of Family Income." Upjohn Working Papers and Journal Articles 91-06. W. E. Upjohn Institute for Employment Research, Kalamazoo, MI.

Basso, G., and Giovanni Peri. 2015. "The Association Between Immigration and Labor Market Outcomes in the United States." Institute for the Study of Labor. Accessed July 7, 2018. http://ftp.iza.org/dp9436.pdf.

Beckwith, Ryan T. 2016. "Orlando Shooting: Read Donald Trump's Speech." *Time*, June 13, 2016. Accessed February 23, 2020. https://time.com/4367120/orlando-shooting-donald-trump-transcript/.

Beinart, Peter. 2017. "How the Democrats Lost Their Way on Immigration." *The Atlantic*. July/August 2017.

Bialik, Kristen. 2017. *Key Facts About Race and Marriage, 50 Years After Loving v. Virginia.* Washington, DC: Pew Research Center, June 12, 2017.

Blalock, Garrick, Vrinda Kadiyali, and Daniel H. Simon. 2009. "Driving Fatalities After 9/11: A Hidden Cost of Terrorism." *Applied Economics* 41 (14): 1717–29.

Boeller, Paul. 1985. *Presidential Campaigns.* New York: Oxford University Press.

Borjas, George J. 1999. *Heaven's Door.* Princeton, NJ: Princeton University Press.

Borjas, George. 2003. "The Labor Demand Curve Is Downward Sloping: Reexamining the Impact of Immigration on the Labor Market." *Quarterly Journal of Economics* 118 (4): 1335–74.

Borjas, George J. 2016. *We Wanted Workers: Unraveling the Immigration Narrative.* New York: W. W. Norton.

Borjas, George J. 2017. "The Wage Impact of the Marielitos: A Reappraisal." *ILR Review* 70 (5): 01077–110.

Borjas, George, Richard Freeman, and Lawrence Katz. 1996. "Searching for the Effect of Immigration on the Labor Market." *American Economic Review* 86 (2): 246–51.

Borjas, George, Richard Freeman, and Larry Katz. 1997. "How Much Do Immigration and Trade Affect Labor Market Outcomes?" *Brookings Papers on Economic Activity* 28 (1): 1–90.

Boubtane, E., D. Coulibaly, and C. Rault. 2013. "Immigration, Unemployment, and GDP in the Host Country: Bootstrap Panel Granger Causality Analysis in OECD Countries." *Economic Modeling* 33: 261–69.

Bove, Vincenzo, and Tobias Böhmelt. 2016. "Does Immigration Induce Terrorism?" *Journal of Politics* 78 (2). https://www.journals.uchicago.edu/doi/pdfplus/10.1086/684679.

Bowen, Catherine Drinker. 1986. *Miracle at Philadelphia: The Story of the Constitutional Convention, May to September, 1787.* New York: Little, Brown.

Bradley Foundation. 2008. *E Pluribus Unum: Bradley Project on America's National Identity.* Accessed September 17, 2020. https://s3.amazonaws.com/media.hudson.org/files/publications/EPUReportFinal.pdf.

Branic, Nicholas, and Charis E. Kubrin. 2018. "Gated Communities and Crime in the United States." *Oxford Handbooks Online.* September 2018. Accessed July 9, 2021. https://www.oxfordhandbooks.com/view/10.1093/oxfordhb/9780190279707.001.0001/oxfordhb-9780190279707-e-8

British Broadcasting Company. 2013. "The Statue of Liberty and America's Crowdfunding Pioneer," April 25, 2013. Accessed February 23, 2020. https://www.bbc.com/news/magazine-21932675.

Brockell, Gillian. 2018. "'An Asylum to the Persecuted': Would George Washington Embrace the Migrant Caravan?" *Washington Post*, November 8, 2018.

Brumfiel, Geoff. 2020. "U.S. Response to China's Talent Plan Is Described as Heavy-Handed." National Public Radio. February 13, 2020. Accessed February 23, 2020. https://www.npr.org/2020/02/13/805537113/u-s-response-to-chinas-talent-plan-described-as-heavy-handed.

Bureau of Labor Statistics. n.d. "Labor Force Characteristics of Foreign-Born Workers Summary." Accessed June 5, 2018. https://www.bls.gov/news.release/forbrn.nr0.htm.

Bureau of Labor Statistics. 2018. "Local Area Unemployment Statistics: Civilian Noninstitutional Population and Associated Rate and Ratio Measures for Model-Based Areas." Accessed June 18, 2019. https://www.bls.gov/lau/rdscnp16.htm.

Bush, George W. 2001. Remarks by the President at Islamic Center of Washington, DC. September 17, 2001. Accessed June 18, 2019. https://georgewbush-whitehouse.archives.gov/news/releases/2001/09/20010917-11.html.

Butcher, Katrin, and David Card. 1991. "Immigration and Wages: Evidence from the 1980s." *American Economic Review Papers and Proceedings* 81 (2): 292–96.

Byman, Daniel. 2019. "It's Hard to Commemorate 9/11 If You Don't Understand It." *Foreign Policy*. September 11, 2019.

Caplan, Bryan, and Zach Weinersmith. 2019. *Open Borders; The Science and Ethics of Immigration*. New York: First Second.

Card, David. 1990. "The Impact of the Mariel Boatlift on the Miami Labor Market." *Industrial and Labor Relations Review* 43 (2): 245–57.

Card, David. 2007. "How Immigration Affects U.S. Cities." CReAM Discussion Paper, no. 11.

Card, David, and John DiNardo. 2000. "Do Immigrant Inflows Lead to Native Outflows?" *American Economic Review* 90 (2): 360–67. http://doi.org/10.1257/aer.90.2.360.

Card, David, and Ethan Lewis. 2007. "The Diffusion of Mexican Immigrants During the 1990s: Explanations and Impacts." In *Mexican Immigration to the United States*, edited by George Borjas. Cambridge, MA: National Bureau of Economic Research Conference Report.

Casselman, Ben. 2018. "Meet the Pro-Trade, Pro-Immigration Economist Running for Congress. As a Republican. In Ohio." *New York Times*, May 6, 2018. Accessed June 18, 2019. https://www.nytimes.com/2018/05/06/business/economy/house-ohio-trade.html.

Centers for Disease Control and Prevention. n.d. *National Vital Statistics System*, "Table 6. Deaths, Percent of Total Deaths and Rank Order for 113 Selected Causes of Death, by Race and Hispanic Origin, and Sex, United States, 2017." Accessed October 20, 2019. https://www.cdc.gov/nchs/data/dvs/lcwk/lcwk6_hr_2017-508.pdf.

Chang, Alisa. "Thousands Could Be Deported As Government Targets Asylum Mills' Clients." *National Public Radio*. September 28, 2018.

Chishti, Muzaffar, Austin Rose, and Stephen Yale-Loehr. 2019. "Noncitizens in the U.S. Military: Navigating National Security Concerns and Recruitment Needs." Migration Policy Institute Policy Brief, May 2019. Accessed June 18, 2019. https://www.migrationpolicy.org/news/us-armed-forces-face-recruitment-challenges-skills-gaps-mpi-brief-examines-noncitizen-enlistment.

Chishti, Muzz, and Charles Kamasaki. 2014. "IRCA in Retrospect: Guideposts for Today's Immigration Reform." Migration Policy Institute Issue Brief, January 2014.

Clifton, Jon. 2017. "Coming to America," Gallup blog, June 28, 2017. Accessed September 10, 2019. https://news.gallup.com/opinion/gallup/212687/coming-america.aspx.

Collier, Paul. 2013. *Exodus*. New York: Oxford University Press.

Corden, W. M. 1984. "Boom Sector and Dutch Disease Economics: Survey and Consolidation." *Oxford Economic Papers* 36 (3): 362.

Crenshaw, Kimberlé, Neil Gotanda, Gary Peller, and Kendall Thomas, eds. 1995. *Critical Race Theory: The Key Writings That Formed the Movement*. New York: New Press.

C-SPAN. 2017. "Total Scores/Overall Rankings: C-SPAN Survey on Presidents 2017." National Cable Satellite Corporation. Accessed October 10, 2019. https://www.c-span.org/presidentsurvey2017/?page=overall.

Daily Beast. 2018. "Fox News Host: Migrant Caravan Looks 'More Like an Invasion Than Anything Else.'" November 2, 2018. Accessed September 10, 2019. https://www.thedailybeast.com/fox-news-host-migrant-caravan-looks-more-like-an-invasion-than-anything-else.

Daniels, Roger. 1991. *Coming to America: A History of Immigration and Ethnicity in American Life*. New York: Harper Perennial.

Daniller, Andrew. 2019. "Americans' Immigration Policy Priorities." Pew Research Center, November 12, 2019. Accessed December 7, 2019. https://www.pewresearch.org/fact-tank/

2019/11/12/americans-immigration-policy-priorities-divisions-between-and-within-the-two-parties/.

Davidson, Michael Scott. 2019. "Clark County Saw Second-Largest Population Increase in Nation." *Las Vegas Review Journal*. April 19, 2019.

Davis, Lance E., Richard A. Easterlin, William N. Parker, Dorothy Brady, Albert Fishlow, and Robert Gallman. 1972. *American Economic Growth: An Economist's History of the United States*. New York: Harper and Row.

Davis, Steven J., John Haltiwanger, and Scott Schuh. 1996. *Job Creation and Destruction*. Cambridge, MA: MIT Press.

Dickerson, Caitlin. 2019. "Border at 'Breaking Point' as More than 76,000 . . ." *New York Times*, March 5, 2019. Accessed September 10, 2019. https://www.nytimes.com/2019/03/05/us/border-crossing-increase.html.

Doing Business 2020. 2020. "Economy Profile of United States," Doingbusiness.org.

Doyle, Don H. 2015. "The Civil War Was Won by Immigrant Soldiers." *Time*, June 29, 2015.

Dubner, Stephen J. 2018. "America's Hidden Duopoly." Freakonomics Radio, October 31, 2018. Accessed September 10, 2019. https://freakonomics.com/podcast/politics-industry/.

Duncan, Brian, and Stephen J. Trejo. 2007. "Ethnic Identification, Intermarriage, and Unmeasured Progress by Mexican Americans." In *Mexican Immigration to the United States*, edited by George J. Borjas. Chicago: University of Chicago Press. Accessed September 10, 2019. https://www.nber.org/chapters/c0104.pdf.

Dustmann, C., U. Schönberg, and J. Stuhler. 2016. "The Impact of Immigration: Why Do Studies Reach Such Different Conclusions?" *Journal of Economic Perspectives* 30 (4): 31–56.

"The Dutch Disease." 1977. *The Economist*. November 26, 1977, 82–83.

Easterly, Jennie M., and Joshua A. Geltzer. 2017. "More Die in Bathtubs than in Terrorism. It's Still Worth Spending Billions to Fight It." CNN, May 22, 2017.

Elis, Niv. 2017. "Trump Triggers Debate on Impact of Immigrants." *The Hill*, August 5, 2017. Accessed July 1, 2019. https://thehill.com/policy/finance/345400-trump-triggers-debate-on-impact-of-immigrants.

Esipova, Neli, Anita Pugliese, and Julie Ray. 2018. "More than 750 Million Worldwide Would Migrate if They Could." Gallup.com, December 10, 2018. Accessed September 10, 2019. https://news.gallup.com/poll/245255/750-million-worldwide-migrate.aspx.

Esses, V. M., J. F. Dovidio, and G. Hodson. 2002. "Public Attitudes Toward Immigration in the United States and Canada in Response to the September 11, 2001 'Attack on America.'" *Analysis of Social Issues and Public Policy*, 2 (1): 69–85.

Ewing, Walter A., Daniel E. Martínez, and Rubén G. Rumbaut. 2015. *The Criminalization of Immigration in the United States*. American Immigration Council Special Report, July 2015. Accessed September 11, 2019. https://www.americanimmigrationcouncil.org/sites/default/files/research/the_criminalization_of_immigration_in_the_united_states.pdf.

Fehner, Terrence R., and F. G. Gosling. 2000. *Origins of the Nevada Test Site*. The Department of Energy, December 2000. https://www.energy.gov/sites/prod/files/DOENevadaTestSite.pdf.

Felzenberg, Alvin S. 2010. *The Leaders We Deserved (and a Few We Didn't): Rethinking the Presidential Rating Game*. New York: Basic Books.

Fiorina, Morris P. 2017. *Unstable Majorities: Polarization, Party Sorting & Political Stalemate*. Stanford, CA: Hoover Press.

Fonte, John, and Althea Nagai. 2013. *America's Patriotic Assimilation System Is Broken*. Hudson Institute Briefing Paper, April 2013. https://s3.amazonaws.com/media.hudson.org/files/publications/Final04-05.pdf.

Forrester, Jared A., Thomas G. Weiser, and Joseph D. Forrester. 2018. "An Update on Fatalities due to Venomous and Nonvenomous Animals in the United States (2008–2015)." *Wilderness & Environmental Medicine* 29 (1): 36–44.

Franklin, Benjamin. "Observations Concerning the Increase of Mankind, Peopling of Countries, etc." 1751.

Frank Soboleski obituary. 2017. Accessed August 5, 2018. https://www.greenlarsen.com/obituaries/Frank-Soboleski/#!/Obituary.

Friedersdorf, Conor. 2013. "The Irrationality of Giving Up This Much Liberty to Fight Terror." *The Atlantic*, June 10, 2013. Accessed September 10, 2019. https://www.theatlantic.com/politics/archive/2013/06/the-irrationality-of-giving-up-this-much-liberty-to-fight-terror/276695/.

Friedman, Milton. 2006. Personal email message sent to Henryk Kowalczyk, October 16, 2006. Accessed April 17, 2019. https://www.freedomofmigration.com/wp-content/uploads/2012/02/Friedman-20061016.pdf.

Frizell, Sam. 2016. "Orlando Shooting: Donald Trump Faces Backlash for Tweets." *Time*, June 12, 2016. Accessed April 16, 2019. https://time.com/4365411/orlando-shooting-donald-trump-tweet-congrats/.

Frum, David. 2019. "If Liberals Won't Enforce Borders, Fascists Will." *The Atlantic*, March 11, 2019. Accessed September 10, 2019. https://www.theatlantic.com/magazine/archive/2019/04/david-frum-how-much-immigration-is-too-much/583252/.

Frye, David. 2019. *Walls: A History of Civilization in Blood and Brick*. New York: Scribner.

Fukuyama, Francis. 2018. *Identity: The Demand for Dignity and the Politics of Resentment*. New York: Farrar, Straus and Giroux.

Gallup. 2020. "Immigration," July 1, 2020. Accessed April 16, 2021. https://news.gallup.com/poll/1660/immigration.aspx.

Gambetta, Diego, and Steffen Hertog. 2016. *Engineers of Jihad: The Curious Connection Between Violent Extremism and Education*. Princeton, NJ: Princeton University Press.

Gates, Robert M. 2019. "To End the Shutdown, Try Thinking Big on Immigration." *Wall Street Journal*, January 18, 2019.

Gehl, Katherine M., and Michael E. Porter. 2017. "Why Competition in the Politics Industry Is Failing America." Harvard Business School, 2017. Accessed April 28, 2019. https://www.hbs.edu/competitiveness/Documents/why-competition-in-the-politics-industry-is-failing-america.pdf.

Gerber, David A. 2011. *American Immigration: A Very Short Introduction*. Oxford: Oxford University Press.

Gibson, Campbell J., and Emily Lennon. 1999. "Historical Census Statistics on the Foreign-born Population of the United States: 1850 to 1990." Suitland, MD: Suitland Federal Center, US Census Bureau, Population Division.

Gimpel, James G. 1999. *Separate Destinations: Migration, Immigration, and the Politics of Places*. Ann Arbor: University of Michigan Press.

Gimpel, James G., and Jason E. Schuknecht. 2001. "Interstate Migration and Electoral Politics." *Journal of Politics* 63 (1): 207–31.

Givens, Terri E. 2010. "Immigration and National Security: Comparing the US and Europe." *Whitehead Journal of Diplomacy and International Relations* 11 (1): 79–88.

Gjelten, Tom. 2016. *Nation of Nations: A Great American Immigration Story*. New York: Simon & Schuster.

Glazer, Nathan. 1993. "Is Assimilation Dead?" *Annals of the American Academy of Political and Social Science*, vol. 530, *Interminority Affairs in the U.S.: Pluralism at the Crossroads* (November): 122–36.

Goldberg, Jeffrey. 2013. "What Conor Friedersdorf Misunderstands About Terrorism." *Bloomberg.com*, June 12, 2013. Accessed April 1, 2019. https://www.bloomberg.com/view/articles/2013-06-12/what-conor-friedersdorf-misunderstands-about-terrorism.

Gould, Joe. 2019. "Dems Warn Shanahan New Border Actions Could Break Civil-Military Law." *Defense News*, May 9, 2019. Accessed July 4, 2019. https://www.defensenews.com/

congress/2019/05/08/democrats-warn-shanahan-military-border-moves-could-spark-posse-comitatus-violations/.

Gralla, Joan. 2007. "Holocaust Survivors Owed as Much as $175 Bln: Study." Reuters, January 18, 2007.

Greenberger, Robert S. 2006. "How Jew-Friendly Persia Became Anti-Semitic Iran." *Moment*, November–December 2006.

Greenfield, Victoria A., Blas Nunez-Neto, Ian Mitch, Joseph Chang, and Jetienne Rosas. 2019. *Human Smuggling and Associated Revenues: What Do or Can We Know About Routes from Central America to the United States?* Rand. Accessed December 8, 2019. https://www.rand.org/content/dam/rand/pubs/research_reports/RR2800/RR2852/RAND_RR2852.pdf.

Guarnere, William, Edward Heffron, and Robyn Post. 2008. *Brothers in Battle: Best of Friends.* New York: Dutton Caliber.

Guild, Elspeth. 2009. *Security and Migration in the 21st Century.* Cambridge: Polity Press.

Haltiwanger, John, Ron S. Jarmin, and Javier Miranda. 2008. "Business Formation and Dynamics by Business Age: Results from the New Business Dynamics Statistics," CES preliminary paper. Accessed May 18, 2010. http://webserver03.ces.census.gov/docs/bds/bds_paper_CAED_may2008_dec2.pdf.

Hanc, John. 2016. "The Plymouth Hero You Should Really Be Thankful for This Thanksgiving." Smithsonian, November 21, 2016. smithsonianmag.com.

Hetter, Katia, and Michael Pearson. 2016. "TSA Security Line Waits Inevitable, DHS Secretary Says." *CNN*, May 13, 2016.

Higgins, Sean. 2017. "The Cuban-born Harvard Economist Who Immigration Critics Love." *Washington Examiner*, August 11, 2017.

Hodgson, Dennis. 1992. "Ideological Currents and the Interpretation of Demographic Trends: The Case of Francis Amasa Walker." *Journal of the History of the Behavioral Sciences* 28 (1): 28–44.

Hsu, Christopher, Sr. 2012. *Faith and Family.* Self-published memoir.

Hubbard, Glenn, and Tim Kane. 2013. *Balance: The Economics of Great Powers from Ancient Rome to Modern America.* New York: Simon & Schuster.

Hubbard, Glenn, and Tim Kane. 2013. "The Great Wall of Texas: How the U.S. Is Repeating One of History's Great Blunders." *The Atlantic*, July 9, 2013.

Hunt, Jennifer, and Marjolaine Gauthier-Loiselle. 2010. "How Much Does Immigration Boost Innovation?" *American Economic Journal: Macroeconomics* 2 (2): 31–56.

Huysmans, Jef. 2006. *The Politics of Insecurity: Fear, Migration and Asylum in the EU.* London: Routledge.

Institute of International Education. n.d. "Number of International Students in the United States Hits All-Time High." iie.org, November 18, 2019.

Isaacson, Walter. 2008. *Einstein: His Life and Universe.* New York: Simon & Schuster.

Jacobsen, Anne M. 2014. *Operation Paperclip: The Secret Intelligence Program that Brought Nazi Scientists to America.* New York. Little, Brown.

Jansen, Bart. 2016. "Hijackings Rare After 9/11 Security Improvements." *USA Today*, March 29, 2016. Accessed April 16, 2019. https://www.usatoday.com/story/news/2016/03/29/hijackings-rare-after-911-security-improvements/82375474/.

Jaumotte, F., K. Koloskova, and S. C. Saxena. 2016. "Impact of Immigration on Income Levels in Advanced Economies." *International Monetary Fund—Spillover Notes* 8: 1–21.

Johnson, Karin. 2016. "International Student Flows to the U.S. Before and After 9/11." *UC Riverside Electronic Theses and Dissertations.* Thesis, University of California, Riverside.

Johnson, Sandra. "A Changing Nation: Population Projections Under Alternative Immigration Scenarios." US Census Bureau, Report P25-1146, February 2020. Accessed May 15, 2020.

https://www.census.gov/content/dam/Census/library/publications/2020/demo/p25-1146.pdf.

Jones, Charles I. "The End of Economic Growth? Unintended Consequences of a Declining Population." Working Paper, February 12, 2020. Accessed February 23, 2020. https://web.stanford.edu/~chadj/emptyplanet.pdf.

Kahn, Patricia. 1996. "The Decline of German Universities." *Science* 273 (5272): 172–74.

Kane, Tim. 2005. "Who Bears the Burden? Demographic Characteristics of U.S. Military Recruits Before and After 9/11." Heritage Foundation, November 7, 2005.

Kane, Tim. 2010. "The Importance of Startups in Job Creation and Job Destruction." Kauffman Foundation Research Series, July 2010. Accessed February 23, 2020. https://www.kauffman.org/-/media/kauffman_org/research-reports-and-covers/2010/07/firm_formation_importance_of_startups.pdf.

Kane, Tim. 2016. "Piketty's Crumbs." Commentary, May 2016. Accessed February 1, 2020. https://www.commentarymagazine.com/articles/kane-tim/pikettys-crumbs.

Kane, Tim. 2017. "National Security Consequences of Cutting Immigration," FoxNews.com, September 20, 2017. Accessed April 2, 2020. https://www.foxnews.com/opinion/national-security-consequences-of-cutting-immigration.

Keenan, Jillian. 2014. "Kick Andrew Jackson off the $20 Bill!" *Slate*, March 4, 2014. Accessed February 23, 2020. https://slate.com/news-and-politics/2014/03/andrew-jackson-should-be-kicked-off-the-20-bill-he-ordered-a-genocide.html.

Kelly, Amita. 2017. "FACT CHECK: Have Immigrants Lowered Wages for Blue-Collar American Workers?" NPR, August 4, 2017. Accessed February 17, 2020. https://www.npr.org/2017/08/04/541321716/fact-check-have-low-skilled-immigrants-taken-american-jobs.

Kennedy, David. 2019. Interview with Jason Willick. "Does America Still Have a Common Creed?" *Wall Street Journal*, November 28, 2019.

Kennedy, John. 1963. "Remarks of President John F. Kennedy at the Rudolph Wilde Platz, Berlin, June 26, 1963." Accessed August 17, 2020. https://www.jfklibrary.org/archives/other-resources/john-f-kennedy-speeches/berlin-w-germany-rudolph-wilde-platz-19630626.

Kennedy, Lesley. 2020. "Building the Transcontinental Railroad: How 20,000 Chinese Immigrants Made It Happen." History.com. April 30, 2020. Accessed July 9, 2021. https://www.history.com/news/transcontinental-railroad-chinese-immigrants.

Khan, Khizr. 2017. *An American Family*. New York: Random House.

Khan, Yasmin Sabina. 2010. *Enlightening the World: The Creation of the Statue of Liberty*. Ithaca, NY: Cornell University Press.

Kirkby, Robert. 2017. "Dark Tales from the Early Days of the American Economic Association." September 4, 2017. Accessed January 8, 2020. http://www.robertdkirkby.com/blog/2017/american-economic-association/.

Klein, Joe. 2019. "How Donald Trump's Obsession with Immigrants Has Shaped His Presidency." *New York Times*, October 8, 2019.

Koch, Alexander, Chris Brierley, Mark M. Maslin, and Simon L. Lewis. 2019. "Earth System Impacts of the European Arrival and Great Dying in the Americas after 1492." *Quaternary Science Reviews* 207: 13–36. https://doi.org/10.1016/j.quascirev.2018.12.004.

Kochanek, Kenneth D., Sherry L. Murphy, Jiaquan Xu, and Elizabeth Arias. 2016. *Mortality in the United States*. Centers for Disease Control and Prevention, 2016. Accessed March 15, 2020. https://www.cdc.gov/nchs/data/databriefs/db293.pdf.

Korea Times. 2011. "Population Is National Power." Editorial, May 31, 2011. Accessed February 20, 2020. http://www.koreatimes.co.kr/www/news/opinon/2013/08/202_88043.html.

Kosten, Dan. 2018. "Immigrants as Economic Contributors: Immigrant Entrepreneurs." National Immigration Forum, July 11, 2018.

Krikorian, Mark. 2008. *The New Case Against Immigration, Both Legal and Illegal*. New York: Sentinel.

Laporta, James, Ramsey Touchberry, and Chantal Da Silva. 2019. "Exclusive: Donald Trump Has Ordered Thousands More Troops to Mexican Border, New Deployment Document Suggests." *Newsweek*, April 16, 2019. Accessed March 15, 2020. https://www.newsweek.com/donald-trump-troops-border-mexican-nielsen-1397532.

Laskin, David. 2011. *The Long Way Home*. New York: Harper Perennial.

Lazear, Edward P. 1999. "Culture and Language." *Journal of Political Economy* 107 (S6): S95–S126.

Lazear, Edward P. 2017. "The Surprising Factor for Immigrant Success." *Wall Street Journal*, June 26, 2017.

Lazear, Edward P. 2017. "Why Are Some Immigrant Groups More Successful Than Others?" NBER Working Paper 23548, National Bureau of Economic Research, Cambridge, MA.

Lederer, William J., and Eugene Burdick. 1958. *The Ugly American*. New York: Norton.

Lee, Erika. 2019. *America for Americans: A History of Xenophobia in the United States*. New York: Basic Books.

Lenard, Philipp. 1936. *German Physics: Bd. Optics, Electrostatics and the Beginnings of Electrodynamics*. Munich: J. F. Lehman.

Lester, Will. 1998. "'Dewey Defeats Truman' Disaster Haunts Pollsters." *Los Angeles Times*, November 1, 1998. Accessed March 15, 2020. https://www.latimes.com/archives/la-xpm-1998-nov-01-mn-38174-story.html.

Library of Congress. n.d. "Irish-Catholic Immigration to America." Accessed May 31, 2020. http://www.loc.gov/teachers/classroommaterials/presentationsandactivities/presentations/immigration/irish2.html.

Library of Congress. 1882. Online record of "An Act to Execute Certain Treaty Stipulations Relating to Chinese." May 6, 1882. Accessed April 16, 2020. https://www.loc.gov/law/help/statutes-at-large/47th-congress/session-1/c47s1ch126.pdf.

Lieberthal, Kenneth, and Michael O'Hanlon. 2012. "The Real National Security Threat: America's Debt." July 10, 2012. Accessed March 15, 2018. https://www.brookings.edu/opinions/the-real-national-security-threat-americas-debt/.

Lincoln, Abraham. 2018. "Proclamation of Thanksgiving." Edited by Roy P. Basler. Abraham Lincoln Online, 2018. Accessed June 19, 2020. http://www.abrahamlincolnonline.org/lincoln/speeches/thanks.htm.

Lu, Xing. 2017. *The Rhetoric of Mao Zedong: Transforming China and Its People*. Columbia: University of South Carolina Press.

Lugo, Luis, and Alan Cooperman. 2013. *A Portrait of Jewish Americans: Findings from a Pew Research Center Survey of U.S. Jews*. Washington, DC: Pew Research Center.

Mahdī, A. A., and E. L. Daniel. 2006. *Culture and Customs of Iran*. Santa Barbara, CA: Greenwood Publishing.

Matthews, Dylan. 2019. "2 Nobel-Winning Economists Speak Out on Our Big Economic Problem: Not Enough Immigration." Vox.com. December 6, 2019.

McGurn, William. 2017. "The Cruelty of Barack Obama." *Wall Street Journal*, September 11, 2017. Accessed March 15, 2020. https://www.wsj.com/articles/the-cruelty-of-barack-obama-1505171158.

Measher, Laura. 2020. "The 2020 Census Continues the Whitewashing of Middle Eastern Americans." NBCNews.com. May 21, 2020. Accessed May 30, 2020. https://www.nbcnews.com/think/opinion/2020-census-continues-whitewashing-middle-eastern-americans-ncna1212051

Merry, Robert W. 2012. *Where They Stand: The American Presidents in the Eyes of Voters and Historians*. New York: Simon & Schuster.

Metz, Cade, and Paul Mozur. 2020. "A U.S. Secret Weapon in A.I.: Chinese Talent." *New York Times*, June 9, 2020.

Migration Policy Institute. 2017. "Immigrant Share of the U.S. Population and Civilian Labor Force, 1980–Present." Online Data Hub. Accessed April 20, 2017. http://www.migrationpolicy.org/programs/data-hub/charts/immigrant-share-us-population-and-civilian-labor-force?width=1200&height=850&iframe=true.

Moser, Petra, Alessandra Voena, and Fabian Waldinger. 2014. "German Jewish Émigrés and US Invention." *American Economic Review* 104 (10: 3222–55.

Mueller, John, and Mark G. Stewart. 2018. "Terrorism and Bathtubs: Comparing and Assessing the Risks." *Terrorism and Political Violence.* October 29, 2018. https://www.tandfonline.com/doi/abs/10.1080/09546553.2018.1530662.

Murray, Robert K., and Tim H. Blessing. 1989. *Greatness in the White House.* University Park: Pennsylvania State University Press.

Nagel, C. R. 2002. "Geopolitics by Another Name: Immigration and the Politics of Assimilation." *Political Geography* 21 (8): 971–87.

National Foundation for American Policy. "Immigrants and Nobel Prizes: 1901–2019," NFAP Policy Brief, October 2019.

Nelson, Steven. "Joe Biden Says Fast Immigration Changes Could Cause '2 Million People on Our Border.'" *New York Post,* December 22, 2020.

Nichiporuk, Brian. 2000. *The Security Dynamics of Demographic Factors.* Rand Arroyo Center. https://www.rand.org/pubs/monograph_reports/MR1088.html.

Nichols, Chris. 2019. "PolitiFact—Rep. Tom McClintock Distorts Number of Homicides by Undocumented Immigrants." Politifact. Poynter Institute, February 21, 2019. Accessed September 1, 2020. https://www.politifact.com/factchecks/2019/feb/20/tom-mcclintock/rep-tom-mcclintock-distorts-number-homicides-undoc/.

Noble, Frederic A. 1907. *The Pilgrims.* Boston: Pilgrim Press.

Nowrasteh, Alex. 2019. "Terrorists by Immigration Status and Nationality: A Risk Analysis, 1975–2017." Cato Institute, May 7, 2019.

Nowrasteh, Alex, and Andrew C. Forrester. 2019. "Immigrants Recognize American Greatness: Immigrants and Their Descendants Are Patriotic and Trust America's Governing Institutions." Cato Institute. Immigration Research and Policy Brief No. 10, February 4, 2019.

Nowrasteh, Alex, and Andrew C. Forrester. 2020. "Do Immigrants Make the United States More Left-Wing?" Cato Institute, July 13, 2020. Accessed September 1, 2020. https://www.cato.org/blog/do-immigrants-make-united-states-more-left-wing.

Nye, Joseph S., Jr. 1990. "The Changing Nature of World Power." *Political Science Quarterly* 105 (5): 177–92.

Nye, Joseph, Jr. 2004. *Soft Power: The Means to Success in World Politics.* New York: Public Affairs.

Ortega, Francesc, and Giovanni Peri. 2014. "Openness and Income: The Roles of Trade and Migration." *Journal of International Economics* 92: 231–51.

O'Toole, Molly. 2018. "Must Reads: John F. Kelly Says His Tenure as Trump's Chief of Staff Is Best Measured by What the President Did Not Do." *Los Angeles Times,* December 30, 2018.

Ottaviano, Gianmarco, and Giovanni Peri. 2012. "Rethinking the Effect of Immigration on Wages." *Journal of the European Economic Association* 10 (1): 152–97.

Padgett, Tim. 2003. "People Smugglers Inc." *Time,* August 12, 2003. Accessed March 11, 2020. http://content.time.com/time/magazine/article/0,9171,474582,00.html.

Parvini, Sarah, and Ellis Simani. 2019. "Are Arabs and Iranians White? Census Says Yes, but Many Disagree." *Los Angeles Times,* March 28, 2019. Accessed September 1, 2020. https://www.latimes.com/projects/la-me-census-middle-east-north-africa-race/.

Peri, Giovanni. 2012. "The Effect of Immigration on Productivity: Evidence from U.S. States." *Review of Economics and Statistics* 94 (1): 348–58.

Peri, Giovanni, and Chad Sparber. 2009. "Task Specialization, Immigration, and Wages." *American Economic Journal: Applied Economics* 1 (3): 135–69. http://doi.org/10.1257/app.1.3.135.

Peri, Giovanni, and Vasil Yasenov. 2017. "The Labor Market Effects of a Refugee Wave: Applying the Synthetic Control Method to the Mariel Boatlift." National Bureau of Economic Research Working Paper 21801. December 2015; revised June 2017.

Pfander, James, and Theresa R. Wardon. 2010. "Reclaiming the Immigration Constitution of the Early Republic." *Virginia Law Review* 96: 359–441.

Pison, Gilles. 2019. "The Number and Proportion of Immigrants in the Population: International Comparisons." INED. Accessed September 1, 2020. https://www.ined.fr/fichier/s_rubrique/28889/563.international.comparison.immigrants.2019.en.pdf.

Poole, Keith T. 2005. *Spatial Models of Parliamentary Voting*. New York: Cambridge University Press.

Public Broadcasting Service. n.d. "Atomic Tourism in Nevada." *American Experience*, undated. Accessed June 5, 2020. https://www.pbs.org/wgbh/americanexperience/features/atomic-tourism-nevada/.

Putnam, Thomas. 2013. "The Real Meaning of Ich Bin Ein Berliner." *The Atlantic*, Septemmber 19, 2013. https://www.theatlantic.com/magazine/archive/2013/08/the-real-meaning-of-ich-bin-ein-berliner/309500/.

Ravenstein, E. G. 1885. "The Laws of Migration." *Journal of the Statistical Society of London* 48 (2): 167–235. https://doi.org/10.2307/2979181.

Rea, Tom. 2014. "The Rock Springs Massacre." *WyoHistory*, November 8, 2014. https://www.wyohistory.org/encyclopedia/rock-springs-massacre.

Reagan, Ronald. 1989. "Remarks at the Presentation Ceremony for the Presidential Medal of Freedom" Speech. Washington, DC, January 19, 1989. Ronald Reagan Presidential Library and Museum.

Rhodes, Richard. 1986. *The Making of the Atomic Bomb*. New York: Simon & Schuster.

Robbins, Ted. 2006. "San Diego Fence Provides Lessons in Border Control." National Public Radio, April 6, 2006. Accessed September 1, 2020. https://www.npr.org/templates/story/story.php?storyId=5323928.

Robinson, Peter. 2004. *How Ronald Reagan Changed My Life*. New York: Regan Books.

Rosenblum, Marc R. 2011. *U.S. Immigration Policy Since 9/11: Understanding the Stalemate over Comprehensive Immigration Reform*. Washington, DC: Migration Policy Institute, 2011.

Roser, Max. 2018. "The Map We Need If We Want to Think About How Global Living Conditions Are Changing." *Our World in Data*, September 12, 2018. Accessed September 30, 2020. https://ourworldindata.org/world-population-cartogram.

Rossiter, Adriana, and Martin Dresner. 2004. "The Impact of the September 11th Security Fee and Passenger Wait Time on Traffic Diversion and Highway Fatalities." *Journal of Air Transport Management* 10 (4): 225–30.

Rytina, Nancy. 2002. "IRCA Legalization Effects: Lawful Permanent Residence and Naturalization Through 2001." Washington, DC: Office of Policy and Planning, Statistics Division, US Immigration and Naturalization Service.

Salam, Reihan. 2018. *Melting Pot or Civil War?* New York: Sentinel,

Saux, M. 2007. "Immigration and Terrorism: A Constructed Connection." *European Journal of Criminal Policy and Research* 13 (1–2): 57–72.

Schneider, Dorothee. 2011. *Crossing Borders: Migration and Citizenship in the Twentieth-Century United States*. Cambridge, MA: Harvard University Press.

Seville, Lisa Riordan, Hannah Rappleye, and Andrew W. Lehren. 2019. "22 Immigrants Died in ICE Detention Centers During the Past 2 Years." NBCNews.com, January 6, 2019. Accessed September 1, 2020. https://www.nbcnews.com/politics/immigration/22-immigrants-died-ice-detention-centers-during-past-2-years-n954781.

Shachnow, Sid. 2004. *Hope and Honor*. New York: Forge.

Shane, Leo. "Trump Again Suggests Sending Troops to U.S. Southern Border." *Military Times*, October 18, 2018. Accessed December 25, 2019. https://www.militarytimes.com/news/pentagon-congress/2018/10/18/trump-again-suggests-sending-troops-to-us-southern-border/.

Sharma, Yojana. 2013. "China's Effort to Recruit Top Academic Talent Faces Hurdles." *Chronicle of Higher Education*, May 28, 2013. Accessed April 16, 2020. https://www.chronicle.com/article/Chinas-Effort-To-Recruit-Top/139485.

Shear, Michael D. 2014. "U.S. Agency Hiring 1,000 After Obama's Immigration Order." *New York Times*, December 26, 2014. Accessed April 7, 2020. https://www.nytimes.com/2014/12/26/us/politics/little-noticed-in-immigration-overhaul-a-government-hiring-rush.html.

Shen, Owen. n.d. "Charting Death: Reality vs. Reported." Accessed July 16, 2020. https://owenshen24.github.io/charting-death/.

Shepard, Steven, and Rebecca Morin. 2018. "Poll: Nearly Half Support Sending Troops to Border." *Politico*, April 11, 2018. Accessed April 16, 2020. https://www.politico.com/story/2018/04/11/border-mexico-troops-trump-poll-512778.

Sheskin, Ira M., and Arnold Dashefsky. 2018. *The American Jewish Year Book, 2018*, vol. 118. Dordrecht: Springer.

Shlaes, Amity. 2014. *Coolidge*. New York: Harper Perennial.

Shlaes, Amity. 2016. "Frank Immigration Talk." *Forbes*, November 30, 2016. Accessed April 16, 2020. https://www.forbes.com/sites/currentevents/2016/11/30/frank-immigration-talk/.

Silverman, Jason H. 2015. *Lincoln and the Immigrant*. Carbondale, IL: SIU Press.

Smith, Adam. (1776) 1902. *The Wealth of Nations*. New York: Collier.

Smith, Noah Smith. 2015. "An Immigrant Won't Steal Your Raise." Bloomberg.com, December 18, 2015. Accessed April 16, 2020. https://www.bloomberg.com/opinion/articles/2015-12-18/an-immigrant-isn-t-going-to-steal-your-pay-raise.

Somin, Ilya. 2017. "Immigration, Freedom, and the Constitution." *Harvard Journal of Law and Public Policy* 40 (1): 1–8.

Sonmez, Felicia. 2018. "Trump Says U.S. Agents 'Had to Use' Tear Gas Against Migrants at Border." *Washington Post*, November 26, 2018. Accessed May 5, 2020. https://www.washingtonpost.com/politics/trump-says-us-agents-had-to-use-tear-gas-against-migrants-at-border/2018/11/26/a2b66a00-f1ba-11e8-80d0-f7e1948d55f4_story.html.

Sorkin, Amy D. 2017. "Donald Trump's Crowd Cheers His Muslim Exclusion Plan." *New Yorker*, June 19, 2017. Accessed April 16, 2020. https://www.newyorker.com/news/amy-davidson/donald-trumps-crowd-cheers-his-muslim-exclusion-plan.

Sowell, Thomas. 1983. *Ethnic America*. New York: Basic Books.

Sowell, Thomas. 1996. *Migrations and Cultures, A World View*. New York: Basic Books.

Spencer, A. 2008. "Linking Immigrants and Terrorists: The Use of Immigration as an Anti-Terror Policy." *Online Journal of Peace and Conflict Resolution* 8 (1): 1–24.

Stern, Ephraim. 2000. "The Babylonian Gap." *Biblical Archaeology Review*. November–December 2000.

Suro, Roberto, Jill H. Wilson, and Audrey Singer. 2011. "Immigration and Poverty in America's Suburbs." Brookings Institution, August 2011. Accessed June 19, 2020. https://www.brookings.edu/wp-content/uploads/2016/06/0804_immigration_suro_wilson_singer.pdf.

Swygart, Glenn L. 2018. "Squanto." *Salem Press Biographical Encyclopedia*. Amenia, NY: Grey House, 2018.

Tapper, Jake. 2014. "Obama, Pushing Immigration Action Today, Said to Have Hurt Effort in the Past." CNN.com, November 21, 2014. Accessed April 16, 2019. https://www.cnn.com/2014/11/21/politics/obama-immigration-flashback/index.html.

Tedesjo, Eva. 2016. "POLITICO50: George Borjas." Politico.com. Accessed September 10, 2019. https://www.politico.com/magazine/politico50/2016/george-borjas.

Tichenor, Daniel. 2016. "The Historical Presidency: Lyndon Johnson's Ambivalent Reform: The Immigration and Nationality Act of 1965." *Presidential Studies Quarterly* 46 (3): 691–705.

Tiron, Roxana. 2010. "Joint Chiefs Chairman Reiterates Security Threat of High Debt." *The Hill*, June 24, 2010.

Treadgold, Donald Warren. 1997. *History of Byzantine State and Society*. Stanford, CA: Stanford University Press.

Trump, Donald J. 2017. *National Security Strategy*. The White House. Accessed April 4, 2020. https://www.whitehouse.gov/wp-content/uploads/2017/12/NSS-Final-12-18-2017-0905.pdf.

Twain, Mark. 1872. *Roughing It*. Hartford, CT: American Publishing.

US Census. 1874. Section III. Accessed June 2, 2021. https://www2.census.gov/library/publications/decennial/1870/atlas/1870d-map-39.pdf?#.

US Census. 1990. "Region and Country or Area of Birth of the Foreign-Born Population, with Geographic Detail Shown in Decennial Census Publications of 1930 or Earlier: 1850 to 1930 and 1960 to 1990." Accessed June 2, 2021. https://www.census.gov/population/www/documentation/twps0029/tab04.html.

US Congressional Budget Office. 2007. "The Impact of Unauthorized Immigrants on the Budgets of State and Local Governments." December 2007.

US Department of Energy. 2013. National Nuclear Security Administration History Bulletin 774, August 2013. Accessed February 5, 2020. https://www.nnss.gov/docs/fact_sheets/DOENV_774.pdf.

US Senate Committee on Homeland Security and Governmental Affairs. 2019. Staff Report, "Threats to the U.S. Research Enterprise: China's Talent Recruitment Plans." November 18, 2019.

US Social Security Administration. 1983. "Report of the National Commission on Social Security Reform." January 1983. Accessed January 7, 2021. https://www.ssa.gov/history/reports/gspan.html.

US State Department, Office of the Historian. n.d. "The Immigration Act of 1924 (The Johnson-Reed Act)." Accessed June 2, 2020. https://history.state.gov/milestones/1921-1936/immigration-act.

UNESCO Institute for Statistics, Education data online. n.d. Accessed July 3, 2020. http://data.uis.unesco.org/index.aspx?queryid=169.

United Nations, Department of Economic and Social Affairs, Population Division. 2019. *World Population Prospects 2019*. Online Edition. Rev. 1.

United Nations Economic Commission for Latin America and the Caribbean. 2019. "Latin America and the Caribbean to Reach Maximum Population Levels by 2058." July 11, 2019. Accessed July 2, 2020. https://www.cepal.org/en/pressreleases/latin-america-and-caribbean-reach-maximum-population-levels-2058.

United States Customs and Border Protection. 2019. "Southwest Border Deaths by Fiscal Year." March 2019. https://www.cbp.gov/sites/default/files/assets/documents/2019-Mar/bp-southwest-border-sector-deaths-fy1998-fy2018.pdf.

United States Department of Homeland Security. 2016. "Statement by Secretary Johnson on Latest Actions to Address Wait Times at Airports." May 26, 2016.

United States Department of Homeland Security. 2017. "ICE Arrests Nearly 2,000 Human Traffickers in 2016, Identifies over 400 Victims Across the US." US Immigration and Customs Enforcement. January 23, 2017.

United States. *Economic Report of the President (2011)*. Washington, D.C.: U.S. Govt. Printing Office, February, 2011.

University of California Los Angeles, School of Public Affairs (2021). Accessed March 5, 2022. 2020https://spacrs.wordpress.com/what-is-critical-race-theory/.

Vought, Hans P. 2004. *The Bully Pulpit and the Melting Pot*. Macon, GA: Mercer University Press.

Wadhwa, Vivek. 2012. *The Immigrant Exodus: Why America Is Losing the Global Race to Capture Entrepreneurial Talent*. Philadelphia: Wharton School Press.

Walker, Francis A. 1896. "Restriction of Immigration." *Atlantic Monthly*, June 1896. Accessed July 20, 2020. https://resources.saylor.org/wwwresources/archived/site/wp-content/uploads/2011/02/Restriction-of-Immigration.pdf.

Wang, Peter H. 1974. "The Immigration Act of 1924 and the Problem of Assimilation." *Journal of Ethnic Studies* 2 (3): 72–75.

Washington, George. 1783. Letter to Joshua Holmes. "Letter to the Members of the Volunteer Association and Other Inhabitants of the Kingdom of Ireland Who Have Lately Arrived in the City of New York, December 2, 1783." From George Washington to Joshua Holmes, December 2, 1783. National Archives. https://founders.archives.gov/documents/Washington/99-01-02-12127.

Washington, George. 1788. Letter to Francis Adrian Van der Kemp. "From George Washington to Francis Adrian Van Der Kemp, 28 May 1788." *Founders Online*. Washington, DC: National Archives. Accessed May 20, 2020. https://founders.archives.gov/documents/Washington/04-06-02-0266.

Watney, Caleb. 2020. "The Global Competition for Scientific Minds Is Heating Up." *National Review*, February 24, 2020. Accessed March 20, 2020. https://www.nationalreview.com/2020/02/us-immigration-policy-global-competition-for-scientific-minds-heating-up/.

Weaver, John M. 2018. "The 2017 National Security Strategy of the United States." *Journal of Strategic Security* 11 (1): 62–71.

Webster, David. 2008. *Parachute Infantry: An American Paratrooper's Memoir of D-Day and the Fall of the Third Reich*. New York: Dell Books.

Weiner, Myron. 1993. "Security, Stability, and International Migration." *International Security* 17 (3): 91–126.

White House. 2018. "National Security Threats—Chain Migration and the Visa Lottery System." *The White House*. February 1, 2018. Accessed July 20, 2019. https://www.whitehouse.gov/articles/national-security-threats-chain-migration-visa-lottery-system/.

White House. 2018. "Our Current Immigration System Jeopardizes American Security." *The White House*. January 16, 2018. Accessed July 20, 2019. https://www.whitehouse.gov/briefings-statements/current-immigration-system-jeopardizes-american-security/.

White House Press Secretary. 2006. "Fact Sheet: The Secure Fence Act of 2006." October 26, 2006. Accessed July 20, 2020. https://georgewbush-whitehouse.archives.gov/news/releases/2006/10/20061026-1.html.

Whitman, Walt. 2005. *Leaves of Grass*, 150th anniversary edition. Oxford: Oxford University Press.

Widener, Andrea. 2019. "Science in the US Is Built on Immigrants. Will They Keep Coming?" *Chemical & Engineering News* 97 (9).

Wildavsky, Ben. 2010. *The Great Brain Race: How Global Universities Are Reshaping the World*. Princeton, NJ: Princeton University Press.

Williamson, Edwin. 2003. *The Penguin History of Latin America*. New Edition. New York: Penguin Books Limited.

Wong, Alia. 2019. "Colleges Face Growing International Student-Visa Issues." *The Atlantic*, September 6, 2019. Accessed July 20, 2020. https://www.theatlantic.com/education/archive/2019/09/how-harvard-and-other-colleges-grapple-student-visa-problems/597409/.

Wong, Catherine. 2019. "Tough US Immigration Policy Could Be the Key to China Winning Technology Race, Says Top AI Investor." *South China Post*, October 30, 2019.

Wong, Kristina. 2016. "National Security Experts Sound Alarm on Long-Term Debt." *The Hill*, May 10, 2016.

Woods, Joshua. 2011. "The 9/11 Effect: Toward a Social Science of the Terrorist Threat." *Social Science Journal* 48 (1): 213–33.

Woolley, John, and Gerhard Peters, eds. 1876. *Republican Party Platform of 1876*. The American Presidency Project, June 14, 1876. Accessed August 20, 2020. https://www.presidency.ucsb.edu/documents/republican-party-platform-1876.

World Bank. n.d. Online database. Accessed July 8, 2019. https://data.worldbank.org/.

Wright, Robin. 2020. "To the World, We're Now America the Racist and Pitiful." NewYorker.com, July 3, 2020.

Yglesias, Matt. 2019. "Immigration Makes America Great." Vox.com, August 12, 2019. Accessed July 20, 2020. https://www.vox.com/policy-and-politics/2017/4/3/14624918/the-case-for-immigration.

York, Alvin. 2018. *Sergeant York: His Own Life Story and War Diary*. New York: Racehorse Publishing.

Zenko, Micah. 2011. "Admiral Michael Mullen: Farewell and Thank You." Council on Foreign Relations blog. September 29, 2011. Accessed July 20, 2020. https://www.cfr.org/blog/admiral-michael-mullen-farewell-and-thank-you.

Zhou, Youyou. 2018. "Chinese Students Increasingly Return Home After Studying Abroad." *Quartz*, July 29, 2018.

Zwetsloot, Remco, Jacob Feldgoise, and James Dunham. 2020. "Trends in U.S. Intention-to-Stay Rates of International Ph.D. Graduates Across Nationality and STEM Fields." Center for Security and Emerging Technology Issue Brief, April 2020, p. 8.

Index

For the benefit of digital users, indexed terms that span two pages (e.g., 52–53) may, on occasion, appear on only one of those pages.

Note: Page numbers followed by b, f, and t indicate a box, figure, or table on the corresponding page, respectively.